Praise for

ESSENTIAL

"*Essential* shows how we, essential workers, were sacrificed during the pandemic—how we were told we were essential but not given workplace protections, how we had to choose between our jobs and keeping our families safe from the virus. *Essential* catalogs the increase in worker militancy during the pandemic, especially by Black and Brown workers who bore the brunt of the virus, police violence, and economic injustice. This book shows us without a doubt that labor struggles are racial justice struggles. Most importantly, *Essential* is a call to action: we need increased workplace militancy to challenge capitalism. As workers, our labor—and our ability to withhold it—is our power."
—Chris Smalls, president and founder,
Amazon Labor Union

"Why the recent surges in union popularity and new organizing all across America? What stake do the rest of us have in these brave workers' success? Jamie McCallum explains how we reached this moment and what the future could hold in an invigorating, urgent book that is, to borrow its title, essential reading."
—Nancy MacLean, author of *Democracy in Chains*

"By combining rich storytelling from the front lines of the pandemic and a deep historical lens, *Essential* brings to life a critical reality: Capitalism is quite literally killing us, and only through worker solidarity across our economy can we protect ourselves and advance our future."
—Sara Nelson, international president, Association of
Flight Attendants-CWA, AFL-CIO

"In the early days of the pandemic, we cheered for essential workers. Today, their labor is again ignored by too many journalists and scholars. Not McCallum, who in *Essential* tells the gripping, deeply researched story of how millions were able to organize for change during the crisis. He reveals what these workers accomplished throughout the pandemic and what remains left undone, showing how worker power can help build us a better world."
—Bhaskar Sunkara, author of *The Socialist Manifesto*

"McCallum has written a wonderfully illuminating book. Its broad topic is rising inequality in the United States. But it takes a distinctive approach, homing in on the circumstances of the worst-off among us—the working people on whom we all depend. McCallum calls them 'the new servant class,' and his documentation of their increasingly dangerous and difficult lives makes a powerful case for the imperative of radical reform. But by underlining the significance of care work, *Essential* also suggests the reforms to which we should aspire: a society based on equality, cooperation, and mutuality."
—Frances Fox Piven, coauthor of *Poor People's Movements*

"*Essential* is a compelling, in-depth look into the heroism of the nation's frontline workers during the pandemic. Millions of long-underappreciated workers—supermarket cashiers, warehouse workers, fast-food cooks, meatpacking workers—were suddenly hailed as essential, but at the same time, corporate America treated them as expendable and exploitable. Well-researched and highly readable, *Essential* examines one of the most encouraging developments during the pandemic: many essential workers took to the streets, went on strike, protested, and organized to demand better treatment, stronger protections, and the respect they deserve. McCallum voices his hopes that this militancy could have transformed America, but he explains why it fell short—and what still needs to be done to lift America's workers and create a far fairer, less exploitative economy."
—Steven Greenhouse, author of *Beaten Down, Worked Up*

"McCallum goes beyond the cliche that the pandemic revealed the existing fault lines and inequalities of our society. Rather, the dangers and burdens borne by 'essential workers' are reshaping the fabric of social relations, creating new forms of exploitation and struggle. Closely observed and passionately written, *Essential* is a necessary intervention."

—Gabriel Winant, author of *The Next Shift*

ESSENTIAL

ESSENTIAL

HOW THE PANDEMIC TRANSFORMED THE
LONG FIGHT FOR WORKER JUSTICE

JAMIE K. McCALLUM

BASIC BOOKS

New York

Basic Books
Hachette Book Group
1290 Avenue of the Americas, New York, NY 10104
www.basicbooks.com

Printed in the United States of America

First Edition: November 2022

Published by Basic Books, an imprint of Perseus Books, LLC, a subsidiary of Hachette Book Group, Inc. The Basic Books name and logo is a trademark of the Hachette Book Group.

The Hachette Speakers Bureau provides a wide range of authors for speaking events. To find out more, go to www.hachettespeakersbureau.com or call (866) 376-6591.

Basic Books may be purchased in bulk for business, educational, or promotional use. For information, please contact your local bookseller or Hachette Book Group Special Markets Department at special.markets@hbgusa.com.

The publisher is not responsible for websites (or their content) that are not owned by the publisher.

Print book interior design by Six Red Marbles

Library of Congress Cataloging-in-Publication Data
Names: McCallum, Jamie K., 1977– author.
Title: Essential : how the pandemic transformed the long fight for worker justice / Jamie K. McCallum.
Description: First edition. | New York : Basic Books, 2022. | Includes bibliographical references and index.
Identifiers: LCCN 2022010468 | ISBN 9781541619913 (hardcover) | ISBN 9781541619906 (ebook)
Subjects: LCSH: Employee rights—United States—History—21st century. | Labor movement—United States—History—21st century. | Medical personnel—United States. | Service industries workers—United States. | Industrial safety—United States—History—21st century. | Industrial hygiene—United States—History—21st century. | Epidemics—Social aspects—United States. | COVID-19 Pandemic, 2020—United States—Influence.
Classification: LCC HD8072.5 .M388 2022 | DDC 331.0973—dc23/eng/20220714
LC record available at https://lccn.loc.gov/2022010468

ISBNs: 9781541619913 (hardcover), 9781541619906 (ebook)

LSC-C

Printing 1, 2022

FOR TESSA

The crisis consists precisely in the fact that the old is dying and the new cannot be born; in this interregnum a great variety of morbid symptoms appear.

—ANTONIO GRAMSCI
Prison Notebooks, vol. II, Notebook 3, 1930

CONTENTS

AN INJURY TO ALL

It was late April of 2020 in New York City, and Kim Moenich, a nurse, was on her way to work. The cherry blossoms sparkled in pink and white, the sun squinted through the rooftops, and it was that magical hour of day when everyone banged on pots and pans. Out their windows, on the sidewalks, leaning out of livery cabs, New Yorkers sang and yelled and raised a ruckus, a show of support for the "healthcare heroes" around the city.

The ritual had begun in Wuhan. "*Jiayou!*" people yelled from their rooftops. Literally "add oil," *jiayou* is colloquially used as a call of encouragement and fortitude. During the COVID-19 pandemic, the Chinese adopted it as a nationwide show of solidarity for the "frontier workers," a remnant term from the lexicon of Maoism.

As the new coronavirus crisscrossed the world, so did the collective rituals of support. In the region of Lombardi, the second global epicenter of the disease, Italians bellowed, "*Bella, ciao*" ("Goodbye, beautiful"), from their balconies. Originally a partisan protest folk song from the nineteenth century, it's been widely adopted as an antifascist anthem since the Second World War. "The day will come," the song goes, "we all shall work in freedom."

When the virus began ravaging their city, New Yorkers began performing their own version of the ritual. Every evening in April at 7 p.m. sharp, from the Bronx to Brooklyn, entire neighborhoods made some serious noise, rattling the quiet air with encouragement that drowned out the constant clamor of ambulance sirens.

Kim enjoyed the serenade and, anyway, she was in no rush to enter the hospital. She knew what awaited her, and she had already seen so much.

In 2013, Kim had traveled to fight the deadly Ebola, a viral hemorrhagic fever in humans and other primates that causes massive internal and external bleeding. It is passed through direct contact with contaminated bodily fluids and kills about half of those it infects.[1] The disease had a catastrophic impact on West African countries during an epidemic outbreak in 2013–2016.

And then came the COVID-19 pandemic here. As a traveling nurse, Kim had witnessed the pandemic unfold across the country. In March 2020, Kim left one post in Atlanta to work in Tulsa, after she'd heard rumors that the city's hospitals were ill-equipped to handle the virus in the event of an outbreak. When the situation seemed under control, she transferred to a hospital in West Palm Beach, Florida, where many attending physicians openly spread COVID-hoax conspiracy theories, even as increasing numbers of people contracted the virus. "They really did not care if their patients lived or died," she said. Unable to be of much use, she requested immediate transfer to New York City, where the virus was killing record numbers of people and public mitigation measures like social distancing proved difficult.

But New York, incredibly, was the worst. "New York was worse than anything I've ever seen," she said. "Worse than Uganda."

As she got closer to the hospital entrance, she worried it would be like the other nights, with more piles of bodies, more chaos, more risk, more mistakes made, more death. She paused another minute to listen to the pots and pans before entering the building. When she walked into the ER, a young woman was already screaming at nurses to save her life. The patient had tested positive for COVID a week earlier and was having trouble breathing. She was passing around a photo of her six-year-old daughter so the nurses knew the stakes. After calming the woman and watching her oxygen level rise, Kim was optimistic and turned her back to attend to another patient.

She didn't get very far. "Then I heard the sound you never want to hear," she said. "Gurgling." The woman's body had entered what's known as a cytokine storm, a condition that destroys the respiratory system. Fluid fills the lungs and begins to rise up the trachea, blocking oxygen and causing fluid to rise even more, producing a sound familiar to experts in lung problems. Kim jumped onto the woman's bed and began performing compressions. In a Tyvek suit, two masks, a face shield, a gown, gloves, and goggles, she felt like she was drowning in her own sweat. "But she was fine just a minute ago," Kim said. "We were going to give her everything we had."

Doctors knew how to fight Ebola, but COVID was just different. What made the COVID-19 crisis in New York worse wasn't the severity of the disease but the chaotic approach to treatment and the conditions under which nurses worked.

Medical professionals didn't know how to treat COVID patients, and there was no accepted emergency standard of care. Doctors and nurses now know that patients were intubated too frequently, and that certain medicines commonly used against COVID could make it worse. "This was combat medicine," Kim said. "Do or die." Kim worked fifteen-hour days, using rest periods to read the latest medical science on COVID treatments. Nurses, doctors, and specialists were learning in real time, from their mistakes as much as their victories.

Their working conditions made everything worse. Personal protective equipment (PPE) shortages were the rule, and Kim kept her N95 mask in a brown paper lunch bag she stored in her locker. She'd been wearing the same one for over a week. The halls of the hospital were lined with ailing bodies begging to be treated. Nurses and doctors were forced to make split-second life-and-death medical decisions without the aid of CT scans. The patients could barely breathe, their hearts beat irregularly; they were feverish and scared to death. The ventilators that night were all full. The negative pressure room, where almost all infectious disease patients were treated, was full.

Occasionally, Kim's patient showed encouraging improvements, swelling hope in the room and demanding that the nurses keep pushing. Her vital signs ebbed and flowed, and she was even able to breathe on her own intermittently. They worked for three hours. "We needed a miracle," Kim said. "And we got fuckin' nothin'."

The woman died of a COVID-induced pulmonary embolism, gripping the crumpled photograph of her young daughter. Kim noticed the cross she wore around her neck and instructed the nurses to gather round her body. They held each other's hands and took a moment of silence. They bowed their heads and, for a brief minute, tried to find peace in the middle of a war zone.

In the course of writing this book, I heard different versions of this story from almost every healthcare worker I spoke with. "In those days we saved the ones we could and made sure the other ones didn't die alone," Kim said. "Oh, and we tried to stay alive in the process."

Such was the reserved humility of those who shouldered an impossible burden. A burden compounded by the insult of having to work with inadequate protective equipment, which increased the risks for caregivers and patients alike, and often for low pay. In the first year of the pandemic, about 3,600 healthcare workers died from COVID-19 in the United States.[2] They were joined by warehouse workers, nursing aides, slaughterhouse workers, delivery drivers, agricultural workers, retail clerks, teachers, grocery store workers, and many others who faced vast risks and sometimes succumbed to them. How many, we will probably never know.

Staying alive was even harder than it sounds. COVID-19 is an occupational disease, and as soon as outbreaks began ravaging US cities, workers began fighting for better working conditions: more PPE, paid sick leave, higher wages, comprehensive healthcare, and other safety improvements. They struck, walked out, held protests, and formed unions. To do their jobs well, they recognized, they needed to fight for higher standards. Compared to previous years, the number of such disruptions was greatly reduced. But that's to be expected when only a third of workers are reporting to a jobsite. Of the major strikes in 2020, half were led by nurses. Kim routinely received job announcements for contracts that hired scabs when nurses were on picket lines, jobs that often paid more than triple the regular wage. She never took them.

"That's the way we improve healthcare," she said. "That's the way we stay alive. You live fighting or die working."

✦

THE PANDEMIC HAS profoundly affected the way we work, and with it, the working class. The three-dimensional nature of the pandemic-induced labor crisis—mass unemployment, remote work, and dangerous in-person work—uprooted our most dearly held assumptions about what employers and employees do, how they do it, and what they owe each other. All these factors contributed to a care crisis, too, both in the home and within the caring professions.

In 2020, the category of "essential worker" became a synecdoche for our risk-intensive economy. Essential workers were called heroes when they left for work and treated like sacrificial lambs when they got there. Between the Scylla of the virus and the Charybdis of the economic crisis, essential workers faced a dilemma of unprecedented complexity, one magnified by their ambiguous status as both hero and victim: go to work and risk their own lives or stay home and imperil their livelihoods. This book is about the workers who faced that impossible struggle, and what it means for the rest of us.

The pandemic illustrated why we should all care about workers' rights, even in good times. Pitifully low pay ensured that nursing home workers had to work multiple jobs, and they carried the virus with them from home to home, infecting the very patients they were working to save. When growers and harvesters work in unsanitary conditions, our food is dirty. If teachers don't have what they need to be successful, children won't either. When delivery and logistics workers log too many hours or spend all day and night behind the wheel, deadly accidents are more common.[3] If caregivers don't have healthcare themselves, work for poverty wages, or have too many patients or not enough PPE, our level of care will be substandard. And if their protests and other attempts to improve their working lives are ignored or opposed, we will make no progress.

In short, the pandemic revealed the extent to which our lives are intertwined with their jobs. Essential workers jeopardized their own health, safety, and security for the greater good. Yet the pernicious conditions they worked under—and obstacles they faced to improving their jobs—undermined not only their personal health but also our collective well-being. By shortchanging essential workers, we performed a collective ouroboros, the ancient symbol of a snake devouring its own tail.

Conversely, when jobs are better, we all benefit. Higher wages, safer staffing ratios, and unions are positively correlated with better health outcomes for patients in hospitals. Unionized workers across essential industries had more paid sick leave, more PPE, and were tested for COVID-19 more regularly, reducing infections and the spread of the disease within and beyond the workplace.[4] Thanks to unions in the airline industry, today we fly on planes without sucking in second-hand smoke and with peace of mind that passengers can't carry small knives on board. Labor unions don't just make jobs better for their members—they've been shown to increase wealth for all workers, decrease the wage gap for families of color, and reduce white workers' racial resentment.[5] Unionized workers in impacted industries kept their jobs at higher rates during the pandemic recession, maintaining their families' standard of living during the downturn.[6] When union nurses in New York hospitals lobbied then governor Cuomo for their members to get a new N95 mask each day, he had no choice but to guarantee one to every nurse, union or not.[7] In nursing homes where workers had unions, residents died of COVID-19 at lower rates.[8] *Their* working conditions are *our* living conditions.

✦

ESSENTIAL WORKERS SEEMED to understand this better than anyone. From the moment the pandemic began, many fought to improve their working conditions, framing their grievances as beneficial to society at large. The relationship between bad jobs and public welfare was undeniable during the pandemic. Yet this link has long been recognized by labor activists. In the early twentieth century, the Industrial Workers of the World, a radical labor union, adopted a slogan: An injury to one is an injury to all. Armed with this ideological and strategic North Star, it organized workers into "one big union" regardless of occupation, race, nationality, skill, or religion. Exceptional as it was, the pandemic actually reflected this long-standing view of the labor movement. As this book illuminates, however, the pandemic also demanded that workers experiment with new kinds of protest actions, form unique political alliances, and push the boundaries of what a union can do.

As a labor scholar, I have studied workers' issues across the globe for almost two decades. I've followed campaigns to improve workers' jobs from South Africa to Europe to India. I've met with clandestine organizers in China, where labor unions are essentially illegal, and in parts of Latin America, where trade union leaders have been common targets of assassination. I've written about why Americans are so overworked today, and why the search for meaning in our jobs might lead to a dead end. When the pandemic began, I immediately recognized some of the vast changes that workers would face. And like everyone else, I was also quite surprised by a lot of what I saw.

Out of what was at first ardent curiosity, I began interviewing essential workers across the world. I soon understood that whatever thin social contract held the American workplace together had been virtually shredded overnight.

My research agenda quickly shifted in scope from the global to the national, starting in US healthcare and eventually working my way through education, food services, retail, and other low-wage service sectors, including logistics, leisure, and hospitality, the industries that defined essential work. In the end I surveyed over seven hundred essential workers and conducted in-depth interviews with about one hundred others. The surveys asked about working conditions, political beliefs, and experience with unions. They gave me a sense of what essential workers were facing, and what they hoped might change, especially in the lead-up to the 2020 presidential election. Through those surveys I also met workers to interview in more detail, which provided an intimate view of their experiences on the front lines.

Most of my interviews were with women and people of color, the groups who bore the brunt of the crisis. Workers of color were laid off at higher rates during the recession, infected with the virus at higher rates as essential workers, and died of COVID at higher rates. Partly for these reasons, they were also some of the most vocal leaders of the pandemic labor movements. Today's working class isn't all burly white teamsters; it's the most diverse section of the American occupational hierarchy. I could include only a fraction of these interviews in the book, but they all helped lay the groundwork for my analysis of how the coronavirus altered the relationship between labor, race, gender, and capital.

Workers routinely voiced conflicting accounts of their on-the-job struggles during the peak of the pandemic. Some blamed themselves and others for not working hard enough, for failing their families, and for not earning enough money to support a dignified life. Anyone who conducts research among the American working class hears these same explanations and appreciates the power they derive from an ideology of bootstrap platitudes and the Protestant work ethic. The majority of workers I interviewed, however, told an altogether different story. That story implicated a systemic failure to uphold the basic premise of a work-centered social contract. In essence, they were signaling a breakdown of the old order, and were frustrated that no ready-made alternative seemed close at hand. Still others voiced what to me was perhaps the most surprising insight of all, that the pandemic workplace wasn't a break of any kind but merely an advance of business as usual in the low-wage workplace. These stories were commonly filtered through racial disparities, as Black and Latino workers were disproportionately exposed to the virus through their jobs, and racist discrimination on the job is a constant feature of employment.

There was no universal workers' experience during the pandemic, just as there is no simple story to tell about how workers view their working lives in better times. That's not to say that workers shared nothing in common. It's objectively clear that they faced a degraded workplace, one rife with more hazards and risks, and mostly without extra compensation. In fact, this common mistreatment was the fuel for a worker justice movement that punctuated essential worksites, a collective response to the Sturm und Drang of the pandemic economy.

"We were sacrificed," says Christian Smalls, a former Amazon warehouse employee from State Island. Christian was fired a few hours after he organized a protest in support of greater COVID mitigation efforts at his jobsite. "It happened to Black and brown workers more. But all of us essentials, we were just used," he said. "Like human shields."

This book combines immersive stories from my interviews with decades of research on labor, politics, epidemiology, and social movements to understand the current state and possible future of the American working class. I explain the shifts in worker militancy during the pandemic, contextualizing it in the history of the long fight for worker justice in America. These struggles happened alongside historic policy changes and government action that also affected the way workers fought back. I also examine the internal world of workers' consciousness—how, in other words, they made sense of their own experiences in relation to others'. This was visible not only through interviews but by analyzing their inchoate movements and demands for change. Their stories are rife with contradictions that refuse to oversimplify the messiness of the pandemic workplace. Yet they offer a framework for understanding essential workers as, to borrow from the historian Benedict Anderson, an "imagined community."[9]

The state of the working class is a bellwether for democracy. When labor gets a good deal, we all win. Just think of the weekend—we only have one because unions and other reformers pushed for a reasonable break from endless toil. Yet those kinds of victories are so rare today. The working life was in trouble long before the pandemic, and recent events pushed it closer to the brink. It's therefore incumbent upon us to figure out where things went so wrong.

✦

THE STORY OF essential workers during the pandemic is part of the long unraveling of the New Deal. The destruction of the welfare state, the attack on unions, and the rise of neoliberalism provide the historical backdrop for this book. As workers' fortunes came under renewed attack in the early 1970s, the historic gains of the New Deal were rolled back decades. Inequality became the defining feature of our economy as we arrived at a second Gilded Age. This was more than unfair—during the pandemic it had deadly consequences. A 2020 study found that in over three thousand US counties, income inequality was associated with more cases and more deaths by the virus.[10]

I pay particular attention to the immediate aftermath of the Great Recession of 2007–2009, when the unemployment rate remained stubbornly high long after the crisis had been declared officially over.[11] The solution to lagging employment growth was an explosion of low-wage service jobs. It was this new servant class of gig workers, low-wage healthcare workers, fast-food employees, maids, delivery drivers, and retail clerks who endured the most intense economic hardship during the pandemic recession. They were deemed essential and worked through the pandemic, or they lost their jobs. Without this longer time frame for context, essential workers appear to be merely the product of the pandemic rather than the outcome of decades of political and economic shifts.

By April 2020, about one-third of US workers were designated as "essential" or "frontline" workers, tasked with laboring in person through the pandemic. Usually these categories overlapped, but there were also millions of retail and restaurant workers who were not technically deemed essential but found themselves on the front lines because their employers fought to remain open during the pandemic.

Frontline workers are more racially diverse than the rest of the US workforce, and about two-thirds are women.[12] They represent parts of the labor force with less formal education, as fewer than half hold a high school diploma. For all these divisions, however, they're unified demographically in an important way: about 75 percent earn wages below the national average.[13] Most had almost no financial cushion or paid sick leave that allowed them to take time off if exposed to the virus at work, while almost all high-wage workers did.[14] Throughout this book I use "frontline" and "essential" interchangeably, but I'm almost always referring to the group who must show up to work in person.

Who was considered essential or not often seemed capricious. Employers carved out niches for themselves as essential, forcing their employees into dangerous workplaces, even though they served no public benefit. Walmart designated its store greeters as essential, putting countless workers at unnecessary risk. I met workers at Dollar Tree who said their company cynically ordered some essential goods just to stay open, even when those products were out of stock. The state of Montana designated elite fly-fishing guides as essential. Kirk Gibbs, an electrician from Syracuse, New York, summarized his status as an essential worker like this: "I'm essential to the pocketbooks of rich contractors and essential for spreading the virus, but that's about it."[15]

Across the world the designations varied even more. In fact, it wasn't always clear what essential workers were essential *for*. Economic stability? Corporate wealth accumulation? Public health? Social reproduction? To ensure a pleasant experience for retail shoppers?

Moreover, who truly counted as a frontline worker in the popular imagination was often determined not by policy or pretzel logic but by shape-shifting public opinions about workers and the state of the pandemic itself. I met some people who worked both as healthcare workers and at fast-food restaurants through the pandemic who claimed they were only deemed essential by the general public in their caregiving roles. This mattered beyond public recognition. Because workers did not have a straightforward relationship to being classified as essential or not, their ability to collectively organize as such when necessary was inhibited.

Still, workers used the rhetorical power of their designation as "essential" to highlight their mistreatment and exploitation. Indeed, the inspiration for this book was not to understand why and how essential workers did their jobs but to illuminate the significance of the moments when they stopped doing them.

In the shadow of the Great Recession, the Fight for $15 campaigns by fast-food workers defined the fitful surges of a labor movement for the new millennium. They identified elite capture of the economy and systemic racism as twin factors of working-class demobilization. In 2011, they were joined by Occupy Wall Street's militant street protests and then waves of public sector strikes as teachers took to picket lines in 2018–2019 across the country, raising the possibility of labor's renewal even in Trump country. This momentum was undone by the pandemic.

Strikes, walkouts, and other large protests weren't as common in 2020, and no national march for essential workers flooded the DC Mall. Successful new union organizing drives also experienced a historic low.[16] Yet the pandemic activism that did happen was perhaps even more important. In some cases, workers forced their managers, bosses, and corporate boards to provide lifesaving safety protocols, more paid sick days, raises, and better healthcare and other benefits. Were it not for workers blowing the whistle, we might never have known the hazards they faced or gotten the kinds of improvements that saved lives. In addition to these much-needed tangible gains for an eclectic class of workers, pandemic-era activism shifted the national conversation about worker justice in ways the previous decade failed to do.

A major consequence of labor unrest during the pandemic was that, against great odds, essential workers helped to transform the political conversation about work in America. They even influenced the Democratic Party's established preference for austerity in ways that were unimaginable before the pandemic arrived.

Why did Joe Biden—who had built his entire career on not being Bernie Sanders—on the eve of his election promise to be "the most pro-union president you've ever seen"? Why did he come out in support of Amazon workers in what was the most hotly debated union election in recent history? Or why did he immediately create a task force on Worker Organizing and Empowerment and pursue the Protecting the Right to Organize Act, groundbreaking legislation that would recast American labor law in workers' favor? "The marching order from the president," said Jared Bernstein, a member of the president's Council of Economic Advisers, "is everything we do in the job market space needs to reflect the importance of unionization."[17]

Biden didn't have a change of heart. He was just reading the pulse of the country, and milquetoast socialism was the order of the day. Long-held popular assumptions about the goodness of unfettered capitalism were being challenged on a daily basis, in the press and in the workplace. The nature of the pandemic raised concerns about essential workers to issues of national security, which gave these workers' struggles a larger audience and deeper significance. Just as Occupy Wall Street changed the conversation about inequality in America—focusing greater attention on systematic wealth concentration, not merely "greed"—labor struggles during the pandemic contributed to a new valuation of America's working class.

Yet a year after campaigning to "get things done," Biden wasn't able to rally even his own party to his signature plans for jobs, infrastructure, climate, higher education, and voting rights. Nonetheless, many of the country's major labor leaders seemed to be waiting for him to do exactly that before taking matters into their own hands. When what was needed was decisive political leadership and militant organizing on a large scale, neither transpired. It wasn't until spring 2022, led by historic movements within Amazon warehouses and grassroots campaigns to unionize Starbucks cafés, that labor seemed emboldened to chart a new course.

The struggles that did happen, however, were especially urgent because the pandemic accelerated a decades-long "risk shift," a phrase coined by political scientist Jacob Hacker, from business and the state toward workers and citizens. This made many Americans' lives and jobs risky, unsafe, and generally miserable. During the pandemic, employers off-loaded responsibilities onto families that were formerly covered by work rules. Nowhere was this more apparent than when it came to healthcare. Our uniquely American work-based safety net meant that when millions of workers lost their jobs, they risked losing their health coverage too. Millions of low-wage workers, including those who were unemployed or temporarily displaced from their jobs, faced hazards that employers willfully ignored, jeopardizing their health and the health of their families.

The pandemic exacerbated America's preexisting crisis of care and underlined workers' role in solving it. "We're striking for our lives," said Marlena Pellegrino, a veteran nurse at Saint Vincent Hospital in Massachusetts, who led the longest healthcare strike of the pandemic. "But also the lives of our patients and the lives of their families. Their care starts with our jobs."

Labor protests thickened the plotline of this book—that our fates are tied to workers having good jobs, at good wages, in safe conditions, with plenty of paid time off. Lousy jobs are bad for all of us, whether we hold them ourselves or not. This simple fact has radical implications. It means we all have a stake in fighting for a new system that ensures workers get what they need to thrive. We can't draw a straight line to get there. But the lessons from history, drawn from the tragic collisions between plagues and people, show us that we need to understand the fault lines in our current system in order to build a better one.

✦

PANDEMICS WERE RELATIVELY common in the ancient world. The Black Death crept across the continents, migrating with merchants by sea and traders along the Silk Road, a series of paths, trade routes, and caravanserais that crisscrossed the steppes of Central Asia. By the time it arrived in Europe, it collided with a society made vulnerable by the horrific conditions wrought by feudalism—famine, poverty, slavery, and the roving armies of the Hundred Years' War. Plague killed a staggering fifty million people, wiping out almost one-half of Europe's population.

Likewise, COVID-19 traversed the circuits of capital of the world economy, emanating from the major trading and travel hubs and passing through labor-intensive nodes in the global supply chain—warehouses, rail stations, air- and seaports, and the rest stops in between.[18] Wuhan itself is often dubbed the Chicago of China because its airport, like bustling O'Hare, is a way station for so much domestic and international travel. The virus ripped across China in a few days, and within two months it was active in seventy-five countries.[19]

As the plague shows us, there have been pandemics across social systems; they're not particular to capitalism. Trade and travel is a centuries-old story, but the manner in which COVID-19 spread is more than just an accelerated version of the past.

Unique features of capitalist society exacerbated the COVID-19 pandemic and caused it to unfold in a spectacularly tragic way. The US has only 4 percent of the global population but suffered about 22 percent of COVID-19 deaths in the first year of the pandemic. By 2022 the share of Americans who had died of coronavirus was at least 63 percent higher than in our peer countries, the result of our inferior healthcare programs and lower vaccination rates, especially among the poor.[20] The most reasonable explanation for this incredible excess death rate is that our social system is designed to let it happen.

Decades of austerity, union busting, low wages, corporate domination, and neoliberal restructuring left our society highly susceptible to the coronavirus. Those deleterious conditions helped spread the disease and concentrate its effects among the underclass, the same people who are filtered by the market into low-wage work or first to be displaced from their jobs during a crash.

Labor under capitalism puts our society, especially workers, unnecessarily in harm's way. The big picture: unchecked capitalist development is responsible for introducing feral pathogens into human populations. The capitalist cocktail of ecological devastation and mass human migrations has given zoonotic disease a great leap forward. Urbanization and the destruction of tropical forests effectively eliminate the border between humans and the pathogens lurking inside wild animals. The subsequent decline of biodiversity combined with the erasure of those ecological borders presents new species as food sources. These processes have long been known as outbreak risks, and the same forces driving climate change will lead to new pandemics.[21] This threat is explicitly accelerated by industrial agriculture and livestock production, which combine novel viruses with unsanitary working conditions, turning our food labor chain into a vector of disease.

Over the last five decades we've perfected the science and art of "just-in-time capitalism," the on-demand supply chains and logistics hubs that make the world economy run. Prior social models—Fordism, for example—would not have spread the virus as far or as quickly because they did not rely on the immediate delivery of parts and services through a globally interconnected web. The absolute necessity of such a web today requires that all the inputs of a particular commodity or service stay operational as long as possible, which helped disperse the virus. Super-coordinated, high-tech systems of production, transportation, and distribution of goods and services were almost overnight transformed into arteries of disease transmission. Global capitalism literally made us sick.

Yet, the pandemic's periodic shutdowns also spread an economic crisis. When domestic automobile manufacturing paused during April and May of 2020, the ripple effect hit hundreds of thousands of workers in parts and materials factories across the globe, many of whom had no unemployment coverage and were thrust into abject poverty. Capitalist society made sure that millions of workers faced the ultimate dilemma: your money or your life.

Understanding how our social system influenced the pandemic is important. After all, the pandemic arrived in the midst of other agonizing crises. For decades, global capitalism had been failing to produce enough good jobs for people to sustain a modicum of human dignity. A family of delusional fascists with control of the US nuclear codes had transformed its beguiled following into a well-funded death cult. Gains made by the civil rights movement were rolled back as police murdered Black people—on camera—with virtual impunity. A repulsive cabal of villainous billionaires were fleecing the American workforce: their time, their money, their unions, their autonomy, their privacy were all under siege. And then, of course, there's climate change and the looming prospect of our species' extinction. If we could have designed the pandemic to wreak the most havoc, launching it in 2019 makes perfect sense. In context, we can see it as a discrete part of a converging general breakdown of the Anthropocene—the inability to sustain human life.

The prism through which you view this crisis depends on your perspective. Philosophers might pay most attention to the abundant moral hazards. Perhaps political scientists see first and foremost the indefensible abuses of power and necropolitical neglect for human life of the Trump administration. Psychologists examine our brains under lockdown. The wealthy see an opportunity. As a sociologist who focuses primarily on labor issues, I saw class war.

We Americans are known for our limited sense of class consciousness, especially among working folks. White supremacy, nationalism, individualism, all key ingredients of the American creed, are obstacles to unity among working people, though the rich seem to conveniently set them aside more easily. The pandemic changed some of that. As janitors lay in makeshift freezer morgues outside the hospitals they used to work in, while the owners of the hospitals were sheltering in second homes in Fort Lauderdale—Italians during the Black Death called homes used by the rich to avoid the plague *villeggiatura*, "country escape homes"—it was hard not to see the world as structured first and foremost by class power.

When employers control access to healthcare, workers either lose it when they lose their job or are more easily bullied into working in

dangerous situations to keep it. When only half the working population has a right to sufficient paid sick leave, the other half lives and
works at the behest of others. When the working poor are denied the
right to Medicaid explicitly because lawmakers will not extend the Affordable Care Act (ACA) provision to grant it to them, as happened
in seven states, they are the captive subjects of a ruling elite. These
developments are the inevitable outcome of a system where one class
places profits over people.

Capitalist employment treats workers with reckless indifference.
An indifference to preventable deaths and working conditions, and
a recklessness rooted in the mistaken belief that our future is not
contingent on workers' well-being.

If the pandemic has shown us anything, it's that we need an alternative. The real antidote to the deadly failings of capitalism is socialism. To get there, workers will need to create a crisis for capital. The
insurgent workers' movements of the 1930s offer a glimpse of what
this could look like. Large and unruly strikes swept through the country's basic industries, challenging the authority of our most powerful capitalists. Strikes shut down production in automobile factories,
steel mills, coal mines, and transportation hubs, forcing employers to
negotiate and, eventually, Roosevelt to intervene. Liberals look back in
awe at what the New Deal accomplished, but they forget it was a compromise with the left flank of the labor movement. Today, labor can't
wait for legislation to ease its woes. The unrest during the pandemic
was inspiring but fell far short of what is needed to force real change.
History holds lessons for charting labor's future.

It was tempting to view the pandemic as a sequel to previous crises.
The coronavirus recession reminded us of 1929, the social unrest of
1968, the virus itself of 1981. Instead, the pandemic is more likely to
be a prequel to whatever climate change and capitalist globalization
bring us next. The risk, then, is not that we repeat the mistakes of
the past, but that we transmit our vulnerabilities into the future. This
book is an analysis of recent events, which can't be changed, and a po-
lemic about what happens next—which is up to us.

◆

I BEGIN, IN Chapter 1, by describing the unique impacts of the coronavirus recession on essential workers. Since the Great Recession that began in 2007, our society has relied more and more on a servant economy of precarious low-wage laborers, who are disproportionately women and people of color and universally underpaid. The unique circumstances of having to contain a deadly virus and maintain social distancing directly determined what happened to this underclass. Some lost their jobs, a few worked from home, and the rest were forced to staff dangerous worksites. This outcome produced the most unequal economic rupture in US history. It also began an uncharacteristically American period of welfare-state generosity. From Trump's CARES Act to Biden's American Rescue Plan, trillions of dollars flowed into the economy, which blocked mass evictions and dramatically reduced poverty nationwide. These policy interventions alleviated the crisis of social reproduction but did not offer an opportunity to substantially transform the welfare state permanently. The likelihood of future pandemics, however, suggests we should learn some lessons from this one and make lasting changes to the way our welfare state operates.

The pandemic economy organized essential workers into a new kind of working class. Chapter 2 describes the process by which essential workers developed class consciousness among themselves as a class premised on its proximity to risk. These workers developed common interests that in some cases bridged status and occupational hierarchies. Yet that process was uneven and incomplete, stymied by polarizing conflicts within it, especially divisions over how to treat the unemployed and intraclass political strife. The pandemic working class was most visible in action, which is the subject of Chapter 3. The pandemic threw working life into tumult, igniting new fires and stoking the embers of pre-COVID class struggles that had been smoldering for too long. Across the country, workers caused uproars large and small, with and without the backing of unions. Their movements also coalesced around new issues particular to the pandemic, and there were unusual examples of cross-pollination between social justice protest movements and organized workplace activism.

At the heart of most of these conflicts was safety. The history of workplace safety in America is inscribed in the history of class struggle. Chapter 4 explains the effect unions have on workplace safety and how they tried to reduce the spread of COVID-19. Unionized care homes reduced infection rates among workers and staff. In schools, unions fought against political leaders to get mask mandates, vaccinations, and safe return programs. In slaughterhouses and poultry processing plants, worker movements were less effective, illustrating the legacy of union busting.

In Chapter 5, I analyze the curious persistence of the "labor shortage" problem alongside the emergence of a pandemic strike wave involving tens of thousands of nurses, heavy-machine operators, coal miners, food workers, whiskey makers, and symphony musicians. Essential workers and the unemployed were ultimately unable to form a coherent class early on, but later high rates of quitting and striking were closely linked. The most popular narratives about the worker shortage—that people didn't want to work or were simply living off generous unemployment benefits—were incorrect, yet the problem resisted a simple alternative explanation. This chapter helps us understand that some of the same structural factors that kept people from working also exacerbated tensions among those who continued to work, leading to wider labor unrest as the pandemic progressed.

I then take a step back from the urgency of the front lines. Whereas the first part of the book explains the way workers navigated the pandemic, the second part reflects on what that means in broader terms. The point is to consider how we might conceptualize the state of the American working class during and beyond the pandemic. COVID-19 marked a new stage of a risk-intensive society and underscored our crisis of social reproduction. Chapter 6 paints a portrait of American society left vulnerable by employers and the state.

I return to Hacker's concept of a risk shift, which refers to spreading preexisting risks onto workers and families. But the coronavirus objectively *increased* the amount and intensity of hazards that people faced. Moreover, past risk shifts have often happened slowly, in the quiet halls of policymaking. COVID, by contrast, was an easily identifiable threat, especially at work, which signifies a qualitative shift from a "risk society" to a "hazard society."

Chapter 7 conceptualizes the pandemic as a crisis of social reproduction. When frontline healthcare workers are in crisis, we're all in crisis. The shocking rise in healthcare labor over the past three decades, surpassing the rate of growth of all other jobs, has paradoxically not translated into a healthier populace. Working-class white men, for example, actually face a declining life expectancy today. The cheering rituals, the pots and pans, the songs, the heroes' welcomes were meaningful symbols of solidarity with our caretakers. Now let's pay them a dignified wage, grant them full workers' rights, and make sure they have the quality jobs they need to keep us all safe and healthy.

Chapter 8 links worker justice to the possibility of social transformation, a *real* recovery from the coronavirus crisis. The public's exposure to the plight—and fight—of essential workers signals a decisive change in attitudes toward worker issues, such as support for unions, universal healthcare, and antipathy toward major corporations. This shift is one mechanism by which worker issues and activism can translate into greater political change that's beneficial to all.

As I finished writing this book, there was widespread hope that vaccines and new treatments for COVID-19 would soon put the biological pandemic in the rearview mirror. At times I was even uncertain about whether I should refer to the pandemic in the past or present tense. What seemed clear, though, is that the effects of the social and economic crisis will outlast the disease. The turmoil of the pandemic turned capitalism inside out, exposing the rotting core of a system that places profit over people, work over workers, and wealth over health. It also showed us faint glimpses of a wondrous alternative, where we care for each other as if our own lives depend on it. We now know that a safer and saner future is only possible on a broad scale if we recognize the interdependent nature of our work and lives. To do that we can reorganize our economy so that essential workers aren't at the bottom of a hierarchy but the foundation of a real democracy.

CHAPTER 1

THE DISPOSSESSED

BEFORE THE CORONAVIRUS OUTBREAK, KENIA MADRIGAL HAD been supporting her family through her job paint-striping parking lots in Houston, Texas. It was difficult on $11.50 per hour, but she made it work, juggling childcare and an ever-shifting work schedule. All that changed in the turbulence of the April 2020 crash. She lost her job, joining twenty-two million others who became newly unemployed in the first two months of the pandemic. Because of either bureaucratic blunders or the de rigueur system failures, she did not receive the $600-per-week unemployment relief check from the Coronavirus Aid, Relief, and Employment Security (CARES) Act for which she was eligible. During that time, she fell behind on rent and by June was two months short.

That same month, the Texas Supreme Court ended the state's pandemic eviction moratorium, pushing thousands of residents out of their homes. A series of stunning news reports followed Houston deputy Bennie Gant of the Harris County Constable's Office as he moved robotically from home to home, carrying out evictions. Kenia was one of them. She had never been late on her rent before. She and her four children, ages eleven, eight, three, and one, were kicked out of their mobile home.

Shelters and churches were full or otherwise unavailable, applications for public housing were closed, and she could not afford a hotel room. With nowhere to go, Kenia moved her family into her small SUV. She took the seats out so her three youngest could sleep in the back while she and her oldest son slept in the two front seats. For three months they endured the crushing Texas summer heat sleeping in a car with a hole in the roof that let the rain in. She herself barely slept, trying to stay alert at night in the event her family was harassed or assaulted.

"The kids used to ask me every day when we're going to get a place," she told me, her voice catching now and then when she spoke of her children. "My oldest, Michael, he was my ride or die. He always told me that we'd get through it together."

Kenia's tragic story speaks to what so many like her endured during the early months of the pandemic, which presented a bewildering assortment of crises—economic, physical, emotional, psychological— that American workers had never encountered before. Yet why so many others avoided a similar fate is of equal importance. The counterpoint to Dickensian stories like Kenia's is the quasi-Keynesian response from the government that saved lives and staved off total economic collapse.

The singular nature of the COVID-19 recession—driven by the need to contain a deadly airborne virus—affected low-income workers in two distinct but overlapping ways. First, the wave of mass layoffs in the early months of the pandemic left millions of workers newly unemployed, perched precariously on the brink of economic destitution. These workers are the focus of this chapter. Second, the "lucky ones" who kept their jobs, the focus of the rest of the book, had their luck effaced by the massive health and safety risks they had to endure, often for a poverty wage. To grasp the uniqueness of the coronavirus recession's impact on essential workers, however, we first need to briefly examine the crisis that preceded it, the Great Recession.

When the housing bubble burst in 2007–2008, it quickly became clear that predatory lending by banks, toxic financial products developed on Wall Street, and poor government regulation of finance industries were to blame. What was initially described as a "financial crisis," as if it only affected Bear Stearns and Lehman Brothers, quickly morphed into a global social breakdown. In the US, the effects were devastating. Rates of home ownership careened down to 63 percent, about 1960s levels.[1] Income and wealth inequality, which had already been expanding, suddenly skyrocketed, setting a new course upward that hasn't slowed since. More than a decade after the recovery was officially declared over in 2009, families affected by the housing market crash had recovered everything but their wealth, which in 2019 was stuck at precrisis levels.[2] Support for labor plummeted alongside a rising movement in 2010 by Republican lawmakers to attack public sector unions.

As soon as the effects of the crash began to ripple outward from Lower Manhattan, iconoclastic critiques by developing-country leaders like Lula in Brazil and Gloria Macapagal Arroyo in the Philippines pinned the crisis on a dying empire's desperate attempt to retain its dominion over the world economy. It was just more confirmation of America's fading status as the global hegemon. The federal government's Troubled Asset Relief Program and Emergency Economic Stabilization Act rescued the unsecured US finance sector and primed the banks to begin their predatory lending schemes again—mission accomplished. At $431 billion, the programs were a steal. From a typical homeowner's perspective, however, they were theft, having largely neglected to aid those who lost their homes or their savings during the crisis.[3] This one-sided bailout policy was the kind of cheapskate austerity politics that linked Obama's neoliberalism to that of his shameful predecessor.[4]

Eventually, something had to give—a homegrown protest movement emerged at the very scene of the crime. I remember snaking through Lower Manhattan with the hordes of protesters clogging the streets during the early days of Occupy Wall Street, traders waving at us from their balconies. Our handwritten signs pointed back up at them with a simple message: "Jump." While Occupy remained largely committed to street protests, some of the energy spilled over into ongoing labor organizing, as low-wage workers went on the offensive to try to double the minimum wage. This movement, the Fight for $15, was directed less at runaway inequality than at the effects of the Great Recession on working-class jobs.

The recovery was characterized by a persistently high jobless rate for workers at every level of the economy. When the jobs eventually came back, they looked quite different. Amid all the Great Recession changes, its most significant economic legacy was the explosive growth of millions of low-wage jobs. The 2007–2009 crisis all but destroyed middle-income jobs and replaced them with jobs that pay far less.

Mid-wage occupations accounted for 60 percent of the job losses during the recession but only 22 percent of the job growth during the subsequent recovery. In contrast, lower-wage occupations accounted for only 21 percent of recession job losses but then constituted 58 percent of all recovery job growth. By 2014, there were almost two million *fewer* jobs in mid- and high-wage industries and almost two million *more* low-wage workers than at the start of the recession.[5] In other words, decent jobs became low-wage work.

During the recovery period, we put people back to work, mostly as fast-food workers and in care services—almost seven million jobs that paid under $25,000 per year. There was also a massive influx of retail sales workers and cashiers, house cleaners, task rabbits, and personal delivery service workers. "These occupations are crucial to the support and growth of major industries across the country," noted the San Francisco Federal Reserve, a statement that seems to presage the "essential worker" designation. "But many of these workers do not earn enough to adequately support their families, even at a subsistence level."[6] Meanwhile, mid-wage jobs were hollowed out while high-paying ones took much longer to bounce back.[7] The recession especially affected heavily unionized sectors like the building trades because home and large office construction stalled after the housing crisis.

In the wake of the recession's economic fallout, Americans scrambled to find work, creating an opening for new start-ups to sell low-wage workers and the unemployed on the concept of a "gig" or "side hustle."[8] Once viewed as temporary, these types of jobs quickly became a permanent feature of the economy. Uber and TaskRabbit were both founded in 2008; they were joined in 2011 by Postmates, in 2012 by Instacart and Lyft, in 2013 by DoorDash, and by Shipt in 2015.

The emergence of the gig economy worsened working conditions nationwide and rapidly expanded the ranks of low-wage, hyper-exploited workers. Gig workers are functionally servants: they can act as your personal chauffeur, bring you dinner, do your grocery shopping, and assemble your furniture, all while the impersonal, app-based transaction lets you hire them without having to assume normal employer burdens, like safeguarding workers' rights. The historic growth of this low-wage servant economy characterized the labor market during both the Obama and Trump administrations.

The advent of a low-wage economy alongside service sector growth presents the impression that these phenomena are inherently intertwined. We're nostalgic for manufacturing employment, which is imagined to be, by default, solid, well-paid work. Such logic suggests there is nothing that policymakers can do to change the poor conditions of service jobs—it's just the inevitable result of deindustrialization.

In fact, there's nothing inherent to service work that makes it so bad. Rather, the development of a low-wage labor market has been a well-executed strategy following the Great Recession. Low-wage work has been mandated by the American business class and its allies in government. To call it a conspiracy isn't far off. In the wake of the Great Recession, a fierce new movement emerged to challenge public sector unions, where the largest percentage of union members are today. Led by corporate-backed organizations like the American Legislative Exchange Council (ALEC), and emboldened by Republican electoral victories in the 2010 midterm elections, this movement struck out to transform American labor law. In 2011 and 2012, fifteen states passed laws that restricted the rights of public employees to collectively bargain. During the same time, nineteen states introduced "right-to-work" laws that try to bankrupt unions by prohibiting them from collecting dues from all workers covered by their contracts.[9]

The decline of worker voice and poverty wages at the bottom of the labor market are compounded by other factors that make for miserable jobs across industries. At-will employment means workers can be fired or threatened with termination without cause. As scholars have tallied it, employers can legally keep you from urinating, force you to urinate, and record videos of you urinating.[10] Or they can do it all illegally and get away with it. You can be legally fired for wearing the wrong color clothing, posting on social media, expressing your political beliefs, or even considering having an abortion.[11] Workers have been fired after donating lifesaving organs to their boss—yes, the same boss who now has their kidney.[12] They can fire you for warning your coworkers that they've been exposed to COVID. In a very real sense, workplaces are dictatorships.[13]

These bad low-paying jobs came to characterize the service economy. In the decade from 2010 to 2020, the economy added 22.5 million jobs, 19 million of them in services.[14] President Trump inherited a country in the midst of the largest jobs expansion on record. And on his watch unemployment sank even lower, bottoming out at 3.5 percent in February 2020. However, the recovery was deeply unequal. By 2017, just 2 percent of overall growth since the Great Recession had trickled down to the bottom half of the population. Almost three-quarters of Americans were actually poorer in real terms. For average workers, real wages barely grew at all during the recovery and definitely failed to keep pace with even the meager increases in productivity.[15] Meanwhile, top-earning households had bounced back much faster, buoyed by a variety of income sources like stock dividends, bond interest, and rising salaries.[16]

We had become so desensitized to low-wage work that it seemed natural that so many people toiled for a pittance. In that environment, there was hardly an uproar that capitalism had simply not produced enough good jobs for those without college degrees, who make up the bulk of the American workforce.[17] In 2019, over one-quarter of low-wage workers qualified for some form of public supplement such as Medicaid or food stamps.[18] But then something remarkable happened: the labor market heated up and wages at the bottom started to rise. The combination of the Fight for $15 movement and a tight labor pool shrunk the reserve army of labor to historic lows. Many states raised their minimum wages. It was a decidedly weird moment of good news after a decade of anemic GDP growth. The ever-buoyant optimism of the political class finally had some hard data on its side.

Then the pandemic hit.

◆

As early as February 2020, the US was experiencing COVID-19 outbreaks in West Coast cities. The Centers for Disease Control and Prevention (CDC) issued stark warnings about an impending economic crisis. But White House National Economic Council director Larry Kudlow broke with the health agency to offer a note of misinformed caution. "We have contained this," he said. "I won't say airtight but pretty close to airtight."[19]

In just a few weeks, the world proved Kudlow wrong. The momentum of global capitalism quickly ground to a foot-dragging creep. Businesses, schools, and churches closed, worksites shut down, transportation networks stopped, supply chains were disrupted, planes were grounded. Workers all along these outposts were stranded, sometimes literally. Hundreds of thousands of crew members on cargo and cruise ships across the world were refused the right to dock and disembark anywhere. I spoke to Ashchaye Mohitram, a seafarer who had been scheduled to end a monthslong stint at sea he'd begun in late 2019 just as the pandemic hit. As it happened, he didn't touch dry land until 2021, well over a year after he'd departed from his home in Mauritius. There were over a hundred other crew members with him on what Mohitram, who turned twenty-eight while stuck at sea, described as a "floating prison."

But Newton's third law of motion kicked in: as the human population became increasingly sick and confined in space, the rest of the earth began to heal itself. Wild boars and pumas appeared in the streets of major Israeli cities. A herd of buffalo occupied the empty streets of New Delhi, India. Dolphins found their way into the notoriously brackish Venetian canals. Even the noxious skies over Wuhan and elsewhere across China turned storybook blue as the lockdowns shuttered the industries that emit infamous levels of air pollution.

But what seemed at the time like a peaceful rewilding of an empty earth was really just a momentary calm before the storm. If the epidemiology of the pandemic was to some extent predictable, the political economy of it was not. It was the worst GDP crash since the thirties, and a cascading series of worsts for unemployment claims. Never before had there been such a collective effort to shut down major parts of global economic infrastructure. Aside from world wars, this was unprecedented.

The International Labour Organization estimated that declines in working hours in 2020 were equivalent to the loss of 495 million full-time jobs worldwide.[20] Over 55 million workers in the global domestic labor pool lost hours or jobs in May 2020 alone.[21] The destruction was largely concentrated within the service sector, with unemployment increasing by an inconceivable 428 percent from February to April 2020 just in the US.[22]

As the graph below shows, all the major economic downturns in the previous half century have been driven by goods-producing sectors like construction, mining, and manufacturing.[23] During the pandemic, industrial output fell by a shocking 12.7 percent, the worst drop in over a century. Still, the pattern of the pandemic recession differed from previous downturns. Because public health depended on limiting face-to-face interactions, exactly the interactions so many service sector workers provide, losses were instead concentrated there.

Within the service sector, leisure and hospitality—the portion of the economy with the highest disparity between CEO and worker pay—accounted for the bulk of job losses.[24] In March 2020, the 459,000 lost leisure and hospitality jobs cancelled out the industry's gains over the two previous years.[25] That plummet, however, was

A Services-Dominated Recession

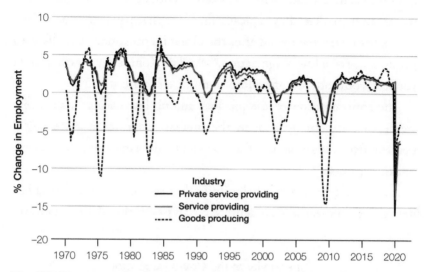

The COVID-19 recession hit the service industry hard, unlike previous recessions that mostly affected goods-producing industries. SOURCE: Bureau of Labor Statistics, with methodology assistance from Jed Kolko

nothing in comparison to the even greater crash in April, when leisure and hospitality alone accounted for 7.7 million lost jobs.[26] Food services and drinking places accounted for nine-tenths and three-quarters, respectively, of the leisure and hospitality jobs lost in March and April.[27] Other areas of the service sector—jobs in the offices of dentists, physicians, and other practitioners, temporary help services, retail trade, personal and laundry services, child day care services, individual and family services, and private education—also saw record drops in employment.

The common feature behind most of these jobs was their poor quality, combining low wages with excessive, inadequate, or variable hours.[28] In other words, most of the newly unemployed had been working lousy jobs, the same kinds of jobs created in droves after the Great Recession.

Joblessness comes with considerable social problems; layoffs render companies less competitive and hollow out middle-class jobs, contributing to greater precarity and inequality in American society. And in recent decades, when workers eventually find their way back to the labor market, they typically find jobs that pay less, which is the opposite of what happened after the Great Depression.[29] Layoffs are a prime cause of a low-wage nation.[30] And as Kenia's case shows, when you lose your job, you often lose so much else with it.

The concentration of the job loss among low earners was so extreme that it actually pushed the median wage *up* a staggering 7 percent from 2019, giving the recession's devastation a deceptively optimistic guise.[31]

As shown by the graph below, no other recent economic crisis has devastated low earners so acutely. Analysis by the *Washington Post*

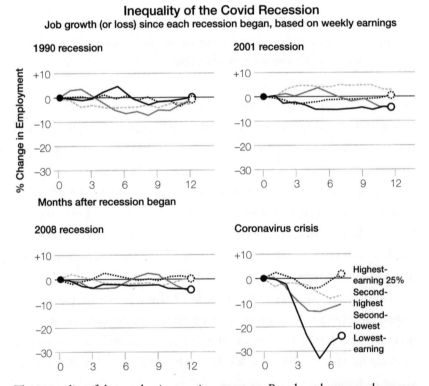

The inequality of the pandemic recession. SOURCE: Based on three-month average to show trend in volatile data. Labor Department via IPUMS, with methodology assistance from Ernie Tedeschi of Evercore ISI, from the *Washington Post*

found low-wage workers lost their jobs at a rate eight times greater than higher-earning workers.[32] By the end of the summer of 2020, the recovery was nearly complete for those in the top quartile, and their home values had rebounded or increased. Meanwhile, those at the bottom were still grappling with staggering losses of jobs, incomes, and healthcare.

This K-shaped recovery, in which some found job stability much more quickly than others, crystallized preexisting disparities in the lives of American workers. As the service sector is overrepresented by low-wage jobs done by a disproportionate number of women and people of color, the pandemic recession resulted in an unprecedented concentration of economic pain among those who already feel it most acutely.

The initial phase of high unemployment, which hit 15 percent at its peak, presented an economic landscape with unique demographic impacts.[33] Unlike in the Great Recession, when men lost their jobs first, prompting culture-warrior diatribes about a "he-cession" or "man-cession," four times as many women as men lost their jobs or dropped out of the labor force in 2020, prompting the equally ridiculous notion of the "she-cession."

Women are overrepresented in the low-wage service economy of restaurants, hospitality, and retail, and are more likely to work part-time, factors that explain most of the disparity. Seventy-five percent of the healthcare workers who contracted the virus early in the pandemic were women, for example. Over the last three decades, women have steadily increased their participation in the paid workforce; in 2019, they held more than half of all jobs. The pandemic recession reversed this trend: by January 2021, women's labor force participation rate had fallen below 56 percent, about the same as it was in 1987. By December 2020, men had gained a net 16,000 jobs while women, nearly all of them women of color, had lost 156,000.[34] Vice President–elect Kamala Harris called it a "national emergency" for women.[35]

African Americans and Latinos also faced higher rates of unemployment during the pandemic. In April, as the overall unemployment rate jumped to 15 percent, the rate was slightly lower for whites, at

14 percent, and higher for African Americans and Latinos, at 16.7 percent and 18.9 percent, respectively. Workers of color faced delayed recovery too. All in all, the record gains Black workers made in the decade after the Great Recession were wiped out in the first few months of the pandemic.

People of color and women lost their jobs at higher rates because they were overconcentrated in the low-wage service sector, where everyone is treated as disposable. But how did they get there in the first place? One possibility is that the progress Black workers had made since the 1980s was redirected by the explosion of low-wage service jobs in healthcare and other personal services after 2000.[36] This process tended to drive down wages by "crowding" marginalized workers into particular occupational categories.[37] These same groups are "crowded out" from better-paying occupations too. This sorting process reduces opportunities for marginalized workers by pushing them into lower-paying jobs, ensuring that certain occupations remain unequally stratified by race and gender. Many of these disenfranchised workers would have been middle-class had the recovery from the Great Recession not biased low-wage service labor. Unpaid care responsibilities, which are still performed overwhelmingly by women, can also act as a crowding mechanism. Whereas men are more available to take longer-hour, higher-paying jobs, women, who are typically burdened by more caretaking responsibilities, are filtered toward more part-time and lower-paying jobs.[38]

More educated workers fared better during the pandemic than those with lower levels of educational attainment. In January 2021, workers with less than a high school diploma were unemployed at 9.1 percent, compared to less than half that, 4 percent, for college degree holders. This pattern reflects trends during the Great Recession. However, today educational disparities are magnified by different abilities to telecommute; those with college degrees are six times as likely to be able to work from home as those without a high school diploma.

The recession was even geographically unequal, which galvanized partisan political squabbles. Conventional wisdom suggested that recovering from the pandemic recession meant controlling the spread of the virus. Yet, northeastern states, which did an overall better job of adhering to social distancing guidelines, still suffered worse economically. Southern and Sunbelt states that did a worse job of controlling the virus saw lower economic fallout. Blue states like California and Massachusetts were hit harder than red ones like Utah and Missouri. This trend persisted even as the COVID-19 infection profile and death rates shifted from blue states early in the pandemic to hot spots in red states during and after the summer of 2020. Why?

Most of the partisan jobs gap is attributable to the composition of the labor market in different places. Blue states continually suffered higher unemployment rates and more anemic recoveries because their economies are based more on the large service sector industries hit hardest by the pandemic. Hawaii and Nevada, for example, thrive on tourism, so it makes sense that they've been hit hard. New York and California are much-visited places as well, and they've seen job losses in the tourism and entertainment sectors. By contrast, manufacturing industries, where losses were less severe, are more likely to be in red states. Overall, job losses were significantly worse in Biden country than in states that Trump won in 2020.[39]

The large metro areas where telework is more prevalent, as in blue strongholds like New York City and the Bay Area, also saw steeper unemployment, as did cities in red and purple states with large remote workforces, like Austin, Boise, and Phoenix. Aside from igniting partisan tensions, the real consequences of this divide were that blue states faced a more dire budget crisis because the pandemic recession destroyed more of their tax base, weakening their economies and blunting their recoveries.[40]

✦

BY MAY 2020, twenty-seven million people either were officially unemployed or lived with an unemployed family member. The government defines an "unemployed" person as someone who has actively looked for work in the previous four weeks, but this definition excluded many throughout the pandemic, including over four million workers who reported in February 2021 that they did not look for work "because of the coronavirus pandemic" and over seven hundred thousand workers who were absent from their job "because their employer closed or lost business due to the coronavirus pandemic." All told, by the summer of 2021, nearly ten million children had lived in a home where one or more adults had lost paid work because of the pandemic.[41]

This overwhelming wave of pandemic unemployment came with dire consequences. A survey conducted by the Social Policy Institute found that those who had recently experienced job or income loss were more than twice as likely to delay medical care or filling prescriptions because they had become too costly.[42] A pandemic job loss in the family also increased the likelihood of food insecurity and a decline in child nutrition.[43]

Unemployment takes a massive psychological toll, as grueling as a death in the family or divorce.[44] One study found that American adults who became unemployed after March 1, 2020, endured two times more "mentally unhealthy days" than their peers.[45] Other studies found that pandemic unemployment came with an increased risk of developing anxiety and depression and lower levels of life satisfaction.[46] Suicidal thoughts and self-harm were positively associated with filing for unemployment during the pandemic.[47]

In its most extreme iteration, parental unemployment during COVID-19 was shown to be "a robust predictor" of both psychological maltreatment and physical abuse of children.[48] I spoke with Kim Taylor, a family social worker in Seattle, who noted a surge in mental health crises in young people, including a shocking rise in suicide risks among six-year-old children. "We'd never seen anything like it," she said. "These effects came on suddenly, but they're not going to just magically go away."

The pandemic provided the perfect opportunity to reevaluate how we treat unemployed people and their families. We squandered it. Our unemployment insurance (UI) system is a dilapidated patchwork of fifty-three separate policies that administers less aid than ever before. It's broken by design. The heart of the problem is the way it's financed—those who pay for it are not the ones who receive benefits. Therefore, there are powerful incentives to pay for as few claims as possible and to decrease the pool of available funds. And that's exactly what has happened in America over the past few decades. There's simply less and less money available, which encourages companies to avoid using it even more, a kind of policy death spiral. For the median state, the minimum weekly benefit is just $50; in six states, the maximum was capped at less than $300.[49] Furthermore, only a small fraction of unemployed workers receive these meager benefits to begin with. From 2010 to 2019, fewer than three in ten did.[50] If you live in a state where the eligibility requirements exclude you or the application process is purposefully designed to trap you in a bureaucratic jungle, then it doesn't matter how high the payout is because you'll never get it anyway. Arizona, for example, rejects 70 percent, and Tennessee 60 percent, of unemployment claims.

During the pandemic, many states simply made UI difficult to access in order to avoid paying. Florida, for example, spent more than $70 million designing a new unemployment insurance website and then limited the hours of the day people could access it. It only pays benefits to one in ten unemployed workers.[51] In 2020, the Trump administration declared that states could deny unemployment insurance claims to workers who refused to return to unsafe worksites. This decision, which was later overturned by the Biden administration in February 2021, was one of the signature ways that workers were given the ultimate ultimatum: work or starve.

Other places are different. Belgium and Denmark use the Ghent system: unemployment benefits are distributed through labor unions, not the government, and unions of course have large incentives to include as many workers as possible. The result is fewer layoffs during downturns. Germans use the *Kurzarbeit* system, a work-sharing arrangement. Under this system, the state subsidizes a portion of a company's labor costs, enabling firms to retain employees during downturns. Work-sharing policies allowed European countries to avoid layoffs and promote legitimate flexibility of hours to save jobs in 2008 and 2020, insulating workers from some of the crash-induced financial pains of the Great Recession and the coronavirus crisis. In May 2020, about one-third of workers in Austria, France, and the Netherlands, and one-fifth in Germany, Ireland, and Spain, were paid through work-sharing arrangements. The historian Adam Tooze, who wrote a book on the global economy during the pandemic, argues this was "the principal means through which the social crisis was contained" in Europe.[52]

In the US, twenty-seven states have work-sharing agreements, which were expanded under Obama after the Great Recession. The federal government increased funding for work-sharing programs in 2020, but implementing the programs proved difficult, and they were vastly underutilized. By late August 2020, thirty million people were receiving unemployment benefits of some kind, but only about 1 percent got them through a job-sharing program.[53]

Europe's "social dialogue" approach to unemployment defined the difference between US and European policies during the crisis. The European schemes are the result of a long-established governance framework that entails coordination among firms, workers, and the state to decide how to handle layoffs. This process is crucial. The European models aren't superior because they're necessarily more generous. But they allowed workers to remain connected to the labor market during the pandemic by avoiding mass firings. This makes the benefits system far simpler and cheaper to administer and allows workers an easier transition back to work.

That's not to say the American political response to the pandemic recession was in any way predictable. In fact, it represented a significant break from austerity, especially when compared to the bank bailouts of the Great Recession. In March 2020, rich and developing countries alike found vast sums of money to buttress civil society against a total collapse. The actions of central banks and the Federal Reserve coalesced with the advice of the International Monetary

Fund, and that was to do virtually the opposite of what neoliberal orthodoxy had promoted for decades. Deficits? None was too deep. Huge bailouts? Check. Stimulus? Increasing long-term unemployment insurance was better than promoting job growth. The idea of a self-regulating market was shelved. Economic reality, in a sense, had a Left bias, and these overwhelming global interventions confirmed the position of the Green New Dealers that the government can actually afford to pay for almost anything.

The first evidence of this was the Coronavirus Aid, Relief, and Employment Security Act, the CARES Act, passed in March 2020. The omnibus bill for extra funding allocations, tax cuts, and direct relief totaled $2.2 trillion. Its long-term value is even greater, as $454 billion in loans to big business could balloon to nearly ten times that amount once disbursed by the Federal Reserve. The Fed used the original money to insure against losses when lending out to big companies. Through mechanisms so convoluted the *New York Times* characterized them as the Fed's "magic money machine," it could actually lend out far more money than it received. Thus, around $454 billion became $4.54 trillion.[54]

The programs created by the CARES Act showed Americans a glimpse of what a more generous UI program might look like— even in red states. The Act's Pandemic Unemployment Assistance (PUA) program was designed to fill gaps in coverage by providing UI to workers who weren't otherwise eligible. One year after the pandemic started, almost eight million workers were receiving PUA benefits who would have otherwise been excluded from UI.[55] Plus the CARES Act included an additional $600-per-week unemployment check, a onetime $1,200 check signed by the president, and a $500-per-child check for families making under $99,000. That far outpaced the European welfare state's generosity. This was a groundbreaking influx of cash to a system where, typically, no state has UI benefits large enough to cover a worker's basic needs.[56] The PUA program showed us another system is possible.

The Act excluded tax filers without Social Security numbers, who are most likely to be immigrants or Dreamers. Others had their checks garnished by banks and other private debt collectors.[57] Still, after a year of stimulus payments, increased food stamps, and expanded unemployment benefits, poverty fell precipitously across the country.[58] Combined with about $150 billion for enhanced hospital care, the CARES Act also expanded the national stockpile of PPE and supported vaccine research development. Chuck Schumer called it a "Marshall Plan" for healthcare.[59]

Why did we get a decent bailout package from Trump? A perfect storm delivered us the goods. Trump, like most Republicans, doesn't care about deficits. Mitch McConnell knew that mass destitution would be bad for the GOP in the upcoming election. And Democrats thought the crisis warranted helping people.

◆

ALTHOUGH THE PROGRAM provided some lasting economic relief for those at the bottom when they needed it most, the wealthiest Americans also received quite a lot. The Senate seized the opportunity to quietly pass into law a suite of tax cuts for corporations and the rich, many of which were previously deemed too brazen even for Trump's 2017 tax law.[60] These cuts created tax exemptions for the super wealthy via big loopholes for corporate interest deductions and loss treatments, allowing large companies to use previous tax losses to get immediate refunds. Combined, these cuts are worth about $258 billion.[61]

The CARES Act also extended previous givebacks, such as the bizarre tax break that benefited people like Jack Knowlton, an owner of elite racehorses. Buried on page 4,911 of the legislation is an allowance for thoroughbred owners to reclassify their horses as "3-year property." This depreciates the value of their horses much more quickly than previously permitted, translating into a tax break that the industry had lobbied for years. Knowlton usually buys one horse per year, but in 2020 he bought four. "During these crazy times," he told me, "we need an incentive to buy horses. And this is a pretty nice write-off."

Nothing says 2020 like Mitch McConnell giving racehorse owners a tax break.

It wasn't easy to sell this kind of vanity-project giveback to millionaire horse owners in the midst of the deepest crisis in almost a century—even some Republican lawmakers objected.[62] But McConnell fought hard to reward one of the most identifiable industries in his state by claiming the legislation would trickle down to the little guys on the backstretch. That's the colloquial name for the mostly immigrant workers who live in dorms and work as groomers, walkers, and exercise riders. "Not a place you or I would wanna spend much time," as Knowlton told me.

These tax cuts for the wealthy were only a portion of the CARES Act's total benefits. The most glaring example of the ways the bailout programs benefited big business was through abuses of the Paycheck Protection Program (PPP). The largest section of the Act, at $669 billion, it provided forgivable loans to smallish businesses, helping to maintain workers' connection to the labor market. The PPP was launched to rescue mom-and-pop businesses, yet analysis by *Pro-Publica* shows that as many as 120 large corporations received extensive support through the program while their profits soared, and they did not repay their loans.[63] The first problem was that the eligibility requirements were vague enough that large, profitable companies could qualify for loans by using the address of a small and needy-looking shell company.[64] The second problem was that enforcement of loan repayment was so lax many companies simply refused to pay their loans back. For a government that polices "welfare cheats" as if they're a threat to national security, it's hard to ignore the obvious blind eye that was turned to wealthy companies unfairly taking a handout.

Even the oversight boards and inspectors general formed by the CARES Act lacked any sort of disciplinary power—they could only report abuses, a diluted mandate weakened even further by the fact that the law also temporarily exempted the Fed from the Freedom of

Information Act, allowing it to keep its minutes and meetings completely secret.[65] Their potential effectiveness was also hobbled by their
lack of independence. Two of the three oversight committees were immediately tampered with by Trump: one had three of its members,
including its head, removed; the other had its powers revoked to request information from government agencies and present reports to
Congress unsupervised.[66]

The third committee, the Congressional Oversight Commission,
was the only oversight body out of the president's reach because its
members were appointed by Congress.[67] Even that didn't guarantee
its success: McConnell and Nancy Pelosi—and later, Schumer and
Pelosi—never got around to appointing a chair, which Bharat Ra-
mamurti, one of the committee's two Democratic members, credited with creating "serious obstacles to performing robust oversight."[68]
To make matters worse, the other Democrat chosen by Pelosi, Rep.
Donna Shalala, not only lacked relevant legislative experience but also
owned stock in an extensive collection of companies seeking loans.
When she sold those stocks, ostensibly to avoid a conflict of interest,
she failed to disclose the sales, in violation of the STOCK Act, which
restricts insider trading by members of Congress. She also had previously served on the boards of both a for-profit healthcare company
accused of overbilling Medicare and a home builder embroiled in the
subprime mortgage crisis.[69]

Consequently, the federal government subsidized big business's
stock buybacks, dividends, and executive salaries, all while failing to
ensure that these same companies didn't fire their workers or force
them to work in unsafe conditions.

The CARES Act shenanigans seem easily assigned to the Trump
administration, but a closer look reveals that these provisions were
decidedly bipartisan and often designed by the architects of corporate
bailouts of the recent past.[70] Although, constitutionally, revenue measures must begin in the House of Representatives, where the Democrats had the majority, the opposition party instead chose to write
the CARES Act in the Republican-led Senate, where the Democrats

would not set the terms of discussion.[71] When it came time to vote, the Senate passed the bill 96 to 0, and the House passed it through a voice vote. Furthermore, when it came time to draft a follow-up law to address the shortcomings of the CARES Act, the Democrats once again deferred the responsibility of crafting the legislation to Republicans. Eventually, Pelosi designed the $3 billion Heroes Act, purportedly, as its name suggests, to support essential industries. Alas, it never got a vote in the Senate.

The situation improved somewhat once Trump left the White House. After weeks of bipartisan ratfucking, a compromise formation of centrists finally hashed out another plan, worth $900 billion. Biden's American Rescue Plan sent out another round of stimulus checks of up to $1,400, brought back reduced unemployment benefits of $300 per week through September 2021, and temporarily expanded the child tax credit.[72] It also protected unionized workers' pensions, provided aid to indigenous communities and Black farmers, funded childcare centers, and finally addressed the budget crises of states and municipalities.[73]

It included surprisingly progressive taxation policies that reduced corporate welfare. In Biden's plan, the lowest three income quintiles received the greatest share (22–23 percent) of the tax reduction. The top 10 percent of the income distribution only received 1.7 percent of the tax benefits, and the top 1 percent saw a tax increase in the bill.[74] Compare this to the American Recovery and Reinvestment Act of 2009. On the surface, it looked similar, with 20–23 percent of the income tax reduction going to each of the lowest three income quintiles and only 3.6 percent of the benefit going to the top 10 percent. Looking at changes to both individual income and corporate tax combined, however, paints a different picture: a quarter of the total tax reductions went to the top 10 percent of the income distribution, and of that, 15 percent went to the top 1 percent.[75]

Nonetheless, the CARES Act and the American Recovery Plan were peculiarly American forms of relief—"welfare without a welfare state," as historian Anton Jäger and sociologist Daniel Zamora put it. The Acts provided assistance without building up any kind of lasting programs or scaffolding for the future.[76] Even in Biden's plan, most of the good the legislation achieved boiled down to temporary cash transfers. The most ambitious part of his proposed legislation, a fifteen-dollar minimum wage, was quickly abandoned under the pretense of the disagreement of the Senate parliamentarian, an obscure unelected advisor whose ruling was nonbinding.[77] This was an enormous missed opportunity to raise the wages of 32 million Americans, most of whom were essential or frontline workers, and lift 3.7 million people (including 1.3 million children) out of poverty.[78] But this policy would do more than pad paychecks for a while. It would change the balance of bargaining power between workers and employers. As such, it was shelved not because it was too expensive but because it would cost elites workplace power.

Neither the Great Recession bailouts nor the CARES Act led to the long-term repair of America's unraveling safety net. Both involved serious giveaways to elites and didn't create the sort of structural change that would permanently alleviate poverty or alter the lives of essential workers for the better. Simply put, the cost of temporarily helping out average Americans during the pandemic was simultaneously helping a few billionaires launch into outer space, which was, sadly, not enough to keep them there.

Before the pandemic, there was one American worth $100 billion. By early 2021, there were nine. At the outset of the pandemic, the ten richest people had $695 billion—now they have more than $1.4 trillion. This gain alone during the pandemic would be enough to send out stimulus checks of $3,900 to every single person in the United States—for a family of four, that would be more than $15,000.[79] And yet these multibillionaires all pay a lower tax rate than the frontline workers who risked their lives in 2020.[80]

◆

KENIA, THE EVICTED mother of four we met at the outset of the chapter, eventually got a part-time job at Sweetgreen, an upscale eatery, but she missed the brief interlude of better pay. After managing to secure childcare during the health crisis, no easy feat, she still couldn't provide for her family and pay rent on her paltry wages behind the counter. Her job was a microcosm of the relationship between rich and poor during the crisis, and it bothered her. "I sold fifteen-dollar juices. That's like double my wage," she told me. "It didn't seem right."

At the heart of the servant economy is the dependence of the upper classes on their servants. During the pandemic, servant workers were forced to fetch, deliver, transport, acquire, and provide the goods and services everyone needed, which required they move around at higher rates to the detriment of their own safety.

Still, those at the bottom also rely on those at the top. Researchers led by Raj Chetty at the Harvard-based Opportunity Insights group found that income inequality has also meant inequality in consumption patterns. As the rich have amassed their fortunes, their spending has driven a greater percentage of the economy. And when they curtailed their spending during the pandemic, it rippled down to job losses for the servant class. We ended up with an odd dynamic in which small businesses and gig-style workers in the wealthiest neighborhoods were hit harder than those in less affluent ones because the rich cut back their spending more than everyone else. Likewise, low-wage workers who largely depended on serving wealthier clients lost their jobs at higher rates.[81]

The servant class in richer neighborhoods performs what economist David Autor refers to as "wealth work," jobs that cater to and service wealthier populations. Massage therapist jobs doubled in the past decade, and the number of personal chefs, those who cook and cater for one family, quintupled. We've added about half a million personal trainers, delivery workers on retainer, drivers, manicurists, dog walkers, maids, housekeepers, etc., since 2010, meaning that the growth rate of this sector outpaced both education and manufacturing. Workers in these fields earn low wages, and their incomes are tied to the fluctuating whims and tastes of the fortunate. Still, it's a growth industry, and this work is crucial to a segment of the population without a college degree.

As fortunes amassed at the top, Kenia, from the bottom, was struggling to get back on her feet and into a home. Even in "good times," evictions increase debts, reduce people's ability to work dependably, strain public services, trigger massive psychological and emotional stress, and create house-sized holes throughout local economies that will only be filled by federal subsidies. According to the Pew Research Center, in September 2020, about a third of those who had experienced household job loss or a pay cut during the pandemic had trouble making the rent or mortgage payments, as opposed to 6 percent who did not have such experiences.[82] The eviction wave of 2020 made it impossible for tens of thousands of people to maintain social distance or shelter in place, thrusting them into public life without access to adequate hygiene.

Research by Kathryn Leifheit at UCLA's Jonathan and Karin Fielding School of Public Health took advantage of the natural experiment in housing policy created by the pandemic to study the relationship between evictions and viral transmission. Twenty-seven states lifted pandemic-related eviction moratoriums from March to September 2020. She found that the increased evictions resulting from ending moratoriums were associated with a staggering 433,700 excess COVID-19 cases and 10,700 excess COVID-19 deaths across the country.[83] Evictions spread the virus.

Kenia was just one of many caught in a desperate situation. In the five states and twenty-seven cities for which Princeton's Eviction Lab has reliable data, in the first year of the pandemic, landlords executed an astounding 278,376 evictions.[84] And official numbers represent only a fraction of the millions of people who are kicked out of their homes each year.

We tend to view eviction as the outcome of poverty rather than a cause of it. But losing one's home, especially during a deadly health crisis, all but ensures the punishment of long-term economic and social hardship. In 2020, the eviction epidemic existed as a parallel horror alongside the coronavirus pandemic. A year later it was only thanks to direct action by the first-time congresswoman Cori Bush, who forced Biden's hand, that the eviction moratorium was nearly extended an extra two months.[85] By one estimate, the extension would have saved or at least delayed 4.7 million evictions in areas where the delta variant was spreading rapidly.[86] Yet just three weeks later, in late 2021, conservative Supreme Court justices ruled against the sweeping moratorium. At that time, census data showed that approximately eight million families were behind on rent and faced the renewed possibility of losing their homes.[87]

In the end, Kenia was not saved by one of her rich patrons, the CARES Act, an eviction moratorium, or even the last-minute heroics of Cori Bush. One of her coworkers, who saw Kenia's family sleeping in their car, started a GoFundMe page to support them. The modest goal of $800 quickly attracted almost $75,000 in donations. It was enough for her to rent a home for her family and pay for childcare so she could keep working. Finally, she caught a break. For the vast majority of low-wage workers, though, luck was in short supply.

Joblessness was one outcome for many low-wage Americans, especially for those in the service sector. They were the dispossessed, their livelihood gone in an instant, sometimes taking their home, healthcare, and future with it. Given how much time has passed, it may be hard to appreciate the anguish and fear that accompanied sudden job loss in March and April of 2020, a time of resounding uncertainty. "It feels like it didn't really happen," said Kenia when I checked back in with her a year later. "Mostly I try to black it out...it was so scary. But at night when I try to sleep, I can't stop thinking about those days in the car, all of us. A miracle must have kept us alive."

The pandemic recession was unique, and unemployment was hardly the only problem facing workers. Not all of the low-wage service sector found themselves suddenly unemployed. They also made up a substantial portion of the new essential workforce. Overall, out of the six broad industries that comprise the bulk of frontline workers, five are within the service sector. And a significant percentage in each of these industries—grocery, convenience, and drugstore workers; building-cleaning-services workers; healthcare workers; childcare and social services workers; and trucking, warehouse, and postal service workers—make less than 200 percent of the poverty line, a common measure of poor earnings.[88]

The next chapter examines the trials of essential workers. No recent time has engendered such a vibrant public debate about working conditions as developed during 2020 and 2021. The ways essential workers performed their jobs, the risks and hazards they faced, their inadequate compensation and legal protection, and their vulnerable economic status were all top news stories. From a labor scholar's perspective, however, these well-trod topics look quite different. In particular, what was missing from the national news stories was what essential workers, as a disjointed and discontinuous whole, could show us about classed society under capitalism. Essential workers represented something greater than the sum of their parts, and in this next chapter, I examine some of the ways they struggled to remake the American working class.

CHAPTER 2

AWAKENINGS

"WALMART KILLED MY MOTHER," ELAINE ECKLUND TOLD ME. "I don't know how else to put it."

Yok Yen Lee was a familiar face to Walmart shoppers in Quincy, Massachusetts. She'd been a greeter there for over a decade. Ecklund said her mom, a Chinese immigrant, enjoyed working hard to make others feel happy. "It wasn't just nurses and doctors," Ecklund said. "Heroes come in all shapes and sizes."

Lee had always been healthy, with no underlying conditions, and she had a lot to live for. She'd been a regular at her gym's Zumba classes and was active enough to keep up with her two young grandchildren. Out of an abundance of caution, Lee used up her allotted sick days in March 2020, when the virus was peaking in Quincy. In mid-April, when she felt the creeping onset of COVID-19 symptoms, she had to request to use her small number of accumulated vacation days to get time off. She went to work while her leave request was pending, greeting every person who entered the store, likely spreading the virus to shoppers and among her coworkers.

When she didn't show up at work or return her daughter's phone calls one day, her family became worried. Her landlord cut the lock to her apartment door and found her on the floor, unresponsive. She was rushed to the hospital and, after a week on a ventilator, she died. She was sixty-nine.

"I never got to say goodbye because she was unconscious," Elaine told me. "She died alone. She wasn't the only one."

In nearby Lynn, another Walmart employee also died of COVID-19, and eighty-one workers tested positive at an outbreak at the Worcester store. By late April 2020, twenty-one Walmart workers across the country had died of COVID-19, and two thousand others had tested positive.[1]

Elaine understood her mom's commitment to service and her community. She said that Lee considered herself "one of the lucky ones" because she hadn't lost her job when the pandemic hit. Elaine saw it differently. She thought her mother shouldn't have been working at all and definitely not while sick. "She wanted to use her vacation days to spend time with us, so she saved them," Elaine told me. "She didn't want to waste them on herself. She should not have been forced to make that choice—of course I don't blame her, I blame the store."

In the days following Lee's death, the store closed amid accusations from Quincy's health commissioner, Ruth Jones, that the company wasn't complying with new COVID-19 guidelines. "We have had consistent problems with Walmart," wrote Jones in a letter to the Massachusetts Attorney General's office. "They have a cluster of COVID-19 cases among employees and have not been cooperative in giving us contact information or in following proper quarantine and isolation guidelines."[2]

Grocery stores' "essential" status exempted them from being required to disclose employee coronavirus cases to local health departments. But Walmart is no ordinary grocery store: it's the largest employer in the world. Any system in which an economy of that size skirts public health mandates is flirting with disaster. Walmart settled a workers' compensation lawsuit with Elaine after her mother's death. Elaine insisted in the settlement agreement that Walmart perform some public acknowledgment of Lee's death.

"They sent me a little plant," Elaine said, "a fuckin' succulent."

By April 2020, there were about fifty million people, a third of the US labor force, who, like Lee, were essential workers tasked with working through the pandemic. Officially the "essential" designation went to businesses, institutions, and government agencies that are critical to public health, safety, economic stability, and national security. Those include government services, defense, healthcare, waste and water management, energy and manufacturing, transportation, information, and financial services, among others.

My survey showed that early in the pandemic, essential workers reported being very concerned about infection risk at work. Black and Latino workers reported more concern than white workers because they were more likely to work in risky roles. On surveys collected by other scholars, essential workers reported they often went to work sick because they balanced their health against their potential loss of earnings or fear from management reprisal. A study conducted by Columbia University scholars in June 2020 found that the median essential worker received zero compensating hazard pay.[3]

We don't know—and likely never will—how many of these workers died after having contracted COVID-19 at work. We do know that they were disproportionately exposed to the risks and hazards of pandemic life at rates far exceeding the rest of the American population. Friedrich Engels, Marx's lifelong collaborator, coined the term "social murder" to refer to a situation in which the ruling class places workers "in such a position that they inevitably meet an early and an unnatural death."[4] The pandemic was just such a case.

Uniquely positioned between a vulnerable public and a ruthless ruling class, essential workers were celebrated for their contributions to keeping the country running, even as they faced extraordinary workplace risks, hazards, and exploitation. Over time, this shared experience led essential workers to see themselves as a group, and they developed what social scientists often call "class consciousness": an awareness of one's class position relative to others in the social hierarchy, and a set of beliefs that help shape class-based organization. Class consciousness is not a simple recognition of fact but the outcome of a process, usually set in motion by a political struggle. During the pandemic, the cognitive dissonance between essential workers' popular designation as heroes and their actual treatment as sacrificial servants inspired collective action and a distinct awareness of their class interests.

At the same time, differences among essential workers strained unity on the front lines. The classic sociological dividing lines of race, gender, and immigration status were in some sense less significant barriers than were other pandemic-specific obstacles: mass unemployment, the ability to telecommute, occupation, political differences and voting behavior, and popular recognition of one's essential status. Across the country, whether essential workers cohered as a group or were rent asunder depended on their ability to overcome the deep barriers that divided them from each other. The process of making and unmaking the frontline class is perhaps the main way we can grasp the relationship between labor and capital during the pandemic.

The workplace struggles that emerged to protect workers like Yok Yen Lee, whom I first heard of through a labor rights organization in Massachusetts, were too late for her. Lee's story nonetheless helped shine a light on pandemic business practices that were all too common. And it inspired some of the resistance that defined the frontline class into the pandemic's future.

"They called my mom a hero but let her die for the company," Elaine said. "That's the definition of an essential worker to me—you talk nice about them but treat them like garbage."

✦

WILLINGLY OR NOT—and that distinction mattered a great deal throughout the pandemic—essential workers went to their jobs when most other people were either unemployed or teleworking from home. The early days of the pandemic were replete with fulsome pronouncements of a great pathogenetic equalizer. "We're all in this together," declared Trump on March 2, 2020, which quickly became a popular lens through which to view the pandemic. Data show otherwise.

Change in Workplace Movement During Covid–19

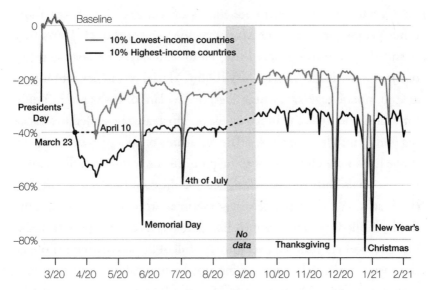

People in low-income areas reduced their work-related travel less than those in high-income areas. SOURCE: Author's analysis of Google Community Mobility Reports and American Community Survey estimates (2014–2019)

Income and occupation were the greatest determinants of our ability to uphold social distancing practices. Not only were we not "in this together," but one group was surviving explicitly because another group was in harm's way.

I collected aggregated location data from Google, which tracks millions of mobile devices as they travel with people to and from work each day. By early March, most of the country was commuting less than they did before the crisis. The graph above shows that those in the highest-income areas were staying home the most, especially during the workweek. Moreover, the rich had a head start on their lockdown period. By March 23, groups in higher-income areas were moving about 40 percent less, but it wasn't until April 10, two and a half weeks later, that those in poorer places caught up. This trend continued for the whole year, far outliving the heart of the lockdown period.

"It's hard to describe the loneliness of working then, when most other people weren't," said Mariel Sander. "Even though I was surrounded by so many people I still felt lonely. Maybe because so many of them were dead." When COVID hit, Mariel was in her senior year at Columbia University, where she'd had a plan to, as she put it, "study for exams and do some binge drinking." Instead, she ended up stacking bodies into freezer trucks. The doldrums of college quarantine life drove her to search for ways to help out in the real world. She took a job in a makeshift morgue designed for thirteen bodies that, during the first wave of the pandemic, sometimes warehoused over a hundred, all piled up cattywampus like garbage. With no space to walk, morgue workers climbed over gurneys full of bodies to access those in the back, sometimes encountering ripped and leaking body bags and amputated limbs. During one of Mariel's shifts, she and her coworkers unzipped a body bag delivered to their basement workstation and realized it was her coworker's uncle. "That was one of those moments when it felt like things kept getting worse, and you just didn't know when it would stop," Mariel said.

Together, Mariel and his niece moved the man's body to a freezer truck in the parking lot. Because the basement was at capacity, the vast majority of bodies were stored in trucks on shelves. The trucks were long and so dark that Mariel carried a lantern with her. "I was literally the light at the end of the tunnel," she told me. That night, April 27, Mariel made an entry in her pandemic diary that she shared with me: "I can't remember the last time I touched someone who was living."

◆

THE LOCKDOWN PHASE of the pandemic, which varied widely according to multiple factors—region, industry, demographics, political orientation, social class—lasted roughly from early March to early June 2020. In New York City, for example, there was a dramatic reduction in movement of the city's working population.

Travel for Work in New York City, February 2020

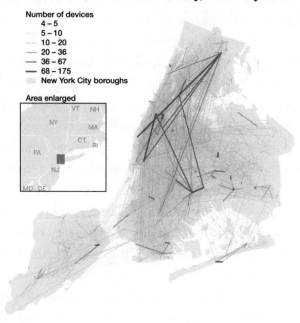

Number of devices
4 – 5
5 – 10
10 – 20
20 – 36
36 – 67
68 – 175
New York City boroughs

Area enlarged

Travel for Work in New York City, April 2020

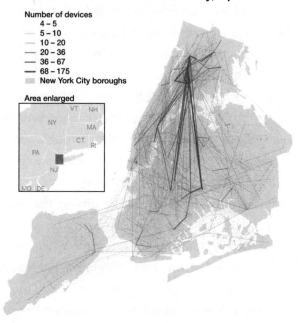

Number of devices
4 – 5
5 – 10
10 – 20
20 – 36
36 – 67
68 – 175
New York City boroughs

Area enlarged

SOURCE: Author's analysis of mobile device location data from SafeGraph, Neighborhood Patterns

The maps above were created using cell phone geolocation data of work-related travel throughout New York City's five boroughs. They show a 66 percent reduction in overall movement from the first map, in February 2020, to the map of April 2020. The lines in February depict an average month of work-related travel; the April map shows the travel patterns of what are mostly essential workers. Generally speaking, different cities' and regions' maps look different based on their respective economies—those with larger populations who could work from home tended to reduce their travel profile more. However, across the world, movement during the pandemic's lockdown phase was directly related to occupation and social class more than any other factors. Those at the bottom of the hierarchy were more likely to hold jobs that increased their exposure to the virus because they had no ability to telecommute.

A May 2020 study of a large grocery store in the Boston area found that employees with customer-facing jobs were about five times more likely to have coronavirus antibodies than workers in other roles.[5] Additional studies have attributed high rates of COVID-19 infection to workplace exposures in agriculture and construction.[6] In a 2020 survey of service workers, 41 percent responded that they were not able to consistently maintain physical distance from others on the job.[7] Researchers at the Harvard Kennedy School collected so much data documenting COVID-19 anxiety among service workers that, to dramatize the magnitude of the problem, they tweeted out a different survey respondent quote every minute for five days straight.[8]

The high dispersion factor of the coronavirus was an early indicator that workplace transmission could be driving the pandemic. At the start of the pandemic, epidemiologists introduced the public to the reproduction, or R, number, which represents the average number of people an infected person goes on to infect. An R value greater than one means a disease is spreading. In April 2020, the R value of COVID-19 in the US was about three, meaning every infected person infected, on average, three more. Within just three permutations, a single individual would be responsible for twenty-seven infections.

Naturally then, it seemed we should take the appropriate steps to re-duce R as far as possible, by social distancing, wearing face coverings, eliminating unnecessary travel, and so on.

Soon scientists argued that knowing the average rate of spread offers only a limited understanding of the real dynamism of the vi-rus. For multiple reasons, some infected people infect many others, whereas some infect none. Scientists represent this variation in spread using the letter K, the so-called dispersion factor. It was believed, for instance, that about 80 percent of COVID-19-positive people did not infect someone else, which means the remaining 20 percent of COVID-19 cases spread the disease far and wide somehow.

Almost all viral outbreaks rely on super-spreader situations, but COVID-19 appeared to be especially dependent on such events to get off the ground. The 1918 influenza had a K value of about 1, whereas SARS, MERS, and this novel coronavirus all had a low K value, about 0.1, indicating that their spread required major events. When there are outbreaks of a virus despite its low risk of random transmission and bans on large public gatherings, evidence shows worksites are the likely super-spreaders.

One report in mid-2020 that studied outbreaks in Utah found that of the 277 reported COVID-19 outbreaks from March 6 to June 5, 2020, 210 (76 percent) occurred in workplaces.[9] In Califor-nia, working-age adults experienced a 22 percent increase in mortal-ity in 2020 compared to previous years. If they worked in food and agriculture, though, that number was 39 percent, or 28 percent if they worked in transportation.[10]

Epidemiologists show that workplace exposure offers a compelling explanation for the racial inequality that characterized the pandemic.[11] Black, Latino, and indigenous people were not only more likely to die of the coronavirus than white people, but they were also more likely to be exposed and infected in the first place.[12] People of color make up a large share of essential workers in high-risk industries and were more often linked to workplace transmission than white employees.[13] California Latinos, for example, had excess mortality of 36 percent in 2020, and that number jumped to 59 percent if they worked the fields harvesting or growing food, where social distancing rules were hardly observed.[14] Black Americans are overrepresented in jobs that put workers in close contact with others and make social distancing practices difficult; they make up 30 percent of bus drivers and nearly 20 percent of food service workers, janitors, cashiers, and stockers, despite being only 12 percent of the national population.[15]

Working conditions were equally dangerous in meatpacking, where almost half of the workers are Latino and one-quarter are Black.[16] Some research suggests that 8 percent of all COVID-19 infections and 4 percent of all COVID-19 deaths in the United States may have originated in meatpacking plants.[17] A CDC report on commercial meat production found that although only 61 percent of the overall worker population were people of color, they comprised 87 percent of coronavirus cases in April–May 2020. The majority of cases, 56 percent, involved Hispanic workers, 19 percent involved Black workers, and 13 percent involved white workers, who made up 39 percent of the overall workforce but are typically employed in managerial positions that allow greater degrees of social distancing.[18] In the summer of 2020, all of the known COVID-19 meatpacking-related deaths were among African American, Latino, and immigrant workers.

Simply put, workers of color are overrepresented as essential workers and were overexposed to the virus. They're also more likely than white workers to live in households with many family members, in multigenerational households, and in families that require childcare, increasing the exposure risks of more people.[19]

Most of the national strategy to curb COVID-19 transmission centered on reducing social gatherings, where the most prolific spreading was thought to occur. Social gatherings do play an important role, particularly gatherings where viral-load buildup increases the probability of infection. So bans on social gatherings, such as holiday and birthday parties, were among the most effective ways to limit coronavirus transmission.[20] Yet, as the epidemiologist Justin Feldman notes, whites demonstrated they were the most likely to attend social gatherings, but they were among the least likely to contract the coronavirus.[21]

Boisterous invocations to social distancing bled easily into Facebook filters and Twitter hashtags like #staythefuckhome, messages that were amplified by dishonest political elites. In a November 2020 press conference, then governor of New York Andrew Cuomo placed the blame for a coronavirus surge on individual failings.[22] "If you're socially distant, and you wore a mask, and you were smart, none of this would be a problem. It's all self-imposed," he said, building toward his Exhibit A: "If you didn't eat the cheesecake, you wouldn't have a weight problem."

Cuomo followed this up with an ad campaign scolding New Yorkers for hosting indoor gatherings, claiming that over 70 percent of coronavirus transmission could be attributed to "living room spread."[23] Likewise, South Dakota's Republican governor Kristi Noem blamed the outbreak within meatpacking plants on workers' dense living quarters.

"Workers definitely transmit the virus to their relatives and roommates at home," Eric Reeder, president of United Food and Commercial Workers (UFCW) Local 293 in Nebraska, told me. "But how do you think the virus got there in the first place?"

While there were good reasons to pause our social lives, doing so involved individual life choices, a microcultural shift. But essential workers can't #staythefuckhome. They have to #gothefucktowork. Allowing them freedom to do otherwise, even to a degree, would require a power shift away from employers and toward workers. Halting social spread is cheap, and all the onus is put on individuals. Large interventions in the way we work and transformations of our economic hierarchies are costly changes that those in power simply can't "afford."

The concept of essentiality calls to mind people who are indispensable to the safety, security, and well-being of the country. Why is it essential that someone says "Welcome to Walmart" every time a patron enters the store during a global health crisis? The answer is because Walmart, and in this case the government of Massachusetts, prioritized the business culture of the world's largest boss over the health of workers and citizens. It was exactly this cognitive dissonance—of being both essential and sacrificial, simultaneously heroic and disposable—that was at the heart of the problem of defining what an essential worker really is.

✦

SCHOLAR BENEDICT ANDERSON argued that nations form as "imagined communities." The members of a particular region might not know each other or ever meet, yet "in the minds of each lives the image of their communion."[24] Imagined communities don't simply form automatically but emerge through shared norms, language, values, cultural codes, and common enemies. A similar dynamic happened among essential workers during the pandemic. Through a knowledge of shared conditions and treatment, an essential worker lingua franca emerged that allowed them to imagine themselves as part of a coherent whole. Occupational hierarchies, economic status, and educational attainment all mattered but, for a brief moment, seemed subordinate to a unique experience only they lived. Sociologist Pierre Bourdieu argued that what he called the "labor of categorization" is a "forgotten dimension of the class struggle." Social classes aren't mere reflections of socioeconomic status. Instead, the struggle to decide who is "in" and who is "out," in effect, is an important aspect of how classes form.

At times, pandemic essential workers pursued the formation of an imagined community of frontline laborers by organizing across professional and occupational lines. Early on, proximity to risk was the minimum price of entry into the class of real frontline workers, as well as the basis for excluding those who didn't share that proximity. Those who worked from home enjoyed a much lower risk of catching COVID and were typically in white-collar industries that might have marked them as members of a different class anyway.

Remote work has been a response to previous disasters. There were telework spikes following anthrax attacks in the wake of 9/11 and after the devastation of Hurricane Katrina. Testifying before a 2004 House committee hearing assessing the benefits of telework "in the post-9/11 world," Congressman Tom Davis stated, "We now realize that telework needs to be an essential component of any continuity of operations plan. Something we once considered advantageous and beneficial has evolved into a cornerstone of emergency preparedness."[25]

So it could be easy to position teleworkers as national heroes too. After all, staying out of harm's way is good for everyone and enhances the safety of those who must travel. But there wasn't that sense of sacrifice among the pandemic work-from-home crowd, who took the transformation mostly in stride. A majority said they already had the technology required to work remotely, had an easy time finding a dedicated home-based workstation, and could meet deadlines and stay productive with few interruptions. About half (49 percent) of new teleworkers reported greater flexibility in how they put in their hours, while just over one-third said telework made juggling work with family responsibilities easier. They didn't even miss their coworkers: 65 percent said virtual communication tools were "a good substitute" for in-person interaction with colleagues. Zoom fatigue, perhaps, was overblown.[26] There was indeed an expanded workplace surveillance state, but most people never knew their bosses were watching.[27] More than half of those with jobs that can be done remotely say they'd like to continue working this way.[28] (The situation was less sanguine for those who had young children home from school during the pandemic. Most working parents claimed getting work done was hard, compared with workers without children.)[29]

Occupation dictated the ability to work from home: only about 4 percent of frontline workers have the option to telecommute, and the vast majority of those are highly paid medical professionals. For this reason, frontline workers often forged an identity that was explicitly predicated on *not* being able to work from home. The "unfreedom," the inability to choose, the requirement to leave the home, made the difference.

Yet there were exceptions. School teachers, who mostly taught remotely in 2020, were often included as true members of the essential working class because their labor was considered socially indispensable and their jobs were crucial to allowing others the ability to work.

At other times, certain kinds of in-person workers were excluded. During my interviews I encountered widespread discrimination against fast-food workers by many other low-wage frontline workers, a reflection of long-standing falsehoods about the intelligence, work ethic, and employability of that labor pool. Even in the same workplace, like a hospital, it was common for workers to construct a hierarchy of essentiality, from ER nurses at one end to specialized technicians who didn't interact with as many patients at the other.

Most workers I met and interviewed derived a sense of pride from being a frontline worker. They saw how public sentiment favored them, probably for the first time, and got a renewed sense of satisfaction and purpose from their roles. Many remarked on the ways they were treated with greater levels of respect on the job yet regretted that it took a global pandemic for customers and policymakers and the general public to see service workers as deserving of appreciation. Early in the pandemic, this positive change in the public's perception of them led many essential workers to feel a stronger sense of solidarity and community with each other.

In March 2020, Bailey Delaplaine was relieved to learn that her job as a welder would be declared a nonessential service. Her work environment was not conducive to social distancing, and the $600 weekly unemployment benefits would be more lucrative than her welding wage. Less than a week later, however, she was back at work. Her employer had lobbied to be considered an essential business, making her ineligible for unemployment benefits, and her company didn't offer hazard pay. She knew of welders in neighboring counties who had been officially designated nonessential and were able to safely shelter in place.

She had no idea on what basis her employer was able to stay open, but she wasn't happy about it. Bailey turned her indignation into action and formed a Facebook group called Give Essential Workers Essential Pay, which had more than ten thousand members at its peak. I met others through her page with stories of their lives as essential workers, as it became an important online meeting place for workers to discuss the state of their jobs and for researchers and journalists to find interview subjects. Bailey's page attracted retail, grocery, and food service workers, the labor pool we only seem to notice when there's a glitch in the service they provide.

The pandemic, however, revealed the significance of a layer of society that most people take for granted. In no sector was this more apparent than healthcare, where intense media brought healthcare workers an unprecedented amount of attention. Nurses stole the show. In May 2020, a painting appeared at Southampton General Hospital in England depicting a young boy in dungaree overalls playing next to a garbage can. Amid discarded Batman and Spider-Man action figures he holds his new toy, Supernurse, replete with a medical mask and nurse's apron and wearing a cape, which is flowing in the wind, one arm outstretched in a Superman pose—Supernurse can fly. The painting is part Rockwellian wholesomeness, part cheesy Hallmark sentimentality. It is entirely in black and white except for a red cross across Supernurse's apron and was accompanied by a note from the artist: "Thanks for all you're doing. I hope this brightens the place up a bit, even if it's only black and white."[30]

The artwork is by Banksy, the notorious guerilla graffiti artist whose true identity remains a mystery, and who is known for his biting social criticism, satire, and off-color humor. The comparatively earnest depiction of a young boy and his toy drew praise from healthcare workers and government officials.

Oddly prescient, before the pandemic, the World Health Assembly designated 2020 the International Year of the Nurse and Midwife to honor the two hundredth anniversary of the birth of Florence Nightingale, the patron saint of professional nursing. Her innovations in sanitation, bedside manner, epidemiology, and statistical data collection transformed the role of the nurse from that of untrained "angel of mercy" into professional caregiver.

Dubbed "the lady with the lamp" for her nightly solo walks throughout the hospital she tended in Scutari, Turkey, during the Crimean

War, Nightingale left behind an ambivalent legacy that can bear heavily on those who have followed in her steps. She established herself as a competent administrator but also as a selfless caretaker. "I did not think of going to give myself," she wrote, "but for the sake of common humanity." Though she is credited with developing the craft of professional nursing, she also preached a gospel of devotion and self-sacrifice, a burden only a pure hero can bear. This established affinity between selflessness and caregiving, the clay with which heroes are molded, produces a tension for healthcare workers, who are not only tasked with keeping people alive but with protecting themselves and upholding professional norms.

This tension, embodied in the discipline of nursing, was also felt widely among all kinds of essential workers during the pandemic, including those who received less media attention for their sacrifices. "If we didn't clean this hospital, you'd have a bug in here that no nurse or doctor could ever cure," said Sabrina Hopps, housekeeper at a hospital in Washington, DC. Sabrina was at a meeting in April 2020 when a supervisor announced the room number of the first COVID-19 patient at her hospital. She instantly recognized it as one she had just cleaned. Without being asked, she immediately returned to the room to clean it again with different germicides that at the time were thought to be more effective at containing the coronavirus. "I knew it had to be done before somebody else gets sick from being in that room," she told me.

Sabrina admitted to feeling "left out" when nurses and doctors began getting accolades for their heroics while the dietary, maintenance, and housekeeping staff were rarely mentioned. "We're heroes too, you know."

Not everyone felt that same pride. Often, it was the resentment of being *forced* to work in such hazardous conditions for low wages that provided the impetus for solidarity among essential workers. Others appreciated the honorific of being called essential, but their resentment toward their working conditions gave them a more ambivalent view of what "essential" actually meant in practice. "Guinea pigs." "Lab rats." "Crash test dummies." "Human shields." "Sacrificial lambs." These are also how many essential workers described their status in the social hierarchy. These metaphors of disposability reflect the deep bitterness and indignation workers experienced.

"I'm not proud to be working here," said Miguel, a janitor at a hospital in Brooklyn. "I hope my son can get a better job than me.... Those people clapping outside? They're not doing it for us. They're doing it because they're happy they're not in here too. They know how lucky they are. And when I hear it, it makes me sick."

Miguel had been bedridden with COVID-19 in April 2020 but refused to check in to a hospital; he felt safer at home. But he was called back to work even before he'd fully recuperated. "I really didn't want to go," he said. "You see? But I'm a 'hero.'"

Across the country, healthcare workers shared Miguel's feeling. They knew what it was like to be face-to-face with a person with a contagious and deadly airborne illness—a hundred times a night, for months on end, without adequate protective gear. I interviewed doctors like Ilya Saltykov, who went from intubating patients to being intubated himself after having contracted COVID-19, wondering if he might die in the same ER bed as his patients just days before. "We didn't sign up for this," Ilya told me. "We're trained, but not for this. There's no training for this."

◆

ULTIMATELY, IT WAS this ambiguous status as heroes and victims that inspired essential workers' indignation. Typically, we think of protest slogans as conveying clear opinions. For many, though, the very moniker "essential" contains an unresolvable contradiction. It was this dialectical quality of the term that inspired protest signs and strike banners:

Don't Call Me a Hero— I'm Being Martyred Against My Will.
We're Essential, Not Sacrificial.
Protect the Frontline Not the Bottom Line.
We Will Not Be Your Body Bags.

The transformation of healthcare workers into hagiographic heroes, however well intentioned, generated powerful resentment. The discourse normalized workers' exposure to risk, substandard conditions, low pay, and even death. Policymakers and legislators cynically celebrated frontline workers as heroes enduring dangerous workplace conditions for the public's benefit while they dodged their responsibility to improve workplaces and workers' lives.

In mid-March, Cuomo tweeted, "Let's show our gratitude to our everyday heroes. I'll start. Thank you to every: Healthcare worker, Grocer, Pharmacist, Police officer, Firefighter, Public transit worker, Childcare worker." Minutes later, #presidentcuomo began trending and a pandemic heartthrob was born, replete with a coterie of "Cuomosexual" sycophants.[31]

All of this was happening at the exact time he was planning cuts to Medicaid, the public health program that insures roughly a third of New Yorkers. The cuts would mean billions of dollars in reductions to hospitals just when they needed more money than ever. They would also mean forgoing a $6.7 billion federal relief package because federal law forbids states receiving national money if they undermine their own Medicaid system. Cuomo also granted hospital executives immunity to spend public subsidies how they saw fit, and he purposefully hid the number of COVID-19 nursing home deaths in his state, trying to minimize the severity of the crisis. (When these revelations became widely known later in 2021, #fuckcuomo started trending.)

Not to be outdone, the Department of Defense chose to salute "healthcare heroes" via Operation America Strong, a fighter-jet flyover display across cities impacted by the virus. Jennifer Berger, a nurse in Baltimore, said she felt the air shake as the Thunderbirds and Blue Angels came roaring near her hospital on May 2, 2020, the day Maryland governor Larry Hogan declared as Healthcare Heroes Day. "We definitely take all the support we can get," she said. "Even though I can think of a million better ways to spend money right now." Each F-16 Fighting Falcon jet costs about $20 million to manufacture, the flyovers cost about $60,000 per hour, and the show went on over dozens of cities. Higher pay, more PPE, and shorter hours would've been better, not to mention less noisy, recognition.

We've been here before. In the two decades since 9/11, thousands of cleanup workers and first responders to the tragedy have died of long-term acute respiratory illnesses. By calling them heroes or martyrs, we obscure why exactly they've died. They weren't killed in battle by an external enemy. They responded to the disaster with inadequate PPE and training, and lacking full knowledge of the risks they were exposed to. Purposefully or not, our government put them in harm's way; their deaths were matters of occupational health and safety, not war and peace.

They were also of hardly any concern to the federal government. The bravery of first responders is often invoked to commemorate the 9/11 anniversary, but it took nearly nineteen years—and the not-so-subtle congressional testimony of comedian Jon Stewart—to pass legislation that would pay for their healthcare. "Your indifference cost these men and women their most valuable commodity: time," Stewart said. "This hearing should be flipped. These men and women should be up on that stage and Congress should be down here answering their questions as to why this is so damn hard and takes so damn long." When Trump finally signed the bill in August 2020, after Senator Rand Paul tried to block it, Stewart quipped, "I think we can all agree I'm the real hero."

Strangely, the aesthetics of war are nonetheless an apt way to recognize the sacrifices made by frontline workers. America's battle troops have faced similar shortages of protective gear, such as body armor or bulletproof vests. Witness then defense secretary Donald Rumsfeld in 2004, trying to rationalize what US troops in Iraq pointed to as aging and insufficient equipment, "hillbilly armor" in their words. Many soldiers have returned from the "call of duty" to face inadequate healthcare systems ill-equipped to handle their physical disabilities and emotional trauma. It's unsurprising that a country that leaves its military recruits vulnerable both on and off the battlefield would similarly ignore the needs of those working amid a deadly virus, enlisted as they were through a de facto economic draft.

Did all of this mistreatment and strange affirmation by the public, recognizable in some form or another to so many different essential workers from different industries, lead to a common self-conception? Answering this question means understanding the difference between a class "in itself" and a class "for itself," which in turn helps us see the pandemic as a unique experiment in what scholars call "class formation."

A class in itself is just a group of workers who share certain objective qualities, like occupation, income, wealth, etc. You can see a class in itself by dividing American society into income brackets and assigning each level a name. The richest brackets might be the "ruling class," those at the bottom "the poor." A class for itself is different. This suggests an active process whereby workers develop a shared set of values and beliefs about their own class position relative to that of others. Crucially, a class for itself might actually span workers across the income distribution if they have similar grievances, goals, or aspirations. In other words, class isn't a static thing—it happens. It might be helpful to think of this distinction as between "the masses," preexisting groups of workers, and "the classes," workers who have recognized a common identity and are prepared to take action against or in solidarity with another class.

"There was an awakening," Tre Kwon, a nurse at Mount Sinai, told me. "Sometimes it just takes a spark. People realized that all of us out there working shared something, a common experience. It was uneven and imperfect, but it happened."

The pandemic provided the spark, spurring frontline workers to understand themselves as a group with common interests. Forged in the crucible of the crisis, a class "for itself" emerged in fits and starts. Newly radicalized, essential workers across the nation launched protests for better working conditions, with and without the support of unions. As the pandemic went on, essential workers increasingly joined forces. Teachers spoke up for food workers, grocery clerks for delivery drivers, meatpacking workers for farmers, doctors for nurses, and nurses for students.

During an April 2020 rally by teachers to oppose reopening public schools, Jillian Primiano, an ER nurse from Wyckoff Heights Medical Center in Brooklyn, called attention to the way nurses understood the plight of teachers being forced back into dangerous classrooms. "As nurses, we know you will be short on supplies and staff as billionaires continue to not pay taxes, throwing us small donations here and there and patting themselves on the back," Primiano told the crowd. "We know that you will bear the brunt of idealistic policies that only look good on paper....They're gonna call you heroes while they don't give you what you need to do your job."

Primiano's exasperation with heroizing essential workers was reflected across many interviews I conducted with workers in different industries.

"Trader Joe's saved my life," said one grocery store worker I spoke to. "But last year I felt it might kill me." After a decade as a sometimes-homeless IV drug user, she landed a job at the grocery chain, which she credits with helping her move on from the addiction cycle and putting a roof over her head. Two decades later the company is still providing for her, including throughout the pandemic, when she became accustomed to the not-all-heroes-wear-scrubs sentiments of genuine solidarity and felt they were a welcome, albeit long-overdue, acknowledgment of the risks grocery workers face. True as it was, it was also something else—"a pernicious label perpetuated by those who wish to gain something—money, goods, a clean conscience—from my jeopardization," she wrote at the time. When I spoke with her, she reflected on her store manager leading employees in a thunderous self-congratulatory stockroom pep rally at a time when workers were discouraged from wearing masks, gloves, or face shields for fear they might scare customers away.

"The hero cult allows us to be put in harm's way," she told me. "It's not that it's not true, it's that it assuages the guilt of society for not doing enough to protect us."

Fighting deadly pathogens isn't typically part of grocery store work, and stores would attract considerably fewer applications if it were listed as a skills requirement. Though nurses and doctors didn't "sign up for this" either, frontline occupations had vastly different levels of preparation for the pandemic. The closure of restaurants drove unprecedented numbers of people to panic shop at crowded stores. By late April 2020, virus outbreaks at Whole Foods Market, Costco Wholesale, Trader Joe's, and other grocery retail chains across the country had resulted in almost 100,000 infections and 178 deaths among workers.[32]

A by-product of this systemic injustice, the grocery store worker felt, was that it placed different groups of workers into a new category, what she called "the behind-the-scenes cogs-and-wheels people." She added: "We're the people just keeping everything running, working, and you do get a sense of pride from that....It was a wake-up call really; it just became very clear that everyone on the front lines has a lot in common." When we spoke, she went out of her way to commend her coworkers and managers. "My boss isn't the problem," she said. "The whole system, it depends on sacrificing ordinary people. That's wrong. It will only change if we stop it. We have to stop fighting each other and start pointing fingers at the top."

Yet this wasn't always as clear to everyone. When the risks became overwhelming, she took an unpaid leave from the store. When she went back to work weeks later, she said the resentment she felt from her coworkers was palpable. Something had changed during the time she was gone from the job. Rather than resenting a system that denied paid leave to workers, her coworkers directed their frustration toward her.

"In a way, I get it—I was avoiding some risks during my time off," she said. "That's what mattered most to all of us."

✦

THE PANDEMIC IGNITED a frontline class consciousness, motivated in large part by the cognitive dissonance of being simultaneously celebrated as heroes and exposed to so much workplace risk. The language of being "essential" was almost always part of the rhetoric of protest. As I'll explore in later chapters, these newly class-conscious workers mobilized and launched organized movements in diverse ways, profoundly reshaping labor politics and the fight for worker justice in America.

Yet even as frontline workers expressed support for each other, forging broad working-class unity proved to be messier and more complicated. Risk and exposure to the virus separated frontline workers from so many other working-class folks, most notably the unemployed. Frontline workers' attitudes toward the unemployed evolved dramatically over the course of the coronavirus crisis. Early in the pandemic, many essential workers sympathized with those who were laid off and viewed their struggles as coterminous. As the pandemic progressed, however, essential workers increasingly doubted that their struggles resembled those of the unemployed.

From March to July 2020, my interviews had no anti-unemployed stigma. It was clear to all that those applying for unemployment insurance were suffering along with everyone else, and that joblessness or destitution in some cases was hardly a balm for not having to work on the front lines. As the economy slowly rebounded, however, and the virus rippled through communities in wave after wave, frontline workers' resentment against the unemployed, who were increasingly portrayed as avoiding risk in much the same way of those working from home, grew.

Bashing the jobless has long been a national pastime, built upon the idea that some people get something—a generic idea of welfare— for nothing. In the early 1980s, Reagan engineered a dramatic turn against welfare premised on racist stereotypes of Black families and especially Black female heads of households, dubbed "welfare queens." Ever since, complaints about welfare generosity have had the effect of racist dog whistles, rallying conservative whites to a program that actually limits their own social support system as well and serving to equate laziness and sloth with "not white" in recent American policymaking. (Never mind that white Americans disproportionately benefit from government support.)[33]

The pandemic inspired a new take. In part because the frontline class was so multiracial, it became harder to link grievances about race and unemployment together. The content of these new complaints wasn't that the unemployed were lazy but that they were unfairly safe. The typically flaunted work ethic was supplanted by a substitute ideology of risk-taking. "It's not that we thought they [the unemployed] should be working, it's that we wished we didn't have to either," Bailey, the welder, said.

This resentment was magnified after the Biden administration extended unemployment benefits in early 2021, guaranteeing a $300-per-week unemployment relief check. University of Chicago economists, traditionally known as the original theorists of neoliberalism, found in a study that almost 70 percent of unemployed workers were getting more money through unemployment than they had made at their jobs.[34] It paid to stay home. The relief programs were necessary and good, and, in many cases, still not enough. But they also served to fracture the working class, dividing frontline workers from the unemployed and preventing broad class solidarity.

"No way somebody sitting at home deserves more than someone out there on the front lines," said Francisco, a slaughterhouse worker from Colorado. "When we say we're essential workers, we mean the people actually working."

This position was widely shared by many essential workers I interviewed, particularly as the economy rebounded. I began asking if they thought it would be better if the employed also received the extra stimulus, on top of wages. More people agreed that it would be acceptable for the unemployed to get some too, but many were still committed to upholding the idea that additional stimulus should not go to the unemployed. "We're not all in this together," Caroline, a nurse from Buffalo, New York, told me. "Some of us are working our butts off and some of us are sitting on them."

Something had changed. Biden's extended unemployment checks were hitting households, contributing to the suspicion that some workers were unfairly avoiding the risks of the pandemic while most essential workers remained mired in the stress of working through it. The frontline working class's resentment of the unemployed ensured that broad working-class solidarity was a bridge too far, thwarting the possibility of collective action among them. The understanding toward the unemployed early in the pandemic—indeed the recognition that *it could have been me*—had given way to bitterness and resentment.

There was a parallel movement among the public too. As the pandemic progressed, many Americans shifted from supporting "our essential heroes" to decrying that "nobody wants to work anymore." They celebrated essential workers so long as they kept the country up and running. And for a while they tolerated the newly unemployed, who had lost their jobs in the crash. But as the economy improved and lockdown periods ended, the public's patience waned, and many Americans began to see the unemployed as lazy once again. Simultaneously, public praise for essential workers who were actually working grew fainter and fainter.

This rapid change in temperament exposes how flimsy and superficial public support for essential workers actually was, underscoring why the cognitive dissonance of those workers was so intense and justified.

Politics also proved to be a large stumbling block to the forging of broad working-class solidarity. Partisanship even pitted some essential workers against one another in their fight against unsafe working conditions. The working class is fairly split, seemingly agnostic as a whole, as to what its collective political values are. Though essential workers of all races skew slightly liberal, the different ways Democratic and Republican voters among them approached the pandemic undercut the essential working class. I conducted a survey of seven hundred essential workers in Wisconsin and Pennsylvania, just before Biden turned both states blue in 2020. Most of my survey respondents reported that they'd become "more liberal" during 2020. They believed Biden was a better candidate to pull us out of the COVID recession, and that he'd be better as a candidate to help workers, though this preference in the data was small.

Working-class partisanship, however, hurt efforts to stop the spread of the virus and frustrated class unity in the workplace. These are linked because workers in conservative places did far less to change the way they work, through social distancing and workplace safety protocols, than did workers in liberal places. This made workplaces with high numbers of conservative voters more dangerous.

It was also widely acknowledged that Republicans were more likely to oppose mask mandates, vaccines, and social distancing measures that would have kept workers and their families safe. They ended social distancing restrictions earlier, including in states with large Black populations, who were disproportionately exposed to the virus as essential workers.[35] These same political biases were reinforced during my interviews with essential workers. Whereas right-identifying workers were more likely to downplay their risk of exposure to COVID-19, liberal workers said the exact opposite.

"They're trying to get us all killed," said Melissa Press, a long-term care nurse from Indiana, referring to her fellow nurses who were Trump supporters. Melissa was a lifelong conservative voter until 2016, when she couldn't bring herself to pull the lever for Trump. The pandemic intensified this change, and the partisan politics of her coworkers began to shift her perception of American conservatism. She said her coworkers flaunted safe practices at work and spread COVID conspiracy theories among each other. "Even when they got COVID they didn't believe it was real," she told me.

This divide might suggest that appeals to unite the working class politically are doomed. After all, debates about workplace vaccine mandates fueled a cultural front of the intraclass war, as many conservative workers refused to be vaccinated and occasionally lost their jobs as a result. They also occasionally lost their lives as a result.

My research suggests glimmers of an alternate future. All of the Republican-voting union leaders I interviewed were strong supporters of workplace mitigation strategies. "You can't be in this position, to help others, to build your power at work, and agree with Trump on COVID," said Tessa Johnson, a nurse and union leader from North

Dakota. "It's impossible." Tessa and her family are committed Trump voters, but she said her experience at work and as a unionist led her to break with the then president on COVID-19 policies. In the fall of 2020, her state had the highest coronavirus infection rate in the world, and its ultra-right-wing governor, Kristi Noem, never issued any stay-at-home orders. When Tessa attended the funeral of a family member who had died of COVID, she was the only one wearing a mask.

"I did my best to make sure COVID wasn't political," she said. "Not everyone sees it that way of course."

◆

TECTONIC SHIFTS IN class politics formed and dissolved an essential working class during the pandemic. The hero status that workers earned conferred a rare degree of respect and appreciation, but it wasn't enough to secure them the kinds of actual benefits they needed to do their jobs safely and with dignity.

One lesson from the pandemic is that we need a new model for actual heroism. Calling workers heroes allowed them to be sacrificed and served to silence dissent. After all, heroes don't complain about poor working conditions; they rise above them. Heroes don't contextualize the current crisis in a history of austerity that undermined the ability of workers to perform in a crisis; they just deal with it. Because heroes are manifestly supernatural, we consider them invincible, by definition not in need of protections.

The variety of sacrifices essential workers made don't fit neatly into the established tropes and canonical forms with which we're familiar. Most sacrifice narratives are about heroic or tragic individuals, not an entire class. In the classic allegory of the Minotaur, the sacrificial citizens were chosen indiscriminately. But essential workers are not simply a random sample of Americans—they're disproportionately poorer, nonwhite, and female. The military are said to make the ultimate sacrifice, but soldiers, whether they want to be at war or not, are at least trained for battle.

Melanie Brown is a fourth-generation fisherwoman in Bristol Bay, Alaska. She can earn up to $60,000 during the monthlong salmon run each year. In 2020, she chose not to work in solidarity with indigenous tribal leaders who pressured Governor Mike Dunleavy to shut down the fishing industry in response to the pandemic. Many others joined her, especially those who had a personal or familial connection to the native Alaskan population. The campaign was ultimately unsuccessful, however, and the bay became full of nets bulging with sockeye—nets that, for the first time in as long as Melanie can remember, were not hers. Melanie worked a side job, and living expenses for her and her two children were lower during the pandemic, so she was able to avoid poverty. Forgoing the money was nonetheless a hard decision, but she felt the sacrifice was the right call given the circumstances. Melanie's great-grandparents, who also fished Bristol Bay, were orphaned when their parents succumbed to the Spanish flu, a viral outbreak that devastated the local indigenous population, a century earlier. "Fishing makes me feel connected to my family," she said. "Not fishing was my way to honor them this year."

True heroes change the world rather than simply acting bravely within it. During the pandemic, true heroism happened when, in the course of doing their already demanding jobs, essential workers stood up and addressed the root causes of the crisis together. We needed nurses not only at the bedside but also at the bargaining table and on the picket lines. Better conditions for nurses—higher pay, more PPE, safer staffing ratios—mean better care for all of us.

"We don't know how to effectively treat COVID-19 yet," Primiano, the nurse, said at the April teachers' rally. "But we do know how to prevent it. Every time rank-and-file workers stand up to demand policies that prevent the spread of COVID-19, you're saving lives that medicine cannot save. If you teachers don't get what you need, you should strike, and healthcare workers and other essential workers should stand behind you…and demand that the working class stop paying for this pandemic with our lives."

Primiano's militant spirit echoes across these pages, though it was far from universal. Essential workers' class consciousness was intimately connected to their treatment by employers but also the public's perception of their labor. And their understanding of themselves as a class reverberated from their interactions not just with management but with customers, patients, and others they served. During interviews, nurses routinely railed against their patients who thought COVID was a hoax; grocery and retail workers against their demanding and unmasked customers; educators against parents who thought in-person learning was the only way to teach.

Still, the moment that created essential workers was discordant and disorderly, and sometimes they became the unruly rabble Primiano was envisioning. Labor unrest is not particularly common in the US. Compared to peer countries, especially those in the Global South, American workers are more complacent and less apt to strike. And certainly the conditions in 2020 were not ripe for rebellion. How can you co-conspire when such significant and important bans forbid even small gatherings? Still, workers found a way. The next chapter looks at labor unrest during the heart of the pandemic, when gross exploitation and unsafe working conditions led to strikes, walkouts, and protests. These disruptions were vital to preserving the health of not only essential workers but all Americans, and indeed, where they happened, they were an important sign that the public was in good hands. A healthy economy is not one lacking open conflict but one where workers have the organizational capacity to express their grievances and win better conditions. Workers who care enough about their jobs to take huge risks to improve them are performing a necessary public service. We turn now to the streets and picket lines of the early pandemic labor movement, where workers took on even more uncertainty in the hopes of better jobs, inadvertently invoking the radical adage: what you risk shows what you value.

CHAPTER 3

THE PANDEMIC PROLETARIAT

For someone who has been publicly derided as "inarticulate," Christian Smalls sure knows how to make a point.

It was late August 2020 when Chris, a former Amazon worker, along with a few hundred protesters, erected a guillotine outside of Jeff Bezos's $23 million DC mansion.

"The point was obviously not to chop off anyone's head," Smalls told me. "The point was to show that we're not backing down until we get unions at Amazon." Chris had worked at Amazon for five years as a pick floor supervisor, most recently at its JFK8 facility in Staten Island. He'd enjoyed the job and his coworkers, regarded Bezos as a stand-up guy, and referred to the company's high-tech workplaces as as "close to a penthouse as a warehouse could get."

When his coworkers began getting sick from COVID-19 in March 2020, he noticed the company didn't increase safety protocols. Instead, it offered "unlimited unpaid time off," which appealed to no one. And you were only eligible for paid time off if you tested positive for COVID. But to get a test in March 2020, you had to be exceedingly sick, and even then people were mandated to come to work while they waited for their results. "It was a breeding ground," Chris said.

He went through the usual channels to air his grievances, and when that predictably failed, he took the next step. Chris organized a walk-out protest and was joined by about sixty of his fellow workers. They demanded their facility be closed and sanitized for two weeks, during which time all employees would be paid their full wage. Two hours later he was fired.

During an executive meeting one week later, Amazon's general counsel David Zapolsky, in notes that were leaked to *Vice* magazine, wrote: "He's not smart, or articulate, and to the extent the press wants to focus on us versus him, we will be in a much stronger PR position than simply explaining for the umpteenth time how we're trying to protect workers."[1]

Zapolsky continued: "We should spend the first part of our response strongly laying out the case for why the organizer's conduct was immoral, unacceptable, and arguably illegal, in detail, and only then follow with our usual talking points about worker safety....Make him the most interesting part of the story, and if possible make him the face of the entire union/organizing movement."[2]

It's hard to imagine a worse calculation. "Amazon wants to make this about me," he responded in a prepared statement. "But whether Jeff Bezos likes it or not, this is about Amazon workers—and their families—everywhere," he said. "Instead of protecting workers and the communities in which they work, however, Amazon seems to be more interested in managing its image....This is not about me. This is about all of us."[3]

Chris's firing and the leaked memo attracted widespread condemnation from activists and politicians, including New York City mayor Bill de Blasio and Senator Bernie Sanders, who called the firing "disgraceful."[4] It also engendered support from other social movements. Smalls, who is Black, soon became not only a leader of a national worker movement but also key in building the bridge from the workplace to the streets as a Black Lives Matter activist.

By the time I caught up with Smalls, he had been unemployed for several months yet was busier than ever. He spent almost every waking moment organizing against Amazon across the country and helping to advise its employees in other countries. "When I signed up for this job it said I needed a GED and I had to lift 50 pounds—that's it.

We ain't the Red Cross. We're not doctors or nurses. We can't be expected to fight a deadly virus while packing boxes."

Chris wasn't an organizer before this. He was the kind of employee who went to work and kept his head down. It was designation as an essential worker that, for him, was a turning point. "They say we're essential, but they fire us for nothing," he said. "But if something was essential to you, you wouldn't let it go so easily. This is capitalism. I see it now."

Chris estimates that his protest cost the company $4 billion. That's the cost of the increased PPE, daily temperature checks, better paid leave, and enhanced sanitation that arrived at Amazon facilities worldwide in early April 2020, in the wake of his protest.[5] "I take credit for that," he said. "I'm proud of it."

The chaotic nature of the pandemic and its attendant recession inevitably produced myriad competing political responses. The shocking magnitude of the federal recovery program described in Chapter 1 was mirrored by the diversity of bottom-up protest movements that rose to challenge the pandemic employment regime. Those challenges were led by a new hodgepodge of a labor movement that was learning to act as a class, a messy and multiracial coalition of old-guard unions and new social movements that were often led by women and people of color. The formal indicators of labor unrest, large strikes, were comparably scarce. But this only requires that we look other places to see where class conflict was really bubbling up.

To make sense of pandemic-era labor activity in a nonsensical year, I propose a schema to help conceptualize how workers fought back during the early part of the pandemic. Worker actions came in three main forms: workplace mutual aid, acts of self-defense, and workplace protests over social justice. At various times, as I describe below, these different kinds of actions overlapped, and they rarely appeared in pure form. A handful of strikes in key essential industries, for example, represent a convergence of all three. This chapter tells the story of the pandemic's first year or so from the vantage point of picket lines, protest marches, and solidarity actions. As the national spotlight swept across essential workplaces, the actions of the frontline class taught us that workers did more than just their jobs. They fought for better healthcare systems, safety protocols, higher wages, a stronger safety net, and better conditions for social reproduction. And the gains they won rippled outward to the rest of society.

◆

MUTUAL AID NETWORKS typically refer to community volunteers to provide resources or services to those in need. As Tocqueville observed, Americans are notoriously cooperative. Yet mutual aid groups have radical European ancestors. In 1902, Peter Kropotkin, the Russian naturalist and anarchist who had renounced his birthright as a prince, published *Mutual Aid: A Factor of Evolution.* Where Darwin saw competition as the driving force for species success rates, Kropotkin identified solidarity among swallows and marmots and preindustrial societies as essential to their survival. A primitive form of communism was the saving grace of the world's dispossessed, who banded together through mutual aid. This social practice, he argued, was undermined by capitalist development—private property, the labor market, etc. It was the work of anarchists and communists to build mutual aid societies and to reignite our base instincts for self-preservation.

Mutual aid is hardly a large-scale solution to social problems, but it has grassroots appeal, and voluntarism is vital to civic engagement. During the pandemic, thousands of mutual aid networks were built in cities and towns across the country. Neighbors shopped for and delivered groceries to their elderly neighbors, offered free childcare to essential worker families, and helped fill social service provision left vacant by the pandemic state.

While many aid networks were led by nonessential volunteers, essential workers also formed mutual aid associations that served the common good even beyond their paid jobs. This activism first emerged in the same place the virus did. In 2018, a Beijing-based delivery driver who went by the pseudonym Xiong Yan attached a unique QR code to the back of his moped. When a driver scanned it, they would be automatically added to a secret group chat on an app beyond the boss's panoptic eye. The welcome message: "Aims: solidarity, mutual assistance, friendship, determination, sharing, and winning together." "No matter if you ride for Ele.me or for Meituan, for Fengniao, Shansong, Dada, or Shunfeng, we're all in the same hustle."[6]

The Drivers' Alliance, a mutual aid network for delivery workers, was born. During the pandemic, the alliance grew to include a few thousand members. Alliance-aligned drivers delivered goods to those in need in outlying neighborhoods where delivery companies rarely ventured. They also drove healthcare workers and other essential employees safely around the city. No one thought these actions would transform the low wages, long hours, and safety risks endemic to the industry. They believed, however, as one driver I interviewed, LeiPi, put it, "it was good to have someone to call."

Starting the network and protesting labor conditions came with a cost. By the time I was writing this book, Xiong had been arrested at least twice for speaking out against delivery companies or the government. Yet it seems the crackdown on mutual aid groups only helped to inspire more.

Similar organizations emerged from the vibrant underground of Wuhan, especially the communitarian punk rock subculture in the Wuchang district. Key members of that scene, many of whom were essential workers, built a citywide volunteer network numbering in the thousands to procure and deliver essential goods and services. Calling themselves Dim Light, another way of saying "beacon," members filled a void where official channels had failed. Originally, they simply responded to hospital workers' social media posts. When they proved they could literally deliver the goods, demand snowballed.

Working in the early hours of the morning, when fewer drivers were on the road, they cultivated relationships with key guards, securing themselves more freedom to travel throughout the quarantined city. LeiPi explained the group secured and delivered tens of thousands of pounds of food, medical supplies, and personal hygiene products, especially tampons, throughout the city. They ferried hospital workers quickly to and from work. They even managed to feed large numbers of domestic pets, who, when the quarantine began, were living in pet day care facilities because their owners were traveling. Somewhere in Wuhan there was a "cat hotel" whose residents were kept alive by enterprising punks.

Through the Drivers' Alliance, Dim Light, and countless other mutual aid networks, Chinese essential workers buttressed their communities in a time of crisis. When the pandemic migrated to Italy, its next hot spot, labor activism bubbled up from below again. There the pandemic inspired a wave of "platform cooperatives," the name often attached to gig-type businesses that are collectively owned and designed for the common good. In Bologna, for example, Consegne Etiche (Ethical Deliveries) formed to bring books and food to people during quarantine. Cobbled together from a group of local shopkeepers, students, and a trade union of couriers, the organization filled a clear mission while also deepening the social fabric of the city that was rent asunder by COVID.[7]

When the pandemic hit the US, American essential workers also formed mutual aid societies to provide goods and services not supplied by the government or corporations.

Gig workers in delivery and transportation industries developed apps to help each other learn how to respond to the neediest situations first, sometimes bucking priorities from the likes of Uber and Lyft. The Gig Workers Collective created a simple map that allows drivers to coordinate mutual aid activities like food delivery and medical personnel transport. "Between the lack of financial security (no sick leave), the number of workers living week to week, and the inability for some workers to take time off due to low income, gig workers are some of the most vulnerable dealing with the COVID-19 outbreak," their website stated.[8]

Factory workers in Marcus Hook, Pennsylvania, moved into the Braskem petrochemical plant on March 23, 2020, with sleeping bags and toothbrushes. The forty-three-man crew didn't come back out until April 20. For twenty-eight days, they worked and lived on the plant floor, producing tens of millions of pounds of the raw material that goes into face masks. "We were just happy to be able to help," Joe Boyce, a shift supervisor at Braskem America, told the *Washington Post*. "We've been getting messages on social media from nurses, doctors, EMS workers, saying thank you for what we're doing. But we want to thank them for what they did and are continuing to do. That's what made the time we were in there go by quickly, just being able to support them."[9]

Inspired by this story, in early April 2020, GE factory workers in Massachusetts, Virginia, Texas, and New York demanded the company's North American facilities rehire its laid-off workers to produce ventilators.[10] Despite the shortage of ventilators and the availability of federal funds for just such an industrial reorganization, GE chose not to make this shift.[11] Ford and GM, however, paid laid-off United Auto Workers union members who "volunteered" to go back into factories to build up the depleted supply of ventilators. On March 20, 2020, Trump invoked the Defense Production Act (DPA) to encourage more of this industrial redeployment, but workers had already been doing it for weeks.[12] The timing was critical: as soon as workers realized they were in a position to produce for the greater good, they took action, before the state decreed it.

Nurses and other healthcare workers established volunteer "flying squads" in underserved neighborhoods to visit needy sick people—those not suffering from COVID—who couldn't, or shouldn't, go to the hospital. Alexa Getty, a nurse in New York City, also recalls being part of a group who wove throughout the hospital when their shifts were over, connecting dying patients with their families via FaceTime. "I held the phone up so they could see their family and say goodbye," she explained. "Then I held their hands so they didn't die alone." This kind of activism is rarely counted when considering the "acts of resistance" that garnered headlines during 2020. It matters, however, because it demonstrates labor's solidarity with underserved communities beyond the workplace.

✦

MOST LABOR ACTIVISM, however, was focused inside the workplace, and most protests came in the form of self-defense. Chris's actions at Amazon are indicative of a wave of pandemic-era labor protests that became commonplace throughout 2020 and 2021. During the early pandemic, protests for better working conditions became a matter of literal life or death, prompting many across essential industries to fight back in unprecedented ways.

In just the first few weeks of lockdown, labor unrest spread like the virus. Autoworkers in Michigan, grocery warehouse workers in Memphis, Whole Foods "associates" in New York, and McDonald's workers in Florida all walked picket lines.[13] Nationwide, workers for Instacart, Amazon, and Target, as well as delivery drivers, also participated in some form of labor slowdown or stoppage, announcing to both their bosses and the world that they were indeed essential—and that their collective power could win them the protections that they and their communities so desperately needed. In Pittsburgh, garbage trucks blocked the entrances to municipal buildings until workers were brought better PPE. This workplace troublemaking wasn't confined to the United States. Municipal workers in Hungary, childcare employees and bus drivers in Norway, teachers and air traffic controllers in Greece, Amazon warehouse workers in Germany, and postal workers in the UK all struck too.[14]

These small and less coordinated actions were matched by highly organized, large, and militant strikes of healthcare workers and other frontline employees.[15] COVID is an occupational hazard, and many of the early protests were direct responses to the presence of the virus in the workplace. When workers walked off the job, they were acting in self-defense. These strikes were significant for three reasons. By getting workers out of dangerously cramped working environments, they were immediate attempts to protect worker safety in the short term. By creating a crisis for management, they promised workers the leverage to make larger demands and to improve workplace safety in the longer term. And they also helped communicate worker grievances to the public. A strike is an act of withholding one's contribution to an employment relationship. The absence of workers at work underscored their necessity—to their employers and the country at large.

"We're up here risking our life for chicken," fumed Kendaliyn Granville to her local news station. She was one of approximately fifty nonunion workers who, on March 23, 2020, walked out of the Perdue poultry processing plant in Kathleen, Georgia, to protest the plant's unsanitary conditions and lack of hazard pay. "We're not getting nothing, no type of compensation...not even no cleanliness." For these workers, the lack of protection against the virus only heightened long-simmering grievances that had been building at the plant. "We're told there's going to be more promotions and more pay for the company, but no one has seen that," said Diamond Gray, another worker who participated in the walkout. "I think a lot of people are just tired and with the virus involved also, I think it's just gotten to the point where enough is enough." In response to their demands for lifesaving protections, the company sent each worker home on March 23 with one free chicken breast.[16]

Elsewhere in the country, even unionized workers were striking without permission. On March 17, 2020, bus drivers in Detroit refused to board their buses until further COVID precautions were implemented. The spontaneous, rank-and-file-led strike—branded a "wildcat" because the drivers launched the protest without official approval from union leadership—shut down all bus routes for the day. Within twenty-four hours, the drivers had won all of their demands, including access to PPE and handwashing stations, increased cleaning protocols, rear door passenger boarding, and a cancellation of bus fares during the pandemic.[17]

About one-third of the strikes during 2020 were led by workers without unions, which probably limited their effectiveness. One reason the Detroit action succeeded was the immediate willingness of their union to back the drivers up. "They called us and asked us to stand by them," explained Glenn Tolbert, president of the local Amalgamated Transit Union chapter, "and that's what we do." In contrast to the poultry workers in Georgia who didn't have an institutionalized body to turn to when they needed it, the drivers in Detroit were supported by the strength of their union, and that made all the difference.

This trend was evident throughout the pandemic, which demonstrated unions' ability to deliver tangible material gains for their workers in times of crisis. The United Food and Commercial Workers union secured an increase in benefits and pay for workers in over a dozen food-processing plants, including $2-per-hour premium pay for Campbell's Soup factory workers, a $1,500 bonus for workers at Smucker's, and premium pay for thousands of grocery store workers. The United Auto Workers union pressured GM, Ford, and Fiat Chrysler to shut down plant operations for two weeks and provide all workers with PPE. Tesla, which does not have a union, was initially held open by CEO Elon Musk, but closed a few days later, facing intense public pressure.

Perhaps no union better exemplified the power of organized labor than the Association of Flight Attendants (AFA), which stood up for its rank and file while its industry struggled to stay afloat. Air travel plummeted by over 90 percent in the month from March to April 2020, and millions of workers were at risk of losing their jobs. Their saving grace was a high unionization rate and strong union leadership that was ready and able to make sure their voices were heard in DC.

"We had so much power with an 80 percent organized workforce," explained Sara Nelson, the AFA president whose militant leadership helped propel the union to national prominence during the pandemic. Nelson, who cut her teeth in organizing as a flight attendant after the massive airline bankruptcies that occurred post-9/11, was ready for the COVID fallout. "I saw this crisis coming, and we said, Hell no, we're going to define how this is gonna go," she told me.

Knowing her fifty thousand members' jobs and livelihoods were on the line, in early March 2020, she went to Congressman Peter DeFazio, chairman of the House Committee on Transportation and Infrastructure, and told him what the flight attendants needed from the CARES Act; DeFazio had been a longtime champion of prolabor airline regulations. At the same time, she made abundantly clear to airline executives that the bailout she was requesting was going to be on workers' terms, not management's. She explained to me her general rap: "The public hates you," and "You're gonna have to work with us if you wanna get this done."

During several frantic days of lobbying from the top, what Sara referred to as "dialing for dollars" because she was asking so many political leaders for money, rank-and-file workers took action too. They launched demonstrations by flight attendants and a social media pressure campaign aimed at shaming airline companies that tried to fire their employees. After a long week, Nelson and the AFA proved that well-organized unions still have political capital that can be used to defend good union jobs. In the finalized CARES Act, $32 billion was granted to the airline industry with the stipulation that it could not furlough workers until September 30. Almost all of the money would go toward keeping flight attendants on the payroll and connected to their health insurance. Additionally, the union made sure that the grants were tied to a cap in executive pay and a ban on corporate stock buybacks. It was one of the first times in history that such a sizable bailout package was brokered on such favorable terms for workers.

The determination of her union's members was critical to this win. "There was just a consciousness in our workplace that you don't have this job without a union," Nelson told me. The AFA fight positioned a major union, led by a woman and with a majority female membership, as leaders in the fight for worker justice during the pandemic. It was just the beginning.

"Striking is a form of self-defense," said Marlena Pellegrino, a bedside nurse at Saint Vincent Hospital in Worcester, Massachusetts, for thirty-five years, whom we met in the Introduction. "We don't want to be out here, but if we are you can be sure there's a major problem in there."

Marlena got her nursing degree at Saint Vincent's in 1986 and started working there shortly thereafter, just before a slew of hospital-sponsored nursing colleges began to close. And although she got her bachelor's degree during her time as a nurse, she never left the hospital, working the same 3:00–11:00 p.m. shift on the same surgical floor for over three decades. "This is the only job I've ever had," she said. "I just like being in the nitty-gritty."

Marlena is the daughter of a bakery and confectionery union activist. She helped jump-start the union at her hospital in 2001 after she and her coworkers noticed patient care standards were slipping. Saint Vincent's is a Catholic hospital, allegedly founded on principles that guarantee high-quality care to the neediest in society. Concerns about patient care pushed the nurses to strike in 2002, a risky proposition for a new union that hadn't yet secured a single change in the workplace. This was the reality for unions then, and it is the reality now: even after workers have won a union election, management has the right to deny them a contract. In an unexpected twist, the 2002 strike was settled only after Senator Ted Kennedy, who was visiting political leaders nearby, spontaneously stepped in. He was sympathetic to the nurses and flew them on his private jet to Washington to sign a deal with hospital management in his office. Kennedy then sent the nurses to a well-known Irish pub in DC, the Dubliner, to celebrate their victory.

During the pandemic, they found themselves in much the same situation as twenty years earlier—understaffed, with patient care declining, workplace accidents increasing, more patients developing bedsores, and management demanding mandatory overtime rather than better staffing. "It felt like the same old stuff again," Marlena said, "except, you know, without Kennedy of course."

Workers wanted all hands on deck. Instead, nurses who showed up to be volunteer "helping hands" in the ICU were forced back home. Tenet Healthcare, the Texas-based corporation that owns and controls the hospital, furloughed many direct care providers to make up for revenue expenditures like increased PPE and testing.[18] The company cut 10 percent of its staff nationwide, even though it received almost $3 billion in federal aid from the CARES Act.[19]

In the year after the pandemic hit, conditions were so bad that a record 110 nurses quit—in a typical year, the average is about 20. The staffing shortage was acute and a direct outcome of the hospital's preference to overwork existing staff instead of making new hires. Staffing shortages are dangerous, and not just during a deadly disease outbreak. "We were doing everything we could," Marlena said. "Every day. All day. They treated nurses like we're in a factory. People die that way, patients and workers. No way. We couldn't take it."

So they struck again. On March 8, 2020, the Saint Vincent nurses became one of the first pandemic-era healthcare strikes. When I spoke with Marlena, who is known as "Mother Marlena" to many nurses, it was day 88 and morale was still high, despite workers having gone months without a paycheck. Management had begun posting their jobs as vacant and advertising them on social media. By day 120, dozens of nurses had traveled to Texas to take the fight to Tenet Healthcare's corporate headquarters. The nurses' rally drew healthcare advocates and other union leaders, including Sara Nelson. "We can't let executives take government money and misuse it, let them make our lives into a commodity, and let them treat essential workers with disrespect," Sara told the strikers and their supporters.[20]

Marlena said that when new workers are hired at Saint Vincent's, veteran workers tell them the story of the earlier strike so they know why the union exists: to improve patient care. "We want safe staffing and better care conditions. That's what this union is for. It's a resource for us, for our patients, and our community. We run the show in that building and we're proud of it. That's why we're on strike."

Most nursing strikes last no more than a few days. The depth of Tenet's commitment to breaking this strike is surprising in the industry. But so is the resolve of the nurses. Marlena herself is intensely loyal to Saint Vincent's as both her alma mater and the only employer she's ever known. She feels a deep commitment to making sure it's better now than when she got there thirty-five years ago. "They think they can break us," Marlena said. "They tried that twenty years ago and it didn't work. It's not gonna work during the pandemic. This shoddy treatment actually made us stronger. We'll be out here one day longer than them."

In the end, one day longer meant 301 days on the picket line. Nurses voted almost unanimously to ratify the contract that Marlena, as a union representative, presented them. No Kennedys intervened, but the final contract was mediated by US secretary of labor and former Boston mayor Marty Walsh. Marlena called it "an enormous victory for our patients and our members." The agreement included raises, retroactive pay, a more affordable health insurance plan, and better staffing rations to improve patient care, the original demand that had sparked the strike. It was the longest nurses' strike in the state's history, and the longest strike of any industry in the pandemic's first year.[21]

Marlena's conception of self-defense is worth emphasizing again. Nurses weren't out there just to improve their jobs. "We're standing up for our hospital, our patients, our community," she said. "This is about all of us." Hers is a broad view of self-defense, one that understands that individuals' self-interests are necessarily reliant on others. Marlena also sees herself and her coworkers as the last line of defense. "We're the ones who can be out here. Patients can't. Sometimes families can't. So we're out here for all of them too."

Four of the eight major strikes in 2020 were led by nurses. The largest was the eight-thousand-strong nurses' strike against Washington's Swedish Medical Center in January. The eight hundred nurses at Saint Vincent's won't even make the official statistics because the US Bureau of Labor Statistics only records "large strikes" of one thousand workers or more. This threshold also excludes nurses' strikes at Cook County Health, Riverside Community Hospital, Montefiore New Rochelle Hospital, Backus Hospital, Santa Rosa Memorial Hospital, Albany Medical Center, AMITA Health Saint Joseph Medical Center Joliet, St. Mary's Medical Center, and more. According to *Strikewave*, over twenty-eight thousand healthcare workers had participated in almost thirty strikes from March to September 2020. They've also founded more than one hundred new unions in twenty-two states.[22]

✦

Given all he faced in 2020, it's no wonder Chris Smalls ended up outside Jeff Bezos's house in August with a personalized guillotine. In May, George Floyd was killed by Minneapolis police officer Derek Chauvin, who knelt on Floyd's neck long after he had stopped breathing. As many as twenty-six million people are estimated to have joined the thousands of Black Lives Matter protests across the country that followed that summer—there was a protest in 40 percent of

US counties. July 6, the peak day of protest, dwarfed the three million who clogged the arteries of cities nationwide for the Women's March in 2017. Black Lives Matter became the largest protest movement in post-Vietnam America.

Heads rolled only metaphorically during the nationwide protests that summer, but street skirmishes with police and right-wing counterprotesters meant the movement took a more aggressive stance than many liberal onlookers were comfortable with. More than three hundred fires burned across Philadelphia, where four hundred people were arrested even before the National Guard arrived. Police precincts burned in other cities, and it seemed like the protest slogan "defund the police" might go mainstream.

Why were the protests so large and militant? It's possible that mass unemployment left people with more time to join the movement. As scholars Frances Fox Piven and Richard Cloward have shown, widespread welfare relief has often been deployed to contain mass unrest.[23] In the summer of 2020, it could have been the opposite. "Nobody has work, and there's no jobs to look for anyway," said Chris. "They got nothin' to do but raise hell and fight back." Another possibility is that the racial dimensions of the pandemic fanned the flames of the Black freedom movement. Black people were disproportionately impacted by the mass unemployment of the pandemic recession, disproportionately put in harm's way as essential workers, dying of COVID at higher rates, and killed by cops at higher rates than people of other races. More than ever, the Black Lives Matter movement and labor struggles were structurally entwined.

Chris was attracted to the bleeding edge of the movement's progressive spirit, a spirit animated by tying worker concerns to political issues outside of the workplace. "Social justice strikes" are often overtly symbolic, which limits their material impact. Cross-movement collaborations are rare but necessary. And they have to begin somewhere. "The start of the pandemic last spring and then the summer's protests worked like the contrasting dye used in M.R.I. scans," wrote the scholar-activist Keeanga-Yamahtta Taylor, "highlighting all of the imperfections in the internal structures of the United States."[24]

Chris emphasized the connection between 2020's worker struggles and social justice protests. He observed that workplaces like Amazon tend to bring the multiracial working class together in one place more often than neighborhoods, schools, churches, or other institutions, which are often structured by neighborhood segregation and other factors. This makes the worksite an especially fruitful place to focus racial justice activism. "These are our people, we have to work with them, and they have all kinds of issues," he says. "The company brought us together, now we gotta finish the job."

These actions took the form of often-spontaneous strikes seeking either immediate short-term gains (safety protections, hazard pay) or more symbolic victories (solidarity with the Movement for Black Lives). When workers go on strike, specifically a strike for social justice, they are subscribing to a theory of change markedly different from that adopted by weekend march goers or hashtag activists. By focusing their organizing on the workplace, social justice strikers are acknowledging (implicitly or explicitly) two crucial ideas. First, capitalism, and by extension the workplace, is inextricably connected to all issues of social justice. Second, by acting collectively, workers can leverage their position within the capitalist system to change it.

These are things the dockworkers of the International Longshore and Warehouse Union (ILWU) understood when, on June 19, 2020, they shut down all of the West Coast ports they controlled, from San Diego to Vancouver, for a full eight-hour shift.[25] The work stoppage aimed to commemorate the Juneteenth holiday, show solidarity with the Movement for Black Lives, and demonstrate the power of labor to make society-wide change. The action's organizers were explicit about their purpose: "The most effective way to stop police terror is by the working class taking action at the point of production," explained Oakland-based organizer Clarence Thomas.[26]

The work stoppage was accompanied by massive rallies at many of the ports. The Oakland rally, which brought out an estimated twenty thousand people, featured several prominent radicals, including veteran activist and scholar Angela Y. Davis, hip-hop artist, filmmaker, and organizer Boots Riley, and of course Chris Smalls.[27]

The ILWU has been doing this for a long time. They integrated their ranks in the 1930s, condemned the Japanese American internment camps in the '40s, refused to handle South African cargo during apartheid, and shut down their ports in opposition to the war in Iraq in 2008.[28] ILWU's radical past demonstrates that labor taking up social justice demands isn't all that new. What's new is a growing number of social justice movements not only taking up the language of labor but recognizing the tactical significance of workplace organizing.

On July 20, 2020, just over a month after the longshore workers' action, tens of thousands of workers across the country walked off the job as part of the Strike for Black Lives. In response to the growing movement against police brutality and systemic racism, the nationwide "strike" was organized by a coalition of sixty different labor unions and social justice organizations. Organizers sought to explicitly link workplace demands like unions for all, healthcare for all, and universal access to PPE with the antiracist demand that communities of color be free from police terror. In over 160 cities, janitors, fast-food workers, nurse's aides, hotel housekeepers, Uber drivers, bus drivers, Amazon warehouse workers, and Walmart staff participated in some sort of work stoppage or slowdown in support of the demands. Many of the actions were not actual work stoppages. They were picking up on the lesson the longshore workers have understood for decades—change happens when workers leverage their economic power.[29]

For many frontline workers—who felt demoralized from the horrendous working and economic conditions brought on by the pandemic—the Strike for Black Lives served as a source of empowerment. "We're supposed to be essential workers taking care of the most vulnerable people in the world, but the owners do not treat us like we are worth what we're worth," explained Trece Andrews, a Detroit nursing home worker and union stewardess who went on strike as part of the day of action. "It meant a lot to be out there, and I want to give kudos to my union for all the hard work they have done to help us to get to this point."[30]

Adriana Alvarez, a McDonald's worker and Fight for $15 organizer in Chicago, went on strike to promote "justice for Black communities." For Alvarez, this justice had to include improving working conditions for essential workers, who are disproportionately Black.[31] Truly antiracist corporations can't just make performative declarations that #BlackLivesMatter. "Every worker must have the opportunity to form a union, no matter where they work," BLM's manifesto declared.

To Alvarez's point, the pandemic proved that workers in *any* sector are capable of forcing change when they act collectively. Professional basketball players demonstrated this when, on August 26, 2020, they shut down the NBA playoffs with an unprecedented league-wide wildcat strike demanding racial justice and an end to police brutality. Three days prior, a white police officer in Kenosha, Wisconsin, had shot Jacob Blake, who is Black, seven times in the back while his three children watched. The horrific scene, captured on video, prompted the Milwaukee Bucks players to refuse to take to the court for their playoff game; they chose instead to stay in the locker room and contact the Wisconsin attorney general to demand justice for Blake. Other NBA teams were quick to join the work stoppage, forcing the league to cancel all playoff games for that evening and the next day as players began meeting to formulate demands and decide whether the playoffs would go on at all.

Inspired by the NBA players, athletes in the WNBA, MLB, and MLS organized strikes in their respective leagues, resulting in a historic sector-wide work stoppage.[32]

For the NBA players, wearing league-approved social justice slogans on their jerseys and painting "Black Lives Matter" on courts wasn't enough. They needed a stronger action to get the point across. "When you talk about boycotting a game, everyone's antenna goes up," explained Andre Iguodala of the Miami Heat, vice president of the National Basketball Players Association. "You have to be willing to sacrifice corporate money for people to realize there's a big problem out there."[33] By putting the team owners' finances under threat, the players could effectively pressure them to make changes in the league and beyond.

In an interview with CNN's Don Lemon, Iguodala made the connection between their labor stoppage and social justice even clearer: "Capitalism and racism go hand in hand. And you can't have one without the other."[34]

After two days of negotiations, the teams agreed to end the strike and continue the playoffs after the league agreed to establish a social justice coalition to advocate for voting access, civic engagement, and meaningful police and criminal justice reform.[35] It's worth noting that the players achieved these wins despite the fact that striking was explicitly banned in their contracts, giving proof to the old labor saying "There is no such thing as an illegal strike, only an unsuccessful one."[36] While calls to top players from Barack Obama and Michael Jordan may have influenced them to end the strike prematurely, stunting its potential to win larger demands, the strike nevertheless demonstrated an increasing popularity of labor stoppages as vehicles for effecting social change.[37]

◆

THE COMPLEXITY AND messiness of the COVID-19 crisis meant labor protests often defied neat categorization. Some worker activism seemed like an alchemy of mutual aid, self-defense, and social justice. Such was the historic strike at Highland Hospital in Oakland, California.

In the late nineties, the Alameda County Board of Supervisors voted to relinquish public control of the county's public health system, including hospitals, clinics, and outpatient facilities that served the poorest of the 1.4 million East Bay residents. The new model allowed an unelected board of trustees to manage the Alameda Health System (AHS) without county oversight. The result was a long-term austerity package—decades of cuts to public services, wage reductions for employees, and according to healthcare workers I interviewed, a decline in the overall standard of care.

Though still a public entity, the system behaved like a private corporation and piggybacked on waves of privatization of health systems across the country. In the new model, the county loaned the AHS Board money for its operating budget, which the AHS paid back through budget cuts. The result was that an unelected cabal began to undo years of public management of the health system.[38]

Workers opposed this model. Highland Hospital employees bargained with management for years for basic improvements in the level of care. John Pearson, an ER nurse and union representative, said he and his colleagues felt forced to send homeless patients, sexual assault victims, and trauma patients out of the ER without appropriate clothing, because they lacked adequate supplies. He described insufficient staffing levels at the hospital and an ER with crumbling walls, pockmarked with holes.[39] More than half of all AHS patients live below the poverty line, and 80 percent of that group are people of color.[40]

Austerity left a legacy that made workers' jobs harder during the COVID-19 crisis and contributed to the spread of the virus. Highland workers were not tested for COVID regularly, even after instances of known exposure. "All of us know that we're going around spreading the virus unknowingly," Pearson said. "We don't want to do that to our patients and each other."[41]

In June 2020, workers began bargaining a new contract, and the hospital used the pandemic to try to extract bigger concessions. At their first bargaining session, management's proposal included over one hundred pages of cuts: wage freezes, the elimination of shift differential pay, changes to shift predictability, an end to guaranteed hours, increasing nurse-to-patient staffing ratios, and a less democratic disciplinary process. The new contract also targeted workers' healthcare, creating new premiums that would hit low-income workers the hardest.

At the same time management was trying to extract concessions, the hospital denied workers adequate PPE. Early in the pandemic, front desk clerks were instructed not to wear masks, citing concerns that masked workers might unnecessarily "spread fear." The gowns supplied to hospital staff who treated COVID patients were stamped

"Not for Medical Use" in boldface type. Nurses were instructed to re-use N95 masks by storing them in lunch bags in their lockers.

"These things are supposed to be used like underwear," Deva Wolf, a labor and delivery nurse told me. "Once and done." But Deva said nurses wore a single mask for weeks when supplies were low, likely contributing to the spread of the virus throughout the hospital as workers moved from room to room and floor to floor.

The lack of adequate PPE got so bad that nurses began manufac-turing their own. Saber Alaoui, a clinical nurse, began using garbage bags as gowns, poking holes in them for his head and arms. "It was make your own PPE day" said the caption under the selfie he posted on Instagram in early April 2020.[42]

Saber was only trying to find some light in a dark situation. His wife was undergoing chemotherapy at the time, and he was trying to be as safe as possible. But the photo went viral, and when hospi-tal management came across it, they accused him of "political theater" and fired him. Saber's family was at risk of losing their healthcare, and his wife had to halt her chemo treatments. A year after fighting for his job, he had still not been rehired.

By that time, nurses across America had been posting pictures of themselves using trash bags as PPE. Hillary Clinton even tweeted about nurses doing so at Mount Sinai Hospital in New York.[43] If Sa-ber was engaging in any kind of PR campaign at all, it was to call attention to mounting nationwide safety hazards endangering the public as much as hospital employees.

"The man was trying to protect his family," Deva said. "And that's when everything started heating up."

The lack of PPE, the lack of testing, the firing of those who spoke out, and stalling contract negotiations all pushed nurses toward a strike.

"The first day I walked that line," Deva recalled, "it felt so therapeu-tic." Over three thousand nurses, specialists, housekeepers, social work-ers, and cafeteria staff struck at eight AHS buildings for five days in October 2020. The picket line became one of the best places to party in Oakland. "There was always food, dancing, celebrations, music," Deva said. Highland workers also made good use of social media to air their grievances. At one point they even performed and recorded their own music video cover of "WAP," the hit rap song by Cardi B and Megan Thee Stallion. (The acronym of the original definitely did not stand for "Workers and Patients.") The workers' version went like this:

> I said picket line, freak, striking seven days a week.
> Workers and patients make that layoff game weak.
> Workers out here on the front line, bosses at home, safe inside.
> COVID breakout, cover your eyes, can't get a test, nowhere to find.[44]

The raucous picket line was also a respite from the demoralizing conditions of working in a hospital during the pandemic. Almost every healthcare worker I spoke with said that her job had been made immeasurably worse by the stress associated with the virus. For Deva, it meant she couldn't do her job the way she was trained without risking her own life.

"I massage my patients, I hug them, I hold their bodies during labor," she said, choking back tears. "But things are different now, we wear all this gear and I constantly feel like I'm not doing a good enough job, like I'm not offering my patients what they deserve. I hate it so much." Deva longed for a time when she could not only do her job safely but also the way she enjoyed and the way she was trained.

"I hear people say, 'Well, this is what you signed up for,' and I respond, I didn't sign up to feel scared and isolate myself from my family. I didn't sign up to help others if it meant putting my own family at risk."

The picket lines drew massive community support, mostly organized by the East Bay chapter of the Democratic Socialists of America (DSA). For months prior to the strike, DSA activists, some of whom are also healthcare workers at the hospital, worked to build a community support network. They held town hall meetings featuring unionists and political candidates, sent mass email and text campaigns targeting county supervisors, and convened dozens of phonebanks to turn DSA members out to the picket lines.

"It was a real political awakening for us," Deva said. "They worked very hard alongside us to make sure this was a fight to improve a community hospital. I mean, who isn't on the side of nurses these days?"

The answer to that question, as Deva well knew, was the AHS Board of Trustees. Rather than negotiate with those on strike, the AHS hired replacement workers, costing them about $6 million. But the strikers had the community, media, and patients on their side, and the pressure worked. They weren't just asking for more PPE or a raise, but for a real voice in how healthcare was administered. The strike created a political disaster for county officials who were seen as mismanaging a broken hospital in the middle of the health crisis. In the middle of the strike, the Alameda County supervisors fired all the trustees governing the AHS.

"We have never seen the kind of chaos as we have seen at AHS with people who are on the front lines," Supervisor Richard Valle told the *East Bay Times*. "Clearly, there's severe problems."[45] In the wake of the announcement, supervisors replaced the trustees one by one and began a process to transition the AHS back under public oversight.

"The workers stopped the privatization process," said Molly Stuart, who led the community support campaign for DSA and also produced the rap video. "They literally fired their boss."

After five days, Highland workers went back to work with a promise for reform from the county supervisors plus a guarantee that the hospital would spend more money on PPE. They had won clear advances toward stronger public accountability for their hospital. And yet workers expressed that the intangible power of the strike might be even more profound. "Using our collective voice was as important as anything else that was accomplished," Deva said. "That's going to help us carry on even post-pandemic as workers. 'Cause it's always a struggle, right? Let's be real. It's always a struggle."

◆

WHAT DOES ALL this labor activism add up to? After all, an aerial view of organized labor unrest in 2020 wouldn't register much at all.

Number of Workers Involved in Major Work Stoppages, 1973–2020

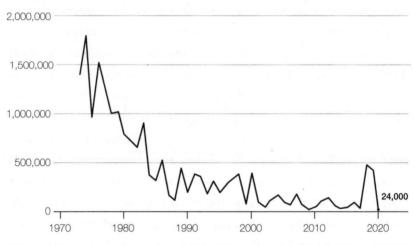

Major strike activity dropped in 2020, following a surge in 2018 and 2019. SOURCE: Bureau of Labor Statistics, "Major Work Stoppages in 2020," February 19, 2021, from the Economic Policy Institute

As the graph above shows, there were only eight "major work stoppages" in 2020, which mobilized a combined total of only twenty-four thousand workers. This was a dramatic decrease from 2018 and 2019 when, buoyed by low unemployment and anemic growth, an average of 455,400 workers participated in major strikes both years, a thirty-five-year high.[46] This 2018–2019 strike wave, propelled by the Red for Ed national teachers' movement, gave many on the Left hope that labor was regaining the power it had lost from the high points of the militant 1970s.

But today only about 10 percent of American workers are union members, less than half the percentage in 1979. The pandemic was a major setback, the lowest level of major work stoppages since 2009, the heart of the Great Recession. Downturns, it seems, are tough times to fight the boss. Multiple factors account for the decline in strike activity. The economy was operating at reduced capacity. With so many businesses closed, there were fewer workers who could strike. The record unemployment levels of 2020 made those who still had jobs feel like the "lucky ones," hardly positioned to speak out. Union organizers, who are crucial to helping workers coordinate a strike, had almost no access to worksites.

Sadly, some major labor leaders seemed to implicitly endorse the status quo, impeding workers' fights for better working conditions. In April 2020, Randi Weingarten of the American Federation of Teachers, Chris Shelton of Communications Workers of America, Mary Kay Henry of Service Employees International Union, and James P. Hoffa Jr. of the Teamsters Union ran an editorial in USA Today with the headline "Coronavirus is a stress test for capitalism, we see encouraging signs."[47] They made a plea to defend "ethical" capitalism from what they called "vulture capitalism." Their "positive examples" included companies like AT&T, Kroger, Verizon, General Motors, and Major League Baseball, all of which have recently been the target of labor disputes. GM had even ended fifty thousand workers' health-care plans in order to break a strike less than a year before the op-ed was published. The report card on so-called ethical capitalism shows it's a sham—much more capitalism than ethical.

It used to be a veritable edict on the Left that the gears of capitalism would eventually be ground to a halt by the very same people tasked with turning them. Capitalism, Marx noted, produced above all its own gravediggers. Today the opposite seems just as obvious. Practically impervious to critique, as seemingly natural as the tides, capitalist political economy produces a working class whose aspirations are necessarily oriented toward pragmatic incremental reforms—a wage hike here, lower insurance co-pays there—that actually fortify rather than dissolve the system itself.

This ambivalence is the crux of the gamble that workers take when they rise up, speak out, or throw down. If they struggle for a better deal, they might end up fired or, in the best case, with a slightly better deal. This calculus strongly favors those who choose to merely accept what they're given. Nothing changes, but at least nothing changes.

During the pandemic this calculus shifted slightly because the stakes were higher at both ends of the spectrum. Striking for greater access to PPE, for example, might mean you could save your life or the lives of those around you. Losing could cost you your livelihood and healthcare in the midst of the largest economic crash in a century. The extraordinarily harsh working conditions during the pandemic didn't lead to an explosion of organizing drives, as happened in the wake of the Great Depression. Yet the pandemic working class faced deadly challenges that, to some extent, put limits on what workers would be able to accomplish collectively. Everything was harder during the pandemic, and that included fighting your boss. Still, workers experimented with new kinds of labor organizing that won material gains, protecting themselves and the greater public.

After all, the Bureau of Labor Statistics (BLS) data above failed to capture the full picture. In order to be recorded by the BLS, a "major work stoppage" must involve at least one thousand workers and last for at least one full shift, criteria that are extremely limiting. In fact, they automatically exclude nearly 60 percent of the private sector workforce, which works for companies that employ fewer than one thousand people.[48] It's notable that the BLS used to track strikes involving as few as six people until 1982, when the Reagan administration cut its funding. Without an adequately supported agency, we are left to guess the actual amount of worker protests each year.

A closer look at labor unrest—at a wide variety of actions, at smaller protests, at nontraditional organizing campaigns—in 2020 and 2021 shows that hundreds of thousands of workers across the country were spurred to action over the course of the pandemic. They utilized new tactics and strategies appropriate to the moment and showcased the ways in which the pandemic served as a period of innovation for the labor movement, all of which happened below the radar of the official statistics. Mutual aid by essential workers filled voids left open by gaping holes in the pandemic safety net. Protests and labor actions combined demands for racial and worker justice, highlighting the way the pandemic affected the multiracial working class hardest. And pitted against an economic system that treated them as disposable, many frontline workers—armed with their newly minted "essential" status—struck back in self-defense. In their own ways, these actions reverberated out, with impacts beyond the borders of the workplace.

◆

THROUGHOUT THE PANDEMIC, this kind of widespread labor unrest contrasted sharply with sporadic bursts of working-class conservatism. As soon as the lockdown period began, small groups of right-wing activists congregated at city halls, governors' residences, and state capitols to demand an end to COVID restrictions and a "reopening" of the economy. While these demonstrations were relatively rare, protestors' extremist rhetoric and tactics attracted an extraordinary amount of media coverage, which magnified their impact and profoundly shaped how the Right approached the COVID crisis nationwide.

While their actions tacitly acknowledged that we all depend on someone else's labor, they were first and foremost centered around the demand that the servant class get back to work. With cartoonish slogans they nonetheless took seriously, the demonstrators broadcast what they believed were their own individual entitlements: "MASSAGE IS ESSENTIAL!" "I WANT A HAIRCUT!"[49] "LET MY PEOPLE GO–LF!"[50]

What looked at first like a spontaneous grassroots movement among economically anxious whites, a "populist" idiom of Trump's America, was soon revealed to be a well-funded right-wing plot to sow doubts about the risks of COVID-19.[51] The vast majority of Americans across the class spectrum agreed that public health concerns should determine workplace closures. To label these protests "populist" is to ignore their funding stream and political coordination. Populism describes political movements by "the people" against an elite. This was the opposite. The protestors quickly attracted widespread media coverage as well as support from powerful right-wing lobbyists. The demonstrations' impact was grossly magnified, and reshaped national politics. The Save Our Country Coalition—a network of conservative think tanks including FreedomWorks, the Tea

Party Patriots, and the American Legislative Exchange Council—was just one of the billionaire-backed drivers of these protests.

Still, authentic anti-elite politics filtered into the workplace during the pandemic. Searing critiques of pandemic profiteering, the comparable safety of the telecommuting crowd, and the deplorable conditions under which essential workers toiled created a kind of workplace populism. In fact, when essential workers were almost the only ones out in public, their rumblings became synonymous with a movement of "the people." Their grassroots labor unrest was an important antidote to the useful idiots of the right wing's astroturf campaigns.

The drama of the pandemic meant we couldn't ignore the kinds of labor activism that rarely grab headlines. By the end of 2021, researchers at Cornell University's School of Industrial and Labor Relations had tracked almost two hundred strikes and almost five hundred other kinds of labor protests that year, a significant uptick from the year before.[52] They included strikes by workers at Volvo and Frontier Communications, by carpenters in the Pacific Northwest, and by graduate student workers at Harvard, New York University, and Columbia. Workers at McDonald's, Burger King, Wendy's, Walmart, Bojangles, and Jack in the Box also walked picket lines or organized short-term walkouts.[53]

As the pandemic slogged on, it prompted essential workers to continue to protest and strike. Workplace safety was almost always their top grievance, and unions played an indispensable role in guaranteeing some lifesaving protections. Still, given the limited scope of unionization today, most workers were left to fend for themselves. If unions are important vehicles of public health, why do we stand in their way? In the next chapter I place the relationship between public safety and the pandemic labor movement in a broader context. Ultimately, our health at work isn't the product of a government watchdog agency or corporate accountability. It happens through class struggle.

CHAPTER 4

NSFW: NOT SAFE FOR WORKERS

THE VARIOUS WORKPLACE STRUGGLES THAT PUNCTUATED THE pandemic were alternately hopeful and desperate, strategic and spontaneous, successful and wanting. They captured the public's imagination in ways that strikes and protests in normal times have not, and workers benefited from that leverage. This was especially true when they fought for safer workplaces.

Worker and public safety are intertwined in most essential industries, but healthcare, meat processing, and education were sectors that drew special attention during the pandemic. In addition to being hot spots for COVID, they were the sites of fierce labor disputes, where unions played important roles in workers' attempts to mitigate the virus. Women, people of color, and migrants are overrepresented in these industries, which is why many of the struggles over workplace safety were also about racial and gender disparity in public health. Examining the ways that labor unions can make good public health policy is crucial to understanding the working class's role in the pandemic.

We typically think that some jobsites are de facto dangerous. Those who work around toxic materials, physical violence, emotional trauma, or in high-paced environments are more likely to experience more regular accidents and mishaps. While being a college professor poses fewer risks than, say, heavy-machine operation, any worksite can include adequate safety protocols. A key determinant of whether or not those safety protocols are in place, or are meaningfully enforced, is whether workers have a collective voice on the job through labor unions. The long attack on labor organizations by employers and government has slowly eroded a major voice for workplace safety protections.

Unions are correlated with good public health. Union members and their families earn higher wages and are far more likely to have health coverage than their nonunion peers.[1] This allows them to visit doctors more regularly for preventive care and to be treated for less serious illness.[2] It's more common for union members to enjoy pensions and better retirement policies, which promote financial stability and health in old age.[3] Research shows that unions have played vital roles in smoking and alcohol cessation, campaigns to reduce hypertension, and movements to reduce stress-related overwork.[4] Because unions offer workers a voice in the workplace, union members may be more likely to point out safety issues or hazards without fear of management retaliation.[5] Other studies have shown that collective bargaining provides opportunities for workers to insert safety protocols into their daily lives on the job and to raise issues critical to their family's healthcare policies. Unions' close relationship with management has allowed them to reduce their members' healthcare costs through new kinds of plans and, in some cases, to build dedicated health centers offering quality care at below-market rates for their members.[6]

COVID-19 is, among many things, an occupational disease. It quickly transformed formerly safe workplaces into veritable Superfund sites, and made unsafe workplaces even more unsafe. During the pandemic, unionized workers across essential industries had more paid sick leave and more PPE, and were tested for COVID-19 more frequently.[7] Research also shows that unionized workers may be less likely to work multiple jobs and to live in settings associated with high COVID-19 transmission.[8] In 2020, researchers found that the presence of a union made it more likely that the US Occupational Safety and Health Administration (OSHA) would conduct an inspection of an alleged violation.[9] These factors reduced COVID-19 infections and the spread of the disease. Stronger unions meant safer workplaces in most cases, though the exact mechanisms by which unions made a difference varied across industries.

Inside the workplace, it's often up to workers to stand up for their own health and safety. OSHA's diminished role—inspecting a tiny fraction of workplace safety complaints, issuing minuscule fines for corporate negligence—meant labor activism filled a gaping void in the effort to protect the public welfare during the pandemic. Strong workers' organizations are a public good. Where workers were unionized or had more power, they saved lives—their own and those around them. When workplace safety was deemed too expensive, and actions to improve it were opposed, workers and those around them often paid the ultimate price. Workplace safety, and public health, are the outcome of class struggle.

✦

"Hell no."

That was what Rosalind "Ros" Reggans thought about the fact that her employer, Infinity Healthcare Management, had received $12.7 million in federal relief funds for its eleven nursing homes in the Chicago area, but workers weren't getting a raise. When Ros first heard, in the spring of 2020, about the money her facility would get, she says she and her coworkers were relieved. They'd been working without proper PPE for months, and residents around them were dying.

"We were losing a lot of people we cared for," she said. "It was truly awful."

Her employer offered hazard pay, but receiving it was contingent upon perfect attendance. Miss one day in a two-week period and you forfeit all the money, a straightforward incentive to work while sick.

Most Infinity employees made less than fifteen dollars an hour, and it was common for them to work several jobs at multiple homes in the area. Ros believed that traveling from facility to facility spread the virus from home to home and from workers to residents. Using cell phone geolocation records and data from twenty-two states, in July

2020 researchers confirmed her hunch, finding that staff who traveled between nursing homes as workers were associated with higher infection rates among residents.[10]

Fed up with her employer's ruthless treatment of workers, Ros and her colleagues began demanding a raise. A two-dollar-an-hour raise would make it possible for nursing home workers to hold one job, and thereby reduce both the spread of the virus between homes and its transmission among workers' families and communities. It would also bring Infinity homes to parity with other nursing homes in the area, reducing the likelihood that workers would leave the company's homes to be hired at others. In addition to a raise, workers wanted more PPE, COVID-related paid sick days, free testing, and early access to vaccines.

"Hell no."

That was the response she and other workers got when they presented their demands.

Ros knew most nursing homes in the area were short-staffed, partly because pay was so low they were losing workers to fast-food restaurants that paid better and were safer. She could have switched to a facility that paid more, but after two decades at her job, at sixty years old, she had made lifetime connections with her colleagues and residents.

"Leaving wasn't an option for me," she said. "I chose to stay and fight—for all of us."

In November 2020, Ros voted to strike along with seven hundred other nursing assistants, dietary workers, janitors, and other staff. At eleven facilities across the state, they walked off the job, facing repercussions from a horrible boss, lake-effect November snow, and an uncertain future.

Ros said the vote to strike was one of the most serious decisions she'd ever had to make. She was one of fourteen children her parents raised in Kankakee, Illinois, what was then an arcadian community barely an hour from Chicago but cultural light-years from the sumptuous tastes of the metropole. Her father asked her to get a job as soon as she became a teenager. Later, when her grandmother fell ill, she got her certified nursing assistant (CNA) license just to help care for her at home for free. She says her work ethic taught her to devote herself to the task at hand by any means necessary. For some, striking is seen as an abdication of that ethic, but Ros decided it was the opposite. "A work ethic means you work hard at the job, but also work hard to make the job better, to improve it," she said.

Striking is always a risk, but there was a greater risk of staying on the job as it was. Employees had been working without a contract since the summer, which meant some of the guarantees that come with a union workplace were thrust into limbo. Moreover, low pay and inadequate protection from the virus were terrifying. Ros was a cancer survivor and worried about her own health as much as that of the residents.

Ros spent practically every waking hour on a picket line: three shifts a day for twelve days straight. She proudly stated that her own facility had only had three scabs, the fewest of any of the eleven buildings on strike. The strike opened up the possibility to discuss issues directly related to the pandemic.

"We weren't just out there for us," Ros said. "We were out there for them," indicating her residents in the home.

Ros and her coworkers won a partial victory, which is usually the only kind there is. They went back to work almost two weeks later with an average $2.00 wage increase plus a $2.50-an-hour "pandemic pay" bonus, more guaranteed PPE, and five paid sick days. "I held my head high the day I went back," she said. "Two dollars is more than a raise. It's a big difference gettin' to parity with other homes because it helps us not to move around so much. Same with paid sick days."

Her union, Service Employees International Union (SEIU), enjoyed an outpouring of public support while they were on strike, including from their own residents. It was easy to understand how those seemingly small victories could translate into safer workplaces, and therefore safer nursing homes. During the pandemic, as residents and workers contracted the virus and died, demanding higher standards was often seen as an act of humanitarian relief.

Ros was at the pandemic's epicenter. Over one million nursing home workers had been infected with COVID by spring 2022, and about two hundred thousand residents and staff of nursing homes and long-term care facilities had died. This meant that resident and staff illness accounted for 6 percent of all cases and almost 40 percent of deaths nationwide. During the pandemic, working in an American nursing home was one of the most dangerous jobs on the planet.[11]

Advanced age and compounding comorbidities made residents particularly susceptible.[12] That doesn't explain the whole picture, however. PPE, N95 respirators, and eye shields for workers were hard to come by, exposing residents to whatever workers brought into the facility. Larger nursing homes with more beds and higher occupancy rates were more likely to have COVID-19 cases and deaths, as were homes where people of color comprised a larger share of the resident population.[13] High rates of COVID-19 cases and deaths within nursing homes were associated with higher levels of community transmission of the virus, a relationship linked by nursing home staff who worked in the facilities and lived in the surrounding areas. Where workers lacked paid sick leave, researchers found that resident mortality and worker infection rates were higher.[14]

Ros said she was "one of the lucky ones" because she hadn't acquired COVID-19—yet. But maybe luck had little to do with it. Unionized nursing homes were safer places to live and work than nonunion homes, as there were fewer COVID-19 infections and lower death rates. A research team led by George Washington University political scientist Adam Dean compared data on COVID-19 cases between unionized and nonunionized nursing homes in New York. Studying the relationship between labor unions and COVID-19 transmission is nearly impossible because the CDC doesn't collect data on job classifications and unions rarely publish their workplace-level membership. Dean's team managed to get the relevant data for New York nursing homes, a major hot spot of the virus. They found that unionized nursing homes had a resident mortality rate 30 percent below that of nonunion facilities.[15] The reason was simple. Union workers had better access to PPE than their nonunion counterparts, which significantly reduced the transmission of the virus among residents.

I joined their research team, and we expanded the study to include all 13,350 nursing homes in the continental US. Healthcare unions represent about 17 percent of nursing homes, higher than the national average union density. We found that unions reduced resident COVID-19 mortality rates by 10.8 percent and nursing home worker infection rates by 6.8 percent.[16] These two phenomena are related, as lower COVID-19 infections among staff meant they would be less likely to transmit the virus to their patients. "It's pretty simple," Ros said. "The safer we are, the safer they are." With more than seventy-five thousand COVID-19 deaths among residents in nonunionized nursing homes during the period of our study, the results suggest that industry-wide unionization would have meant approximately eight thousand fewer resident deaths.

Our results were most significant during the winter 2020–2021 COVID wave, which was concentrated in the Northeast, where union density is comparably strong. The results were weakest during the summer 2020 wave, which was concentrated in the South, where restrictive right-to-work laws have ensured that union density in nursing homes is abysmally low. In effect, those conservative policies may have decreased the difference between union and nonunion nursing homes.

In nursing homes, this "union effect" disproportionately protects women of color because they're overrepresented in that labor pool. Moreover, Black workers are more likely to work in frontline occupations or perform tasks that involve higher risk. CNAs interact with patients and visitors, and kitchen staff have no ventilation, are overworked, and are pressured to work while sick. Whites are more likely to be managers or charge nurses, or to work in offices with doors that close. In my interviews with workers, I frequently heard of a stark racial divide among staff in nursing homes.

"Black people are put in harm's way in nursing homes," explained Gloria Duquette, a Jamaican immigrant who works in three different nursing homes in Bloomfield, Connecticut. "The bosses are white, the supervisors are white, but most of us direct caregivers are Black. Unions have rules in place for fairness, for balance. So it makes it harder for supervisors to play favors with white workers or discriminate against Black workers."

Gloria noted a clear difference among the homes she worked at, only one of which was unionized. It was no coincidence, she said, that the nonunion homes had more COVID outbreaks. "Unions were on top of things early, right from the start, supplying us with PPE even before management," she told me. "With the union we actually have a voice, a chance to make changes, to demand better conditions, more PPE, sick time off, and whatnot. We can talk to our supervisors like adults....At [the nonunion homes] we have no mechanism for that. We're just told what to do."

The presence of and struggles by unions in nursing homes demonstrate one way that organized labor reduced the spread of COVID-19 during the pandemic. It was more complicated in other industrial hot spots. Workers in meatpacking plants offer a cautionary tale.

◆

SAN TWIN REMEMBERS her mother, Tin Aye, as someone who took great personal risks so that others could find justice. In her native Burma, she was a committed human rights activist and member of the Karen ethnic minority who often took up arms alongside students, workers, peasants, and others against the dictatorship of Ne Win. The military state's response was to kill by the thousands and torture or starve tens of thousands more. While pregnant with her only child, Tin fled to a Thai refugee camp, barely escaping with her life.

In the camps, she taught courses on women's rights and gave birth to San. San's father returned to Burma during that time and was murdered by the dictatorship for desertion, his body found floating naked in a river. Eventually, after fifteen years, her family was able to get out and landed in Denver, Colorado, as part of a resettlement agreement. To make money, Tin took the only job available to someone with her language abilities, in the Greeley plant run by the world's largest meatpacking company, the Brazilian-owned JBS Foods. She worked shoulder to shoulder with other Karen immigrants, cutting and packaging meat on a shift that spanned from 1:00 p.m. to 4:00 a.m., including transit.[17]

It was a clean break from the past, and her family felt for the first time that the vague notion of the American Dream they'd heard so much about might finally be within reach. "She was deeply loved at the job," San told me. "Everyone called her 'mom' or 'sister.'" This fictive kinship with her coworkers and managers didn't protect her from brutal exploitation. Despite surviving harrowing dangers in her life, she was unable to escape the hazards of her job at an American slaughterhouse.

Upton Sinclair called the early twentieth-century meatpacking industry "the jungle" because lawlessness reigned. Modern meatpacking facilities are slightly different—they're run by crooks who make all the laws. A cursory review of OSHA reports offers a grim portrait of the industry: "Employee's arm amputated in Meat Auger." "Employee killed when arm caught in meat grinder." "Employee decapitated by chain of hide puller machine." "Employee killed when head crushed by conveyor." "Caught and killed by gut-cooker machine."[18] The modern slaughterhouse is the Triangle Shirtwaist Factory of the heartland.

At the JBS plant where Tin worked—which slaughters 5,400 head of cattle daily—gory industrial accidents and deaths are high above the national average, and contagious diseases spread like gossip because workers are crammed body to body in freezing and unhygienic conditions.

Tin was sixty years old in March 2020 when she began coughing uncontrollably and dutifully went for a checkup. But, according to her daughter, the company doctor diagnosed Tin with a common cold and sent her back to the line. Then she urinated on herself after being denied a bathroom break. Her fever climbed. Her daughter begged her not to go to work, but she said she couldn't afford to take time off.

Tin's family believes the company did not communicate to employees the importance of staying home while sick, nor did it provide enough financial support for workers to take a sick day, leading some to identify a "working while sick" culture. On the day of the first confirmed COVID-19 case at the plant, in March 2020, the company offered all employees complimentary meat. "FREE 5 lb. ground beef roll to every employee as your [*sic*] leaving work today," it posted on its Facebook page. "We want to say a big thank you to all of our employees that continue to come to work during this time to help feed the world."[19]

The plant's union, the United Food and Commercial Workers, is the largest body that represents labor in the industry. Only 15 percent of workers industry-wide have a union, but that's slightly higher than the national average. As the pandemic unfolded, union leaders at the plant pressed for more PPE, social distancing, and sick time. Instead, workers were offered a bonus if they worked a week without missing a shift, the same policy Ros had in her nursing home. A Weld County analysis found that 64 percent of the workers from the plant who tested positive had "worked while symptomatic and therefore were contagious to others."[20] Predictably, hundreds of workers and their families began flooding local emergency rooms and hospitals with COVID-19. Saul Sanchez died first, one week after he was diagnosed in late March. Six others followed in quick succession. Eventually, Tin couldn't ignore her COVID symptoms anymore and checked herself into a local hospital.

San went into labor with her first child at the same time; she drove herself through a snowstorm to the hospital, where she tested positive for COVID-19. Her son, Felix, was delivered later that day by emergency cesarean. San and Tin spoke by phone, each from a different hospital bed just miles apart, and rejoiced in the good news of Felix's birth. Tin, calling from the ICU, dropped the phone toward the end of the call. "That was the last time I ever heard her voice," San said. Her mom slipped into a coma and was placed on a ventilator. She never came off it, dying on May 17, 2020, without the chance to lay her hands on her new grandson.

When we spoke in mid-2021, San's family had not yet been contacted by JBS, and the company had not assumed any culpability for failing to protect its employees. JBS hung a large photograph of Tin outside the plant in her memory. "It makes me sick when I drive by it," San told me, her voice trembling. "They're still using her even after she's dead."

The month after Tin died, the plant's processing lines sped up to increase output, and cases continued to rise. Anthony, who preferred I use only his first name for fear of retaliation, claimed the company temporarily made some adjustments following a wave of worker deaths. Cows were spaced six feet apart and the lines were slowed down. However, the distance between the cows was quickly returned to the standard two feet.

In response, Greeley workers spontaneously walked off the job, a strike unsanctioned by their union, the UFCW. The walkout drew some bad press for the company and a wave of community support in the company town. "We were spreading the virus in town, too," Anthony said. "A lot of people wanted it shut down for their own safety and ours. But they also knew that nobody was gonna pay for that," he said. "That's why they supported us." Some workers whose jobs entailed extra face-to-face contact got a small pay bump after the walkout. Anthony's job, for instance, required "wrestling with another guy to get some of these bones out of the cows," he explained. "It's really rough work, hard to wear a mask."

Anthony said it has long been common practice for people to work while they're sick. "We're all here looking for that second chance, or to provide for our families. We can't afford a day off," he said.

Following the wave of deaths in Greeley, OSHA conducted an investigation in September 2020. The outcome lumped insult on top of the tragedy for local families. The US Department of Labor fined JBS $15,615 for failing to comply with minor safety regulations. A local news outlet calculated that amount as 0.0000026 percent of the company's $50 billion annual profits, or $2,230 per death.[21]

Meanwhile, conditions were arguably even worse in poultry processing, where unions are even scarcer. In an Iowa facility owned by Tyson, managers allegedly placed bets on how many workers would contract the virus, even as they went to great effort to restrict their own time inside the plant. The lawsuit filed by workers in November

2020 describes a "cash buy-in, winner-take-all betting pool for supervisors and managers to wager how many employees would test positive for COVID-19."[22]

"We weren't even as useful as the chickens," said Beatrice, one poultry worker I spoke to. "We were their sacrificial lambs. The more we squealed the worse it got."

In pork processing, those employed in slaughtering, cutting, and "conversion"—the term for turning pigs into pork product—were disproportionately affected by COVID because most of those jobs were not changed to accommodate social distancing. In contrast, salaried managers moved cubicles, built glass shields between their desks, juggled offices, and brought in box fans.

Consequently, outbreaks swept across the Midwest among line workers in plant after plant, threatening the viability of the nation's food supply. The virus also spread far outside the plants' walls. Researchers found that the presence of a large meatpacking plant in a US county increased per capita COVID-19 infection rates by 110 percent compared to those counties without such facilities. Workplace transmission radiated out to the rest of the community. The same study estimated that 334,000 COVID-19 infections in the United States came from beef, pork, and chicken processing plants.[23]

Over fifty-nine thousand meatpacking workers had been infected with COVID-19 by mid-2021, and almost three hundred had died.[24] That's nine times as many infections as in all of Europe's slaughterhouses, despite the US employing only one-third more workers.[25] European meatpacking plants are smaller than those in the US, which allowed producers to more quickly shut down plants with outbreaks and shift production to other locations. US workers process about one thousand pigs per hour, compared to just four hundred on average in Europe. Speed is the single largest cause of accidents in the industry, not to mention the fact that the faster the line, the more jammed together the animals and workers are.

Which raises the question: Why are US meatpacking and poultry workers so weak when the industry is so essential? One would think that workers who feed the country would enjoy a degree of structural power, a built-in bargaining chip when it comes time to talk wages and safety conditions. A look back at the history of the domestic meatpacking industry reveals a pattern: When workers are organized, working conditions improve. When workers are without unions, as most are today, they're as sacrificial as the animals they're processing.

In 1905, muckraker Upton Sinclair published *The Jungle*, a novel based on several weeks of undercover work in a Chicago beef-packing plant. The book, which documented the plant's horrific labor and sanitation practices, presented a scathing portrait of the industry's brutality at the turn of the century. "It was to be counted as a wonder," Sinclair wrote, "that there were not more men slaughtered than cattle."[26] The plight of the factory's mostly immigrant workforce was largely overlooked by the book's readers, who were more concerned with the accounts of feces, vermin, and human body parts contaminating the meat they were consuming. "I aimed for the public's heart, and I hit it in the stomach," Sinclair later recounted.[27]

The novel made waves, eventually leading to the passage of the Federal Meat Inspection Act in 1906.[28] But reforms did little to improve workers' wages or conditions. As Sinclair, a committed socialist, understood, workers' lives don't generally improve when public sympathy inspires top-down reforms—workers' lives improve when they build bottom-up power to challenge their bosses on the shop floor.

This didn't happen until almost thirty years after *The Jungle*'s publication, when, finally spurred to action by a combination of gruesome working conditions and the militant spirit of the Depression era, meatpacking workers organized the Packinghouse Workers Organizing Committee (PWOC). The PWOC was a combative, Left-led organization that gained considerable power by organizing across racial and craft lines.[29] Its outspoken support of civil rights and workplace democracy allowed it to counter management attempts to divide the workforce by race and skill level.

In the ensuing decades, the union gained considerable power organizing the era's major meatpacking firms in the large midwestern cities where they were based. By the early 1960s, a full 95 percent of meat-packers outside of the South were unionized. This level of organiza-tion paid off: workers' wages were comparable to those in the auto and steel industry and significantly higher than those in the rest of nondu-rable manufacturing.[30]

Then, bolstered by the emergence of refrigerated trucks in the 1960s, which reduced their dependency on trains, meatpacking plants fled the densely unionized cities for the unorganized rural counties on their pe-riphery.[31] Since the union's strength came from its ability to organize workers, their families, and extended networks in densely populated urban hubs, the geographic reshuffling of the industry hamstrung the union's ability to build power, stacking the deck in favor of management.

In this new environment of low union density and monopsony buying power, a new breed of meatpacking plants emerged that suc-cessfully de-skilled the meatpacking process and heavily recruited im-migrant laborers. By turning the work of slaughtering and processing into a virtual assembly line (more accurately, a disassembly line), where workers were tasked with simple, repetitive jobs, the plants aimed to make workers easily replaceable. By employing workers who, as a re-sult of their legal resident status, had precarious living situations, the plants exploited the vulnerable for their own gain. Both moves, while effective, put front and center the vile logic of the industry: profits are everything, workers are expendable.

Between 1983 and 2019, union density in meatpacking was cut in half.[32] Unsurprisingly, as the workers became more disorganized, their real wages fell.[33] Meanwhile, the industry has once again become heavily concentrated among a few giant processors. As of 2021, four top firms control half of the market, with JBS, the multibillion-dollar meatpacking behemoth that oversaw the worker deaths in Greeley, leading the pack.[34]

This trend, what historian Daniel Calamuci calls the "return to *The Jungle*," showcases the simple fact that worker safety is contin-gent on worker power, a lesson that should have been learned long ago, just after *The Jungle* was published, from the tragic history of workplace dangers the book described. The degree of worker power fluctuates across Europe, but on average it is far greater than in the US, meaning American meatpackers also perform faster work for less pay. The declines in worker safety are correlated with adverse health for consumers too. Many of the most infectious and deadly zoonotic diseases—those we get from contact with sick animals—have emerged only recently, alongside the rising corporate consolidation of the industry and the increasing complexity of the global meat supply chain. Avian flu H1N1, severe acute respiratory syndrome (SARS), West Nile virus, Nipah virus, and bovine spongiform encephalopathy (BSE) are all products of the last two decades.[35]

The strength of nursing home unions to make a positive impact on public health stands in stark contrast to the weakness of those in meat and poultry processing. The sustained attack on food unions helps explain the difference, a history shared by virtually all other unions too. Yet, unions and their allies have always been at the forefront of workplace safety fights. Those fights began long ago, and were often led by pioneering women policymakers, organizers, and scientists.

✦

ON MARCH 25, 1911, Frances Perkins, then thirty-one, was having tea at a friend's house when she heard commotion from the street outside. A blaze had engulfed the Triangle Shirtwaist Factory down the street, and Ms. Perkins gathered up her skirts and ran toward the smoke. When she arrived, workers, mostly young women, were gathered in the windowsills ten stories up as flames lapped at their backs.

"They began to jump," Perkins said later. "The window was too crowded and they would jump and they hit the sidewalk....Every one of them was killed, everybody who jumped was killed. It was a horrifying spectacle."

Forty-seven people jumped to their deaths that day. One hundred others were burned alive or died from asphyxiation. Bosses had locked the exits to the stairwells, a common practice then to ensure workers didn't take unauthorized breaks, preventing workers from being able to flee the fire.

Perkins had been an advocate for the working poor before the fire, but that single day transformed her thinking about what real change looked like. "The New Deal began on March 25, 1911," she later said. Her memory of that day convinced her that "something must be done. We've got to turn this into some kind of victory, some kind of con-structive action." Perkins and other leaders who had a direct expe-rience with the fire, including New York governor Al Smith, helped pass workplace safety laws in New York State they hoped would es-tablish a template for the rest of the country. But though there were some improvements, there were also continued atrocities. One of the Triangle Factory owners, Max Blanck, who escaped charges of man-slaughter at the subsequent trial, was later fined twenty dollars for locking doors to another factory he owned.

Perkins climbed her way through the political ranks in New York State alongside Franklin Roosevelt, and as president, he appointed her labor secretary in 1933. As a key New Dealer, she was central to the creation of the Social Security system and jobs programs like the Ci-vilian Conservation Corps, the Federal Works Agency, and the Public Works Administration. The Fair Labor Standards Act (FLSA) was probably her highest accomplishment, establishing as it did the coun-try's first minimum wage law and overtime law.

National workplace safety regulations, however, remained elusive. The Triangle Factory fire was only one of countless industrial acci-dents that, over time, slowly gathered momentum for worker safety legislation. It remains symbolic of a larger process, however, partly because the victims were mostly young women and because the death toll was so high. It was the deadliest workplace tragedy in New York City's history until the terrorist attacks on the World Trade Center ninety years later.

As much as Perkins's legislative legacy has a connection to the fire, she was unable to enact wide-reaching worker safety laws. Nor was she the first to try.

Two years before the Triangle disaster, a young Polish immigrant and Jewish socialist named Rose Schneiderman had led a strike at the factory as part of a wider protest against the very same safety concerns that led to the fire. As many as thirty thousand New York shirtwaist workers stayed out of factories for three months. Rather than address their concerns, management called in private guards to beat the strikers as Tammany Hall and city officials looked the other way. Clara Lemlich, another prominent face of the strike, suffered six broken ribs during one such attack.

It wasn't until later that public indifference turned to rage, and protests and impromptu memorial meetings organized by reformers popped up across the city. At one such meeting at the Metropolitan Opera House, an argument broke out between working-class Lower East Siders and the haut monde in the box seats who sought only modest reforms. Rose stepped into the fray, delivering a speech in her characteristically diminutive voice that belied the rage on her tongue.

> I would be a traitor to these poor burned bodies if I came here to talk good fellowship. We have tried you good people of the public and we have found you wanting. The old Inquisition had its rack and its thumbscrews and its instruments of torture with iron teeth. We know what these things are today; the iron teeth are our necessities, the thumbscrews are the high-powered and swift machinery close to which we must work, and the rack is here in the firetrap structures that will destroy us the minute they catch on fire. . . . I can't talk fellowship to you who are gathered here. Too much blood has been spilled. I know from my experience it is up to the working people to save themselves. The only way they can save themselves is by a strong working-class movement.

Rose was later elected president of the National Women's Trade Union League in 1926. In 1933, she was the only woman to be appointed to the National Recovery Administration's Labor Advisory Board by President Roosevelt, a post that positioned her to work with Perkins on the landmark New Deal legislation.[36]

Perkins, from a middle-class family, viewed legislation as key to safeguarding worker rights, while Schneiderman, the daughter of immigrants, believed that legislation is pointless without strong unions to defend it in the workplace. In the end, their respective careers brought them both closer to workers and men in power, and their theories of social change were more aligned than is often thought. Policy is only useful to workers when they have the power to defend it.

Such was Perkins and Schneiderman's effect that their living enemies recognize their potency even today, decades after their deaths. In March 2011, almost one hundred years to the day after the Triangle Shirtwaist Factory fire, Maine's anti-union Republican governor Paul LePage removed a thirty-six-foot-wide mural from Augusta's Department of Labor's building and remanded it to a secret location. Among the mural's eleven panels are scenes from Maine's labor history, one of which contains a portrait of Perkins, who was born in Maine, and Schneiderman. At the same time, he renamed the building's conference rooms, two of which were named after Perkins and Schneiderman. (Muralgate caused quite an uproar that raged for months, but eventually the artwork was hung prominently in the atrium of the Maine State Museum.)

The workplace safety issues that most concerned Perkins and Schneiderman were the accidents of early industrial America—the mills, mines, and factories that disfigured, maimed, or killed multitudes of workers, and whose tragedies abated only when unions were able to force changes to the speed or process of goods production. Important though these issues were and continue to be, they did not represent the whole threat posed by dangerous worksites.

Deadly microbes, chemical agents, airborne pathogens, and infectious diseases have long been less visible workplace hazards that evaded reform movements. That we have *any* current legislation that offers workers protections from these elements, however insufficient, is the result of Alice Hamilton's founding of the field of occupational medicine.

Hamilton decided to pursue medicine as a way to be useful on her family's religious missionary trips. But she soon found it rewarding as a way to support herself and gain independence as a female professional as well. Early in her career, in 1897, she accepted a teaching position at a women's medical school in Chicago and became a resident of Jane Addams's famous Hull House. The settlement house brought the well-off, immigrants, and poor together, giving Hamilton an insider's view of poverty-induced health defects among the working class. She lived with and treated the working poor and immigrants for diseases resulting from commonplace working conditions. It was at Hull House she was encouraged to pursue a particular life of the mind that combined rigorous research with a social agenda.

"Life in a settlement does several things to you," Hamilton noted in her 1943 autobiography, *Exploring the Dangerous Trades*. "Among others, it teaches you that education and culture have little to do with real wisdom, the wisdom that comes from life experiences."[37]

Hamilton noticed that peer-reviewed journals paid scant attention to occupational illnesses.[38] "When I talked to my medical friends about the strange silence on this subject [occupational safety] in American medical magazines and textbooks," she wrote, "I gained the impression that here was a subject tainted with Socialism or with feminine sentimentality for the poor." By then a pioneering bacteriologist and pathologist with a social reformer's heart, she set out roaming America in search of toxic factories and chemical mishaps on industrial farms. She descended into deadly mines to track diseases, all places women were routinely forbidden to go. The numerous reports she submitted to the US government about workplace hazards directly influenced industrial safety laws.

In 1924, while a delegate to the Health Committee of the League of Nations, she visited Moscow for six weeks at the invitation of the Soviet Public Health Service. There she toured the first hospital in the world devoted to occupational diseases. She was more impressed, however, to see that female scientists were regarded more equally by the state and their male peers than they were in the United States. At the time, she was teaching industrial medicine at Harvard Medical School, having become its first female professor in 1919. She held her position on the condition that she not attend the Faculty Club or football games, or march in the commencement procession. (Or, as it turned out, attain tenure.) Rampant sexism, as commonplace as lead paint, was a workplace hazard she was never able to avoid.[39]

Active in social causes after being forced to retire at 65, she died in 1970 at 101, three months before Congress passed the Occupational Safety and Health Act, the landmark legislation dedicated to safeguarding workers.

◆

HAMILTON WOULD HAVE welcomed that development. Since its inception, the number of workplace deaths and the rate of on-the-job injuries have declined by 65 percent, and with a workforce twice as large.[40] And just as surely Hamilton would have lamented OSHA's sorry state fifty years later. The main body charged with upholding the act for which it is named was a workplace hazard itself during the pandemic.

Despite overwhelming pressure from Congress and a lawsuit by the American Federation of Labor and Congress of Industrial Organizations (AFL-CIO), OSHA refused to make any emergency protocols specific to occupational exposure to COVID-19 or regulations about airborne infectious disease during the first year of the pandemic. (That wouldn't come until June 2021.) Instead, it issued voluntary guidelines diluted with phrases like "if feasible" and "when possible," devoid of any enforcement mechanism. Under Obama, the agency had more swiftly mandated specific changes to emergency protocols to protect workers from swine flu (H1N1) at workplaces.[41] Trump's administration, by contrast, exerted no pressure on OSHA officials to do the same with COVID.

By and large, during the first year of the pandemic, the duty to regulate workplace safety was left to states, whose capacity and willingness to do so varied greatly.[42] The striking decision by Trump and then labor secretary Eugene Scalia not to issue any coronavirus-specific safety rules for companies to comply with left workers unsafe.[43] As the virus spread, workplaces became breeding grounds. Yet OSHA conducted 44 percent fewer workplace inspections from March to December 2020 compared to the same time period in 2019, when there was no raging pandemic.[44] During the first five months of the pandemic, OSHA received 7,943 complaints but issued only four citations.[45] The inspections it did carry out were usually conducted remotely, as per COVID protocols, which allowed employers to avoid disclosing violations.

Meat processing workers were especially impacted by these failures. When OSHA found that Smithfield Foods was negligent in its Sioux Falls plant, which was forced to close temporarily after four workers died of COVID-19, it fined them a measly $13,494. Pennsylvania meatpacking workers at Maid-Rite Specialty Foods had to sue OSHA just to get the watchdog to show up to investigate a complaint. The workers accused the company of mishandling sick workers, failing to inform those who'd been in contact with COVID-19-positive coworkers, and offering bonuses that incentivized sick workers to show up. As was the case with the meager fines imposed on JBS after Tin and seven others died in Greeley, OSHA allowed companies to pay a pittance for multiple workplace fatalities.[46] Far from punishing corporate exploitation, investigations had the unintended—but totally predictable—consequence of encouraging companies to continue putting workers in harm's way.

"The companies aren't afraid of OSHA," UFCW president Eric Reeder told me while he was meeting with meatpacking workers in Nebraska. "OSHA's afraid of them."

There's a positive correlation between COVID-19 complaints and deaths. Researchers at Harvard University's T.H. Chan School of Public Health found that a rise in COVID-19 deaths in certain areas occurred approximately two weeks after an OSHA complaint was filed in that area. This finding suggests that worker concerns were an accurate barometer of threats posed by the virus, and that the failure of OSHA to respond contributed to workplace transmission.[47] Despite this, workers who voiced concerns about COVID protocols at their workplace faced frequent retaliation from their employers for exercising their health and safety rights. When these whistleblowers took their complaints about the retaliation to OSHA, the body tasked with handling these grievances, they were ignored. Of the 1,744 retaliation complaints OSHA received by October 2020, fewer than 20 percent were even investigated, and only 2 percent had been resolved in the time frame studied.[48] To sum up: overall, OSHA failed to adequately investigate workplace hazards and then failed to protect workers who stood up to demand greater workplace safety.

However much OSHA bungled the job, it must be remembered that lawmakers adhered to a stark partisan divide on what a workplace safety organization should do, hampering OSHA's efficacy. Democrats largely argued it should protect workers in frontline industries. OSHA has "failed to develop the necessary tools it needs to combat this pandemic, and it has failed to fully use the tools it has," said Rep. Alma Adams (D-NC), chairwoman of the House Education and Labor Subcommittee on Workforce Protections. The agency has appeared "invisible," she added, during opening remarks at a House hearing in June 2020. In contrast, Republican lawmakers largely warned against OSHA's safeguarding of workers because they feared it would hurt plans to reopen businesses. At the same hearing, Rep. Bradley Byrne (R-AL) argued that creating an industry safety standard "would be an unproductive burden for businesses already struggling to reopen, potentially exposing them to unnecessary liability risks."[49] The magnitude of the partisan discrepancy on this issue is almost without precedent—one side tried to protect workers during a global health crisis, the other made them a bull's-eye.

OSHA's annual budget, set by a Republican-controlled Senate, says it all. At less than $600 million, it is clear that we don't spend that much money on enforcing worker safety and health because the government doesn't care that much about worker safety and health. The Environmental Protection Agency (EPA) budget, for example, is roughly $11 billion. OSHA's staffing levels are lower than they've been in forty years. With only nine hundred inspectors, it would take 165 years to visit every establishment in its jurisdiction just once.[50]

Still, the past practice of the agency shows it can make a difference when it is better funded. These days, every hospital in America has a container designated for disposal of sharp blades, and they offer free vaccinations against hepatitis B. Why? Because during the AIDS epidemic, the agency created a bloodborne pathogen standard to improve safety protocols around the disease. The result has been fewer needlesticks among healthcare workers and plummeting cases of work-related hepatitis B.[51] The same standard was useful years later during the Ebola outbreak because it prepared hospitals for particular kinds of precautions, especially those hospitals likely to receive Ebola patients.

Under Obama, the advent of swine flu (H1N1) encouraged OSHA to begin developing a new standard around infectious airborne diseases, like flu, tuberculosis, or methicillin-resistant *Staphylococcus aureus* (MRSA). This new series of good practices would have come with requirements for businesses to contain occupational contagion, implement worker training programs, and provide greater on-hand quantities of PPE. If nothing else, such a standard would have provided much-needed guidance on the complicated task of maintaining some degree of economic activity while keeping workers safe. The progress made toward developing that standard abruptly ended when Trump took office and slashed the department's funding.

✦

CONSERVATIVE LAWMAKERS PUT workers at inordinate risk by underfunding the government organization tasked with protecting them. Not content to stop there, they also tried to prohibit workers from improving workplace safety standards. A good case study is Iowa, where Governor Kim Reynolds argued that the state should not "prioritize" lives over livelihoods, adding in May 2020: "For our state, recovery means striking a balance between getting life and business back to normal."[52] With employers and the state given the green light to "balance" the lives of their employees with profits, workers were left to fend for themselves.

Therefore, as soon as Mary Heeringa learned that Governor Reynolds was not going to adopt a statewide mask mandate in Iowa schools, she made a plan to ensure that her school district, at least, would have one. Heeringa, a librarian and teacher and president of the Bettendorf Education Association, took notice of the safety checklist developed by the statewide teachers' union, which included mandatory face coverings. She read it at a public school board meeting and then took the checklist to the various committees responsible for a safe return in the fall and made sure they supported a mask mandate too. Heeringa's work paid off and her district adopted the practice, which, she claimed, was widely successful. The main holdouts were actually several school board officials, who brazenly walked through the district buildings maskless—until Mary confronted them during livestreamed school board meetings.

Our research team, which showed unions reduce the spread of COVID-19 in nursing homes, also looked at the relationship between unions and mask mandates in Iowa, a very red state. The CDC advised mask wearing inside schools but, without a statewide mandate, only 60 percent of Iowa school districts required them. Why did some schools have them while others did not?

As states began mandating that public schools reopen, Dr. Anthony Fauci, head of the National Institute of Allergy and Infectious Diseases and a prominent member of the White House Coronavirus Task Force, told teachers they would "be part of the experiment" to learn more about how the disease spreads. As even he probably anticipated, this unfortunate bit of sarcasm didn't go over well with a lot of educators, who objected to being guinea pigs. Why not send corporate lobbyists back into small, crowded, poorly ventilated rooms with sneezy kids for low pay instead?

In the absence of robust federal standards, teachers' unions played an essential role in securing safe classrooms for communities. For example, our research found that districts with stronger teachers' unions were more likely to adopt mask mandates.[53] Independent of the extent of community spread, what really mattered was whether a teachers' union was able to fight for safety protections like masks and win.

Partisanship influenced unions' ability to protect schools. We found that the greater the percentage of registered Democrats in a union, the more likely it was to have a mandate. Some teachers told us that the union might have tempered that partisan divide, though. "We [the union] were the ones who pushed for the mandate—and we got it," said Nancy Grisham, a teacher of twenty-six years in Iowa schools and president of her local union. The district and superintendent were pushing for masks to be "encouraged but optional" in the schools, she said. "We said 'no,' it's gotta be the rule."

Grisham was a committed Trump supporter when I spoke with her just before the November 2020 election. She believed mask wearing was a matter of "personal choice" except at work. She made a crucial distinction between Trump supporters she knows who were in the union and those who were not. "The union is important to us," she said, "because it really shapes your outlook on what matters at work."

Mask mandates protect more than teachers and students. Schools that required masks in 2020 saw an incredible 37 percent drop in COVID-19 cases, and research shows that masks slow community spread.[54] Strong unions were an important mechanism by which teachers helped mitigate the impact of the virus in the workplace and beyond.

Teachers' unions were effective not only in Iowa and not only through mask mandates. In Los Angeles County, after more than a year of remote instruction, teachers and students were called back to the classroom in March 2021. The plan to reopen schools included a phased agreement negotiated by the union, the United Teachers Los Angeles (UTLA), with the district.[55]

There was significant pressure to open schools earlier, but the union led the movement to not do so until case numbers dropped, vaccinations increased, and safety measures were reliably in place. The union fought for and won the right to return only once workplace-specific vaccination levels were high and high-tech air filters were installed in classrooms, and after they'd secured better PPE and paid time to prepare for the return to in-person learning.

"Every step of the way, UTLA educators have kept our students and communities safer, from the call to close down schools early in the pandemic to holding the line against an unsafe return," UTLA president Cecily Myart-Cruz said. "While the improving COVID-19 situation is still fragile, we believe this agreement puts [Los Angeles Unified School District] on the path to a physical reopening of schools that puts safety first."[56]

For Erica Alvarez, a veteran English teacher in the district, the power to bargain such a strong agreement for a safe return was forged years earlier on picket lines. In 2019, LA teachers joined the Red for Ed strike wave that had been kicked off in West Virginia the year before. About 375,000 teachers walked a picket line across the country, the largest number since the mideighties, pushing for higher wages, racial justice demands, and local political reforms.

In LA, the union won sweeping changes that extended beyond the typical purview of contract negotiations, a strategy called Bargaining for the Common Good, whereby unions use their seat at the table with management to secure community-wide victories.[57] Pretty soon the schools had additional counselors and librarians, smaller class sizes, a 6 percent pay raise with no healthcare concessions, political support for a statewide moratorium on additional charters, plus the extension of a program to phase out racist "random searches" on students and the establishment of an immigrant defense fund.[58] Perhaps most important to the discussion about the pandemic, they also won the right to have a full-time nurse in every school. This proved remarkably prescient, as the schools' 2021 reopening coincided with an unexpected rise in cases of multisystem inflammatory syndrome in children (MIS-C), a rare but serious complication associated with COVID-19 and children.

Alvarez described the 2019 strike as "transformative," both personally and professionally. Not only did she witness the power of collective action but also the experience prepared her and her coworkers to act together during the pandemic.

There were trade-offs with their victories in 2021. To win high safety standards, the union compromised elsewhere, agreeing to an extended workday. Erica thinks it was worth it. "Nothing mattered more to us than the safety of our kids," she said. "That's what the union fought for. And that's why the return-to-work plan looks the way it does."

Chicago teachers fought a similar battle. Kenzo Shibata opened his email one morning in January 2021 to find out he'd been called back to work as a teacher at Chicago Public Schools (CPS). His classroom was slated to have thirty students, few of whom were eligible to receive a vaccine. At that time, Kenzo's wife had stage 4 breast cancer, and his family had been taking social distancing measures very seriously. That included his decision to continue to work remotely.

"Without the union I would have been back in the classroom— definitely," he told me. In defiance of orders from the Chicago mayor Lori Lightfoot and Janice Jackson, the CEO of Chicago Public Schools, thousands of teachers refused to report to in-person classes the following Monday. The teachers' union's six-hundred-member House of Delegates voted to continue to teach online, refusing to enter the school buildings. The work-from-home action came on the first day that kindergarten through eighth-grade teachers were scheduled to go back to classrooms. Some preschool and special education teachers had already been mandated to return to their classrooms, two of whom had since contracted COVID-19, leading most of the others to join in the larger work-from-home protest. CPS officials regarded it as an "illegal strike."

Although district officials argued that the union was acting contrary to what families needed and wanted, only 19 percent of eligible students had returned to school in the first wave. Lightfoot tried to get teachers back into buildings in fall 2021. When the union threatened to strike, the mayor backed down. Ultimately, it was the city government that stopped teachers from being able to work, not the union. When teachers failed to report to their in-person classrooms, the city locked them out of their Google Classroom accounts, making it impossible for them to meet with students virtually. Teachers who refused to return were also threatened with disciplinary measures and pay cuts.

Across the country, optimism swelled in the late spring and administrators began planning a post-pandemic school year to start in fall 2021. The delta variant of COVID-19 thwarted these plans. So, as it turns out, did leaders like Iowa's Kim Reynolds. She outlawed mask mandates across the state, meaning Mary Heeringa's union no longer had the strategic leverage it had in 2020. It advocated masks, but it couldn't mandate anyone to wear one.

The Centers for Disease Control and Prevention and the American Academy of Pediatrics both recommended masks be worn. At the same time, conservative lawmakers in other states began banning masks.[59] In August 2021, only ten states had statewide mask mandates, compared to thirty-eight states the year before. Even before vaccines were available to young children, public health mitigation standards were being slashed.

Heeringa noted that her union was at a disadvantage in 2021 because of the governor's statewide ban on mask mandates. But in other conservative states, unions sometimes still won important victories. Dallas, Austin, and Houston school districts, with the support of their unions, implemented a mask mandate in their schools, defying Texas governor Greg Abbott's ban.[60] Texas teachers, like those in Iowa the year before, showed what unions can do to make good public health policy when governments don't.

However, nationwide, unions' approach to vaccines was more nuanced. As the country prepared for a possible broad return to in-person schooling, American Federation of Teachers president Randi Wein-garten was clear that her union would oppose a vaccine mandate for classroom teachers, making face-to-face teaching more dangerous for everyone. "Vaccinations must be negotiated between employers and workers, not coerced," said Weingarten. National Education Association president Becky Pringle even took a stand against prioritizing teachers to be vaccinated. "We don't want to be in the business of putting a hierarchy in place, because some of our members are being bullied into returning back to classrooms," she told the *New York Times*.[61] "That's not safe, we don't want to support that."

It was an odd stance. On the one hand, the union had floated the possibility that the delta variant posed a serious enough health risk to force more remote instruction. On the other, it opposed mandating the strongest public health action that would allow for the reopening of schools. Combine this with mounting data showing the educational drawbacks of remote schooling and the union's stance looked, even to their ardent supporters on the Left, self-defeating.

The teachers' union was hardly alone. In the summer of 2021, SEIU, the country's largest healthcare workers' union, took to the streets of New York City to demand that NewYork–Presbyterian Hospital "educate, not mandate vaccines."[62] SEIU also publicly fought vaccine mandates for public sector workers in California. Elsewhere, they quietly opposed them, knowing their full-throated opposition would anger some key political allies. Still, within workplaces, they strove to get as many workers vaccinated as possible.

"I was against it," said Gloria Duquette, the Connecticut nursing home worker we met earlier in this chapter. She wasn't alone. These workers had initially very high rates of vaccine refusal, especially among Black and Latino workers. "They [her employers] wanted us to get it. We don't trust them," Gloria explained. "So when they say 'get this shot,' of course we're going to say no."

Unions helped convince nurses, however, to get vaccinated. Unions ran public health workshops in different venues. They produced webinars for workers in multiple languages with doctors from a variety of backgrounds. Union stewards showed the videos in break rooms using workers' laptops and phones. Unions organized groups of workers to get vaccinated together, as a social event, with food and drinks. And unions across the country negotiated paid sick leave with employers that made it possible for workers to get the shot and recover as needed, instead of having to miss a payday for vaccine recovery; nonunion workers often don't have a way to communicate issues like that to management. "After the union came in, told us what it [the vaccine] was all about, I got mine straightaway. I trust doctors, just not my manager," Gloria said. Other workers I interviewed said exactly the same thing and credited the union with convincing them to get the vaccine.

But why would unions stand against a perfectly reasonable public health policy, especially unions representing those who work in education and healthcare, the two industries with the biggest potential to kick off more outbreaks? By the fall of 2021, vaccination rates of staff at union nursing homes in many parts of the country were below 50 percent. Though residents were vaccinated at higher rates, it's hard to avoid the fact that unvaccinated nursing home workers could still easily spread the disease among a vulnerable population.

Opposition to flu vaccines has a long history among nurses' unions. COVID-19 should have been treated differently, however, because the disease is so much more contagious and lethal. Teacher and healthcare union opposition to vaccine mandates rests on a liberal idea of individual bodily autonomy. That works for abortion but is inappropriately applied to infectious diseases that affect the health of the larger society. More importantly, it's a political stance typically opposed by unions, which view public health and workplace safety as social goods that require collective action to achieve.

"Vaccines are the most effective way to protect essential workers," Mary Kay Henry, president of the Service Employees International Union, said in a tweet. "But workers need adequate paid time off, protective equipment, pandemic pay and equitable access," she wrote.[63] That message might have resonated in unlikely places. Blue counties have higher vaccination rates than red counties. And counties where a larger percentage of union members reside are statistically correlated with higher vaccination rates. These positive effects of union density on vaccination status, however, are stronger in counties with high levels of support for Trump in 2020.[64] This reveals a more complex relationship between unions, public policy, and partisanship than we typically expect. All this is to say that despite their objections to vaccine mandates, union membership was a powerful force for vaccine take-up.

◆

AS WORKERS STRUGGLED *for* the common good over the course of the pandemic, defending themselves and their communities, employers often stood firmly *against* it. When workers at Amazon banded together to demand higher safety standards or hazard pay, bosses fired workers and opposed their unionization campaign. As teachers fought to get their students vaccinated, the pharmaceutical companies that had developed vaccines lobbied the government to retaliate against any country attempting to produce their vaccines without approval, a mission backed by Bill Gates.[65] As nurses fought for better patient care ratios, Alteon Health, a major medical staffing company, slashed pay and benefits to medical professionals on the front lines.[66]

Our most vaunted institutions were complicit as well. Take, for instance, the decrepit Supreme Court's 2022 decision to thwart Biden's vaccine-or-test mandate at large private companies. Biden's mandate proposed that the eighty-five million private sector employees at businesses with one hundred or more workers would either be vaccinated or tested weekly for free. A week later, a federal court struck down a similar mandate that applied to three million employees of the federal government. The rulings prohibited OSHA from doing the job it was tasked to do, undoing broad public health policies that were widely popular. The Republican-appointed justices were, in effect, prolonging the pandemic and endangering essential workers.[67] "As disease and death continue to mount," wrote the liberal Supreme Court judges in their dissent, "this court tells the agency that it cannot respond in the most effective way possible."

If unions are ever to get the kind of public relations face-lift they so desperately need, today they should broadcast what is perhaps their signature accomplishment over the decades: unions have long kept us safer and healthier. Their collective bargaining agreements are vehicles to providing health insurance that allows people to see doctors with more regularity at lower cost. A voice on the job, with protections against unjust dismissals, means union workers are freer to speak out when they see safety violations.[68] Finally, in states where so-called right-to-work laws have eroded the power of unions, workers are 14 percent more likely to die of an occupational hazard.[69]

During the pandemic, unions played a critical role in minimizing the spread of the virus. As Adam Dean and I wrote in the *Washington Post* about our research on mask mandates and teachers' unions, after more than a year of debating how the country can protect essential workers, it turns out that allowing essential workers to unionize may actually enable them to protect the country.[70] Our findings have implications for policymakers who have a goal of reducing the spread of the virus—for the public good, make it easier for workers to organize unions.

We can't expect that unions would be able to completely negate the incredible power of corporate America or fill the void of government negligence. Still, worker power is good for public health inside and outside workplaces, critical to mitigating the risks and hazards of capitalist employment. Workplace safety should be an enduring concern whenever the pandemic recedes, if for no other reason than to safeguard us against the next one. Yet, as vaccines helped drive down cases across the country, our attention turned to another curio of the pandemic political economy: Where were all the workers?

We spent the first year concerned with the safety of the frontline class. Then at exactly the same time vaccines became universally accessible in the US and wages began to rise, labor was suddenly in short supply. It's not just that people weren't coming back to work; they were quitting like never before.

The persistent labor shortage was more of a puzzle. It wasn't caused for the reasons most people think, and it didn't end the way most conservative lawmakers thought it would. It had elements of a collective problem but also involved a great deal of individual risk and benefit calculation. The labor shortage was one of the most unpredictable and perplexing moments of the pandemic because it tangled in a knot the convoluted relationship between bad jobs, structural barriers in the labor market, worker activism, and antipathy for work in general.

CHAPTER 5

QUITTER'S PARADISE

Work is a scam. We spend far too much time doing it, and most people aren't paid anything close to the amount of value their labor creates. In the last few decades, those who have added the most hours to their workweek have seen their incomes stagnate or decline. Meanwhile, those who have kept more or less the same hours have grown far richer by earning higher salaries, not by working harder or longer. We've designed our society so that you have to work to survive, but millions of jobs don't pay a living wage. It's a scam—literally.

Nonetheless, one of the biggest scandals of the pandemic economy was the possibility, plastered across newspaper headlines and on the doors of major restaurant chains, that nobody wants to work anymore. Indeed, quit rates were high. And in many industries that had previously survived on an endless supply of low-wage labor, workers seemed suddenly hard to find. In response, there developed a popular assertion that the persistent labor shortage was a direct outcome of workers living high on the hog of Biden's extended unemployment benefits. This claim does not hold up to scrutiny.

As the previous chapter attests, for over a year many workers faced dirty, contaminated workspaces replete with deadly airborne pathogens, often without adequate protective equipment or a raise. It would be forgivable if, after working through a pandemic in such conditions, they didn't want to do it any longer. And in many cases they didn't, but that doesn't explain the labor shortage. What *does* explain the labor shortage is far more complicated. The labor shortage first appeared as a cynical ruse, an invented crisis that served a conservative agenda to roll back the lingering programs of the pandemic welfare state. The unusually generous unemployment insurance payments dispersed through the CARES Act and the American Recovery Plan were still sloshing around in the bank accounts of low-wage workers, an important barrier between joblessness and poverty. But a few months after the jobless benefits of both parties officially ended, a more confounding picture emerged that suggested an actual worker shortage in several service industries, like restaurants, hotels, and healthcare.

This time the labor shortage collided with a nationwide strike wave, peaking in October 2021, which seemed qualitatively different from the earlier labor unrest during the heart of the pandemic, examined in Chapter 3. What do all these facets of the pandemic economy have in common? To answer that, we must first dispatch with a (very) brief history of labor shortages.

◆

A LABOR SHORTAGE happens when employers can't find enough willing workers at the wage they're offering. In May 2021, there were 10 million job openings and 8.4 million people looking for work. Technically speaking, that's a labor shortage. On cue, that month the *Wall Street Journal* editorial board had had enough and ran an op-ed with the headline "Worst Worker Shortage Ever."[1]

That's a bold claim, considering the fraught history of worker shortages. When the British were short on indigenous workers to enslave, for instance, they kidnapped twelve million Africans and forced them to work on American plantations. That was a worse "worker shortage." In Europe, the widespread privatization of land in the form of enclosure laws during the sixteenth century pushed people off their plots and into cities, where they had no choice but to avail themselves of factory labor, an early solution to a scarcity of industrial workers.

As the system migrated across the Atlantic, even Abraham Lincoln impugned "wage slavery," modern indentured work rules that ensured employers had the labor they wanted.

That's not to say things didn't get dicey in 2021 too. The history of labor shortages repeats—first as farce, then as tragedy. It was a farce because so much of the presumed shortage was really just employers refusing to raise wages. It was also a tragedy because labor shortages in healthcare contribute to declining standards of care, mistakes by workers, and unnecessary patient illness and death. Neither dynamic was caused by the pandemic, though COVID revealed long-standing economic weaknesses that are now in even more desperate need of attention.

After Biden's extension of unemployment benefits in early 2021, employers began howling about the sorry state of the American work ethic, which included a nationwide program of shaming people into going to work. Signs were plastered on café and restaurant doors across the country urging customers to be patient with the staff, who were overworked thanks to the layabouts getting by on Biden's expanded unemployment plan. The work ethic is a powerful weapon and is easily wielded with precision. Whether it was jealousy, resentment, misunderstanding, or political disagreements, complaints about the unemployed did serve to fracture the spirit of the pandemic working class, pushing many workers to side with employers. After all, short staffing in hospitality, retail, and dining did add stress, danger, time, and workloads to those who were still working.

The debate about the labor shortage unfolded in waves. First, even before Biden's extended UI policies went into effect, many employers argued that they needed to import foreign laborers to staff low-wage jobs, as they had done in the past, because native-born workers were unwilling to work them. Much of this happened through their industry lobbying group, which is called—I'm not making this up—the Essential Worker Immigration Coalition (EWIC). The EWIC defines essential workers as that mass of "lesser skilled and unskilled" labor that always seems in short supply, even when they're not. Its main political goal is to make it easier for domestic employers to import foreign workers on terms favorable to business instead of raising wages. In all of the top fifteen industries the EWIC was looking to recruit labor for, wages stagnated or declined during the decade of 2004–2014.[2] The neoliberal trade agreements of the nineties helped fuel an economy that relies on migrant workers to staff fields and factories. It's no wonder then that 70 percent of all immigrants in the US labor force were essential workers in 2020. As one of the main programs that grants employers access to a pool of temporary workers abroad, the H-2B visa program facilitates this modern-day corvée labor regime.

The program is predicated on the spurious assumption of a constant labor shortage, even in good times. Research shows that workers who come to the US on H-2B visas work in rough conditions for long hours at low wages and are typically provided substandard housing.[3] In February 2020, notably before the pandemic hit the US economy, the Department of Homeland Security authorized forty-five thousand additional H-2B visas as a result of lobbying from states with large seafood processing companies that rely on migrant labor.

A year into the pandemic, however, there were no signs of labor shortages in major H-2B industries. In fact, there was the opposite: high unemployment in every one of the top ten jobs receiving H-2B migrant workers.[4] The law states that H-2B workers can only be used "if unemployed persons capable of performing such service or labor cannot be found in this country." Powerful employers and the business lobby successfully argued that additional workers were necessary instead of raising wages because they prefer workers who are pliable, expendable, and cheaper. In the midst of widespread claims about labor shortages, there were almost two million Americans looking for work in major H-2B industries, many of which were categorized as essential, such as food processing. Rather than hire these workers, employers lobbied to import record numbers of migrants instead.[5] Employers steal their wages, abuse them, and work them when they're sick. During the peak of the lockdown period, Trump extended visas for current H-2B workers and made it easier for employers to hire more. How exactly did we show our appreciation? Some H-2B workers were fired simply for going to the hospital to get a COVID test.[6]

Employers who relied on migrant labor often pointed to the fact that Trump's harsh immigration restrictions had contracted their usual labor pool. The US issued just over half the usual number of visas in 2020 as in 2019. But the H-2 category of visas, which are specifically for work, fell by the smallest amount. Many migrants who were brought to the US to work were frequently unable to do so because their cheek-by-jowl housing conditions meant they were often sick or required to quarantine.

Businesses moved on to other ideas.

"What if we just cut off the unemployment?" suggested conservative pundit Laura Ingraham glibly. "Hunger is a powerful thing."[7] To her credit, the threat of starvation has in the past been a vital work incentive in the American economy. So, in a massive economic experiment, in June 2021, twenty red states went with a carrot-and-stick approach and cut workers off from unemployment checks. To be clear, this meant that about half of American states, all red, turned down financial gifts from the federal government that were propping up their consumption levels, keeping their economies going when so many people couldn't work. They voluntarily slowed their own recovery and risked their constituents' livelihoods just to try to force them into bad jobs. One group of business owners in Springfield, Missouri, was so incensed by the worker shortage that they purchased billboards around town reading, "Get Off Your Butt!" and "Get. To. Work."

The billboard campaign flopped. In October, three months after Missouri ended its emergency unemployment benefits, the state's jobless rate remained nearly three times its pre-pandemic level.[8] The same was true across other red states; they had unemployment numbers basically equal to those of blue states, which were still paying expanded benefits. Six months after that, when all of the lingering expanded unemployment benefits had ended, because blue states stopped paying them on Labor Day, the result was the same. The labor shortage persisted.

The National Restaurant Association, a lobbying body of corporate chain restaurants sometimes referred to as "the other NRA," has fought against higher wages for decades. It has spent tens of millions lobbying to keep the federal tipped minimum wage at $2.13 per hour. A UC Berkeley study, however, found that about half of laid-off restaurant workers didn't receive any unemployment insurance at all because their base pay was so low they didn't even meet the minimum eligibility requirements. And for those who did opt to go back to work at $2.13, tips were far below their pre-pandemic rate.[9]

Employers began to get creative. Maybe, it stood to reason, children could step up. After all, they were not receiving UI benefits, because they were never laid off, because they weren't allowed to work in the first place—because they're children. Nonetheless, Wisconsin's Republican-dominated senate approved a bill to allow children as young as fourteen to work late-night shifts in order to fill low-wage jobs. To be fair, this is only an extension of past practice. The state has been whittling away at child labor laws for years, striking down maximum hours restrictions for minors; in 2017 it replaced any mention of "child labor" with "employment of minors."[10]

A similar law trying to solve the labor shortage with children earned bipartisan support in Ohio. Yet, even without any official change to child labor laws, franchise restaurants across the country had been advertising job vacancies for underage teens for months. An Arkansas restaurant owner offered to pay his teen employees to do their homework before their shift in an effort to retain them.[11] To staff a Subway restaurant, one franchise owner pulled her own teenage daughter out of high school to work. A Pennsylvania pizza parlor hired kids to cover open shifts it couldn't fill with adults. "I wouldn't be open without my teen employees," owner Keith Fetterman told a local news outlet. "With the stimulus money and the weekly increase in unemployment (benefits), I found some older people didn't want to work."[12]

No hard data showed unemployment benefits were the cause of the labor shortage. Sure, some people were living off expanded UI checks, waiting out the pandemic or applying to graduate school or working from home. That's what the checks were for. But job growth in the spring and summer of 2021 was concentrated among low-wage workers. If UI was driving the labor shortage, we would have seen the opposite, because it would have impacted low-income workers the most. Disappointing job growth in April, for example, was commonly attributed to high UI. If that were the case, we would have seen a decrease in hiring, but we saw the opposite. Actually, sluggish growth that month had to do with high quit rates and layoffs.[13] This isn't to say UI didn't matter. UI can make it prohibitive for employers to slash wages because workers have a safety net and are less likely to simply take any job at the lowest price. In other words, UI benefits tilted the economy ever so slightly in workers' favor.

And that was the problem.

Economists were clear. "Overall, our evidence suggests that employers did not experience greater difficulty finding applicants for their vacancies after the CARES Act, despite the large increase in unemployment benefits," found one prominent study in July 2020. Another study: "We [researchers] find no evidence that more generous benefits disincentivize work either at the onset of the expansion or as firms looked to return to business over time."[14]

In other words, the labor shortage was a farce.

Capitalist societies like ours have a ready-made solution to labor shortages: raise wages. If you want a yacht but you are only willing to pay $5,000 for one, that doesn't mean there's a yacht shortage. There's just a shortage of yachts at that price. If you were willing to pay, say, $500 million, you'd have a yacht surplus, or just one of Jeff Bezos's megayachts.

The same principle applies to the labor market. When wages rise, workers will enter the labor market and the labor shortage will disappear. It's theoretically possible that workers could demand wages so high that employers could not afford to pay them. But that's not happening. Real wages for everyone but the most affluent have barely improved in decades. In fact, we're long overdue for a massive wage bump. Meanwhile, corporate profits have soared to new heights. As labor's strength at the bargaining table has been systematically diminished, corporations have been able to extract far more profit and time from workers who earn comparably less in real terms than they did in the midseventies.

In the midst of a labor shortage, it's easy to see why this incredible store of cash might come in handy for corporate America. They can use it to raise wages and incentivize people—adults, preferably—back to work. Some of them did this. Amazon, Chipotle, Costco, JPMorgan Chase, Starbucks, Bank of America, and Sheetz gas stations, to name some of the big ones, all upped their hourly wages. A desperate McDonald's franchise even began paying people just to walk in for an interview.

Still, the labor shortage persisted. In the spring and summer of 2021, the labor shortage became increasingly concentrated in just a few areas: leisure and hospitality, restaurants, and healthcare. In all of these sectors, employers, government, and industry lobbies had kept wages low for decades. In a survey of almost three thousand restaurant workers conducted by One Fair Wage, a nonprofit that advocates for an end to subminimum wages, about three-quarters said they were looking to leave the industry because of low wages, and 78 percent said a "full, stable, livable wage" would entice them to stay. Average compensation clocks in at about $20,500 a year.[15]

For most workers, wages still hadn't risen enough. But it didn't matter to Jane.

"It's like everyone forgot how much restaurant work sucks," Jane said, a former server at Wolfgang Puck's glitzy Spago in Beverly Hills. "It's just not worth it. Of course I'll take some unemployment for a while. It's not like I won't have the opportunity to be a waitress again—it's that I don't want it."

On a good night before the pandemic, Jane made $400. Though demand for high-end cuisine was returning in the summer of 2021, Puck couldn't find the staff to fully open, even as the pandemic receded. A Spago pizza will separate you from $75, and it's a hundred bucks more for a steak. Add in alcohol and tips, which were still high at fine dining places, and the math shows that servers would earn far more than on Biden's UI plan. Why weren't they following the money?

Jane's answer went like this. "Customers suck. Chefs suck. Getting harassed all night to take your mask off sucks. I learned something this past year, that's that I never want to wait a table again if I can help it. Trust me, it's not just me."

Gianni Verdi, a server of twenty-one years at mostly fine dining places in New York City and Providence, felt similarly. He said he's used the unemployment benefits to plan an exit from the industry. Noting that line cooks were among the most likely to die from COVID, he said he didn't feel safe in the industry anymore. "The restaurant industry business model is built on paying workers shit," he said. "So when workers have been realizing their true value and demanding more [during the pandemic], these businesses don't know how to pivot, especially the non-corporate ones."

I heard many similar stories from many servers who simply had had enough, and who would rather forgo decent pay for a little time out. Stories from the trenches of the service economy illuminate another dimension to labor shortage hysteria: not only were employers having a hard time hiring the unemployed, workers who had jobs were quitting like crazy. It wasn't just restaurants. In April 2021 alone, retail establishments lost 650,000 workers and nursing facilities shed 20,000 care workers, the result of a historic quit wave that came to be known as the "Great Resignation." In July, that record was broken. In August, it was broken again, when a total of 4.3 million people left their jobs.[16] It kept rising to 4.5 million quits in November 2021, about 3 percent of the entire workforce.

The popular impression was that American workers were taking cues from the original slacker himself, Bartleby the scrivener, Herman Melville's recalcitrant low-level clerk who, when told repeatedly to work, responded simply, "I would prefer not to." In November, the *Financial Times* even published a piece on the explosive growth of Reddit's "antiwork" forum, as if millions of unemployed Americans might suddenly be tempted by the allure of anarchism.[17]

Actually, the historic quit rates were concentrated in sectors such as retail, food service, hospitality, and healthcare, where exposure to the virus combined with low wages and long hours led to unsafe working conditions and poor quality of life. Moreover, the data show that the rate of hires actually outpaced quits, meaning those leaving jobs were out to get a better one at higher pay.

Employers began complaining in the press that workers were "ghosting" them for interviews, a term borrowed from dating lingo. But the mismatch of empowered workers and lousy jobs was more than just bad romance. Soon other signs began appearing on the doors of shuttered restaurants and businesses across the country. "We all quit! Closed!" read one posted on a drive-through kiosk at Wendy's. "Closed indefinitely because Dollar General doesn't pay a living wage or treat their employees with respect," said another. "Attention Chipotle customers: Ask our corporate offices why their employees are forced to work in borderline sweatshop conditions for 8+ hours WITHOUT MASKS. We are overworked, underpaid, understaffed, and underappreciated. Almost the entire management and crew have walked out until further notice." At Wendy's: "Please be Patient. Management has chosen to operate this location short-staffed. #Thereisnolaborshortage." "Capitalism will destroy this country," said another sign. "If you don't pay people enough to live their lives, why should they slave away for you?"

Workers flipped the right-wing script. Journalists began covering their version of the story, which was that almost all labor shortages can be solved by money. How much money, exactly, became the terms of the new debate. In the fall of 2021, modest to substantial wage hikes in many industries still weren't enough to lure people back to work in the midst of a deadly pandemic, even after higher unemployment benefits expired.

What was happening? It might mean that wages were simply not high enough. Wages overall had risen almost 5 percent across the economy, but in restaurants, where the shortage was concentrated, this translated into just one dollar per hour. Other workers were soaked up by platform companies, which expanded their reach during the pandemic, and offered socially distant work with more flexible schedules. These workers were typically self-employed and left more vacancies elsewhere. I met a few former food industry workers, for example, who started working for DoorDash, delivering food from their old restaurants, which were understaffed. Bailey, the welder we met in Chapter 2 who started the essential workers Facebook group, became self-employed using OnlyFans, the platform that became popular among sex workers during the pandemic. "I have a good gig now," she told me. "I'm not going back to work for somebody else like before. That was awful."

It's possible that slowed flows of migrants were causing shortages in certain industries, but Biden had reversed Trump's ban on legal migration, allowing people to cross borders to work. Some people were forced out of jobs by refusing to comply with vaccine mandates, but that wouldn't be a prime cause of such a huge worker shortage. Two other explanations, however, are more interesting.

The first is that the Great Resignation was partly the result of a Great Reassessment. Liberals heralded the idea that the pandemic prompted a sweeping reconsideration of the role of work in our lives. The alleged conclusion reached by many was that wages aren't high enough, work isn't good enough, and our limited time on this burning planet shouldn't be spent in a cubicle or some other dead-end job, lest we shuffle off this mortal coil while clearing out our in-box. An April 2021 Pew Research Center poll found that two-thirds of the unemployed had "seriously considered" changing their field of work, a far greater percentage than during the Great Recession.[18] Harvard economist Lawrence Katz calls this a "once in a generation 'take this job and shove it' moment."[19]

Take Jesse Short, a bartender for twenty-five years. He volunteered in the early days of the pandemic to help his restaurant produce and distribute meals. Due to poor treatment, however, even as an essential volunteer, he turned away from the industry for good to focus on songwriting. "Risking your life so some rich guy can eat his beef tartare and not tip you during a pandemic isn't really worth it," he told me.

As it turns out, a lot of people weren't eager to jump back on the hamster wheel. Even those who are ready to go back to work now understand that jobs don't have to look the way they did before the pandemic, having witnessed the possibility of remote work and flexible schedules. In mid-2022, even many low-income workers were also more financially stable than they were before the pandemic, giving them more leverage to be picky about the conditions on which they reenter the labor force. Maybe some people, in other words, just don't want to work anymore.

There's no doubt we need to grapple with work's existential place in our lives. Yet, this doesn't explain much of the reason for quits or reluctance to join the labor force. The Great Reassessment didn't happen on the scale imagined, nor equally along the class ladder. Did essential workers spend 2020 and 2021 reconsidering the inherent value of work, pursuing passion projects, or applying to graduate school? "We dreamed big for sure," Meredith, a CNA told me, "but those dreams require money to come true. Not everybody has that." It's irresponsible to exaggerate the degree to which the ideological bubble around work was punctured, because it underappreciates its strength and its staying power.

The second explanation has the most hard evidence. The US Census asked people why they weren't working and people told them. The results show that the persistence of the labor shortage was mainly the result of the combined effect of unattractive low-wage jobs and the consistent pandemic constraints that made it difficult or impossible for many people to work.

The graph below charts weekly responses to a household survey administered by the US Census Bureau. It asked people why they were not working and gave them a handful of explanations to choose from. The results show that people who responded "I did not want to be employed at this time" represent an infrequent explanation. By contrast, those who said that caregiving responsibilities—for children,

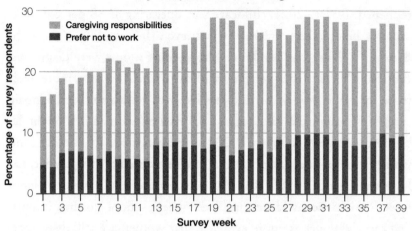

Caregiving responsibilities are the most common reason people report for not per-forming paid work during the heart of the pandemic. SOURCE: Author's analysis of the US Census Bureau's Household Pulse Survey (employment tables), May 20, 2020, to October 20, 2021

the elderly, and those with COVID—kept them from working were far more common. In fact, the frequency of those with caregiving re-sponsibilities trends upward for most of the thirty-nine weeks this data covers. The survey also shows that those earning $25,000 or less were three times as likely to miss a week of work due to their own COVID symptoms or those of a loved one in their care than those who made $100,000 or more.[20] The labor shortage was mainly a crisis of care felt by the working class.

The widespread unavailability of childcare, eldercare, and care for the disabled especially kept working mothers from going back to work or forced them to quit their jobs. Even with schools more likely to be open at the end of 2021, frequent closures from COVID outbreaks, or the need for families to periodically quarantine, meant consistent work was off the table. The school day, after all, does not align with the workday.

When the essential worker classification schemes went public in March 2020, about one-third of US states did not include childcare providers as essential services and closed them down. Many never reopened. By late 2021, childcare was operating at 88 percent of its capacity before the pandemic, which even then could not meet the demand.[21] When the pandemic hit, working moms were disproportionately affected. They were more likely to lose their jobs, more likely to be forced to quit them, and less likely to return to them. Unpaid caregiving responsibilities pushed 2.3 million women out of the labor force between February 2020 and February 2021.[22] By that time, women's labor force participation rate registered at 56 percent, the lowest rate since 1988.[23] The gap between men's and women's labor force participation widened in places where school closures intensified caregiving needs, more evidence that women are still disproportionately burdened by caregiving concerns.[24]

Babysitters were scarce, as were in-home day care centers and more established businesses. Some had gone out of business altogether, unable to weather the lockdown period. This is because it's hard to attract workers to the industry when wages are so pitifully low. The median salary for a childcare worker was $12.24 per hour in 2020, or $25,460 per year, according to the Bureau of Labor Statistics. In many places around the country, especially in rural America, where the shortages were particularly acute, workers' wages hover just over the federal minimum wage. Pay raises for childcare workers would invariably mean higher costs for parents, who already spend about 10 percent of their earnings on childcare.[25] Low childcare availability contributes to other labor shortages as well, since parents can't go to work or don't have the time to even focus on remote jobs.

The same problem permeates the home care industry, where demand outstrips supply and wages are a significant barrier to finding workers. The New York State population, for example, is expected to grow by 3 percent overall in the next decade, but the number of those sixty-five and over will grow by 25 percent, about half of whom, according to the CDC, are disabled. The need for personal home care aides there is huge, but labor shortages, which predated the pandemic, leave many families burdened with unpaid care responsibilities and older folks increasingly institutionalized in nursing homes. By the time this book is published, New York State will need to add fifty thousand personal home care aides just to keep up with the need, which is a 45 percent increase since 2013.[26] PHI, a care worker advocacy organization, estimates that between 2018 and 2028, home care will add far more new jobs than any other occupation in the state.[27] Despite this rapid growth, there's a current labor shortfall of twenty-five thousand workers that will grow to eighty thousand by 2025. Today it's common for home care aides to leave the profession for higher-paying jobs in fast food, retail, warehouses, and customer service. The problem is not that McDonald's might finally pay fifteen dollars an hour, but that home care work is vastly undervalued.[28]

Research by the CUNY School of Labor and Urban Studies finds that dramatically raising wages would fill nearly twenty thousand vacant home care positions each year and would create nearly eighteen thousand jobs in other industries by boosting economic activity in adjacent fields.[29]

In short, the "reopening" of businesses en masse didn't correlate with the conditions that allowed people to go back to work, even if they wanted to or needed the income. Before vaccinations became easily accessible in the US, health risks kept people from returning to dangerous jobs at poverty wages because they were scared of contracting the virus or transmitting it to others. The surge of hiring in the early reopening phase also created a basic reallocation problem. Once millions of people are fired, they simply can't be rehired easily and quickly. Restaurants, where two-thirds of the entire industry lost their jobs, are a perfect example. As restaurants closed or were predicted to close, servers, cooks, and others had to move on with their lives. People found other jobs, former jobs weren't available again, schedules and hours changed, and other mismatches between job seekers and employers complicated rehiring efforts.

The jobs that were hardest to fill had few remote options, making them unfeasible for those who needed schedule flexibility or had atypical COVID exposure risks. At the same time, jobs that did have remote options were attracting workers who were, pre-pandemic, working in brick-and-mortar establishments, leaving more vacancies there.

Yet despite the alleged desperation of employers to hire, they seemed to be quite picky. Unemployed Action, a group that provides resources to unemployed workers, posted tweets from its members. They show the other side of the labor shortage: workers looking everywhere for a job, with no one to hire them.

"They ended our unemployment in June and I have put in 187 applications and resumes with 0 call backs."[30]

"I've been hustling freelance jobs that pay crappy and applying for literally hundreds of jobs on LinkedIn, ZipRecruiter, Indeed, Glassdoor. I'm panicking I'll have to accept two or three lousy jobs to make half of what I did before the pandemic. This has been a nightmare."[31]

"I am beyond frustrated. I used to be able to quickly land an Accounting / Bookkeeping/ Office Manager position…now I need a degree? I've been doing this over 20 years…what???"[32]

"I had my first interview today after a year applying everywhere. Unfortunately it's only part time and the amount they are paying I'll have to work 3 jobs to comp what i was making pre pandemic. UI should last til we can find a *decent* job!"[33]

Labor shortages in low-wage jobs contributed to disappointing job news for Black people across all industries, despite hiring surges across much of the economy. The August 2021 jobs report recorded an uptick in Black unemployment. William Spriggs, chief economist at the AFL-CIO, argues that the only logical reason for this decline is blatant discrimination. "Once again the Black labor force shows employers are the problem….Employers don't mean they can't find anybody."

A combination of discrimination and low wages in key essential industries held back a fuller recovery, greater access to care, and employment prospects for women and people of color. For all the talk of employers bending over backward to find workers, many erected plenty of unnecessary barriers to getting a job. Most employers kept criminal background checks and regular drug tests in place, meaning that smoking pot off the clock could cost you a job. Cutbacks in spending on public transportation also reduced the ability of some to get a job.

Unemployed Action is a fledgling attempt to give voice to those frustrated by the labor market as a result of these factors. In scope or goals, however, it's only a faint echo of an earlier time of labor organizing among the unemployed.

In 1928, American Communists declared—as they are apt to do—that capitalism was on a course for an inevitable collapse. In preparation, members of the Communist Party began organizing Unemployed Councils (UCs) in cities across the country, recruiting hundreds of thousands of the unemployed to their ranks. When the Great Depression hit, the party's prognostication and planning paid off. Through the UCs, the Communist Party provided three things for the unemployed: immediate relief, an outlet for political mobilization, and the political education they needed to become and remain dedicated members of the party long after they regained employment.[34]

The UCs were highly successful on multiple fronts. In terms of providing immediate relief, they were able to prevent evictions through direct action against landlords and the police. In 1932 alone, New York City UCs moved an estimated seventy-seven thousand families back into their homes after they had been evicted. They also provided meals and case-by-case grievance assistance to thousands. In terms of mobilization, they were able to get millions of unemployed people into the street for large-scale demonstrations aimed at garnering public support and pressuring the Roosevelt administration to provide government aid for the unemployed.[35]

Crucially, UCs coordinated their actions in solidarity with the employed. After auto factory layoffs in Detroit, UCs led marches to protest the abysmal benefits of furloughed workers and read a statement pledging that they wouldn't scab if the remaining employees chose to strike. In 1934, the UC-inspired Lucas County Unemployed Council mobilized its members to support the Toledo Auto-Lite strike. The unemployed refused to scab and instead encircled the factory and helped striking workers fight off the National Guard.

Some on the Left argue that organizing the unemployed is a strategic dead end. Unlike workers, whose central location in capitalist production makes them a key asset, unemployed people have no leverage over the system as a whole. Depression-era UC organizing showed that this isn't necessarily true. By providing relief, political education, and the chance to taste political victory, the Communist Party and other organizations turned unemployment into a radicalizing experience. In other words, organizing the unemployed turns potential strikebreakers into fellow travelers.

◆

THIS HISTORY HAS perhaps never mattered more than during the fall of 2021, given that the ongoing labor shortage was accompanied by another anomalous curiosity of the pandemic economy—a strike wave. By January 2021, six workers at the Hunts Point Produce Market had died of COVID. Described as the "nerve center" of New York City's food supply, the market supplies more than half of the fresh produce that New Yorkers consume. To compensate for the risks associated with working through the pandemic, employees launched the first strike in the pandemic's second year. They wanted an extra dollar per hour and more PPE. Some strikers said that although they worked to put food on the tables of the city's residents, their own kids sometimes went hungry. After a week of raucous pickets that drew major support from the Left, they settled on a $.70 raise, their largest in thirty years.[36]

Small walkouts and protests erupted throughout 2021. But most establishment labor leaders seemed focused on what Biden would be able to do to help unions, or on convincing Joe Manchin to switch sides on the filibuster debate. Neither plan was destined to win.

In the meantime, militant action was brewing among the rank and file. In the fall of 2021, workers went on offense. Ten thousand workers walked off the job at John Deere plants across Illinois and Iowa. They joined the monthslong strike at Warrior Met Coal in Alabama and the nurses' strike at Saint Vincent's in Worcester, led by Marlena, whom we met in Chapter 3. Food workers at Frito-Lay, Nabisco, and Kellogg's were on strike over long hours, bad conditions, and low pay. There were graduate student workers on strike at Harvard University, as well as symphony musicians in San Antonio and whiskey makers in Kentucky, shutting down orchestras and bourbon production. By the end of October 2021, taxi drivers in New York City were on the second week of an indefinite hunger strike in the wake of nine driver suicides. Almost sixty thousand camera crew workers in Hollywood had authorized a strike, as well as thirty-seven thousand healthcare workers at Kaiser.

What was going on? As we saw in Chapter 2, there was a conflict between essential workers and their unemployed brethren, whom they saw as unfairly safe from the virus while the rest of them were risking everything to keep society running. As vaccines became more common, and the general public more accustomed to mingling, proximity to risk slowly became less important to the development of essential worker class consciousness. So, perhaps, did politics, the other stumbling block to working-class consciousness, as men in MAGA hats joined younger workers from Bernie's movement on some of the major picket lines.

As we saw in Chapter 3, large strikes weren't common during the first year of the pandemic, yet that year was punctuated by diverse labor actions, many by nonunion workers, or seemingly spontaneous walkouts, known as "wildcat strikes" because they weren't officially sanctioned by workers' unions. There was a lull in the action after the economy began reopening. Essential workers fell out of the headlines and back into the humdrum of their jobs. Then in the fall of 2021, there was an explosion.

The changing reality of the coronavirus crisis produced a new wave of pandemic labor unrest. Dubbed #Striketober, it seemed like the boiling point of long-simmering discontent. This mass outpouring of resistance sat awkwardly astride the labor shortage. On the one hand, the quitters and the strikers had nothing in common. Many people were quitting just to get a better job someplace else at higher wages, a purely individualistic and opportunistic solution to a lousy job. High quit rates typically suggest workers have leverage and confidence in the labor market, not that they're signing up for class war. In fact, the very idea of a Great Resignation suggested just that workers had become so resigned to bad jobs they were willing to simply walk away, if only for a while. In the absence of a powerful workers' movement to help turn that resignation into organization, quitting belied labor's historic weakness.

On the other hand, the persistent labor shortage also meant workers enjoyed a moment of greater leverage over employers who were short-staffed. With workers harder to replace, labor seemed to be taking advantage of the bosses' crisis. The Great Resignation helped fuel the Great Discontent.

As a labor activist myself, I'll admit that waking up each morning to new reports of workers on strike brought me much joy. Yet the labor historian in me had to square the current moment with the uprisings of the past. In the late nineteenth century, massive, unruly strikes brought entire industries to a halt. Traveling along rail lines and through shipyards, news of workers' unrest begot more unrest. In the early twentieth century, the Seattle general strike—a five-day work stoppage by sixty-five thousand workers across the city in 1919, inspired to some extent by the Russian Revolution—helped define a new era of politicized labor protest. This spirit was rekindled decades later as industrial workers shut down automobile plants across the Midwest in a wave of "sit-down" strikes in the thirties, replete with armies of passionate supporters outside the factories willing to defend the strikers from attacks by the police and National Guard. This activity eventually caused such a crisis for capital and the state that the Wagner Act, which legalized collective bargaining and became a backbone of the New Deal, seemed unavoidable by 1935.

In the 1970s, industrial monotony and overwork stirred a decade of occasional wildcat strikes, the last high-water mark for "job days lost," the official statistic that tabulates strikes. A 1972 report published by the Department of Health, Education, and Welfare found that "dull, repetitive, seemingly meaningless tasks...are causing discontent among workers at all occupational levels. Worker dissatisfaction, measured by absenteeism, turnover rates, wildcat strikes, sabotage, poor quality products and a reluctance of workers to commit themselves to work tasks is crippling productivity in the workplace."[37] In 1979 alone, the same year Johnny Paycheck's ode to quitting, "Take This Job and Shove It," topped the charts, there were 235 work stoppages involving more than one thousand workers.

The 2018 and 2019 public school uprising was the most recent manifestation, when a wave of strikes broke out in schools concentrated in rural Trump country, earning the movement the moniker Red State Revolt. About one million schoolteachers in West Virginia, Oklahoma, Colorado, New Mexico, North Carolina, California, and Kentucky walked picket lines during those two years.

The Red for Ed inspiration is clear, as it was basically a series of copycat strikes in the same industry. The pandemic wave was different because strikes took place across divergent industries and did not seem to be the result of other strikes. Instead, this new wave was inextricably linked to the political and social turmoil of the pandemic. The strikes were in many ways responses to the Biden administration, the labor shortage, and indeed, the poor health of the country. Among essential workers, there was a rejuvenated indignation in fall 2021, which manifested as something like a renewed sense of working-class consciousness.

The rage was focused largely on a few issues that were present before the pandemic, but which were magnified during and after it, such as low wages, long hours, and rotten jobs. Surprisingly, one of the most salient was labor time. The length of the working day used to be the central concern for organized labor, though it was eclipsed by other concerns over wages and conditions when the eight-hour day became normalized. The downward trend in hours reversed course in the 1970s, when annual hours began to rise again. Unions have since failed to revisit the cause, a happenstance I referred to as "labor's forgotten fight" in a previous book.[38]

The pandemic may have awakened that dormant impulse to gain greater control over labor time. John Deere strikers cited mandatory overtime that could stretch shifts to twelve hours as one of the reasons they walked off the job. Kellogg's employees pointed to the taxing seven-day workweeks they had to endure, and Frito-Lay workers decried what they called "suicide shifts," extended workdays with only eight hours of rest in between.[39] The Kentucky whiskey makers at Heavenly Hills went on strike in part because their new contract aimed to eliminate caps on their healthcare premiums, alter their work schedules, and cut overtime.[40] Nabisco workers struck over the elimination of premium pay for weekend work.

Union actions were also directly related to worker shortages and supply chain disruptions in other sectors. Strikes or sick-outs by bus drivers in North Carolina, New Mexico, Maryland, Florida, Indiana, Georgia, Pennsylvania, and New York left families scrambling to get their children to school on time. "We call ourselves CNAs with CDLs," said one special education driver in North Carolina, invoking a designation as a care worker as well as a transport worker.[41] Drivers cited poverty wages as the main reason for the labor shortage their industry was facing.

Broken supply chains throughout the pandemic began as a result of a spike in consumer demand for home-based durable goods, many of which we import. In fall 2021, however, the supply chains weren't clogged by buyers. They were left unattended by a dearth of workers to transport, unload, store, and deliver consumer goods. That shortage, in turn, resulted from declining wages and standards. Trucking companies, which claimed they were short eighty thousand drivers, couldn't find enough willing drivers at prevailing rates.[42] Those wages had been slowly eroded by decades of deregulation, first by Carter and then by Reagan, which undermined the power of the union to create better trucking jobs. Though truckers hadn't struck, the driver shortage was one more way in which poor wages hurt workers and rippled out to problems for the rest of us. Think of it as chaos theory for labor: shortchange workers in the US, and you get supply chain disruptions from China.

By the end of the year, there had been 250 strikes, far more than in any year since before the Great Recession.[43] Yet only 17 of them were large enough to meet the threshold of a major strike as tabulated by official government statistics. Did #Striketober accomplish anything? There were the immediate gains of the individual strikes. Deere workers rejected the first two contract proposals from their union's leadership because they included provisions to eliminate retirement benefits for new hires.[44] By allotting different pay and benefits to different employees, a company can undermine the solidarity of the workforce, a classic divide-and-conquer tactic. Eventually, they settled with a contract that doubled their raises, provided a better pension, and eliminated one of the hiring tiers. This was #Striketober's success story.

Kaiser Permanente workers won the elimination of a proposed two-tier wage provision in their contract.[45] The striking food manufacturer workers won wage increases and more reliable and humane schedules. Overall, however, the lasting impact of the fall 2021 strikes will probably be less quantifiable. "The main thing we did was to show that American workers still have power," said Randy, from Iowa, who spent three weeks on the picket lines and was proud to vote down the union's first contract offer. "Our union is strong, but it's just made up of guys like me, just regular people," he said. "Without us, nothin' works."

As a group of strikes, they accomplished something of greater significance. They deepened the hardship for capital that had been set in motion by the labor shortage. Workers can only win when they create a crisis for employers and governments. Strikes, especially large ones, and especially alongside many others, force businesses to make hard choices. If settling the strike favorably to workers entails fewer costs—economic or political—than hiring scabs or prolonging it, then labor has the upper hand. The labor shortage provided just such a context and unions stepped through the window of opportunity. Such favorable objective conditions can be easily exaggerated, however, if we don't look beyond the headlines. Where labor didn't seize the moment, there were major setbacks. Unions shed 241,000 members in 2021, and overall union density continued its downward spiral.[46]

✦

THE LABOR SHORTAGE was really a surplus of bad jobs. And the strikes were a direct response. Employers' reluctance to raise wages shows they have become dependent on a low-wage nation. We must break their habit.

Proponents of "individualism" like Laura Ingraham, mentioned earlier, or other commentators like her, don't actually believe there are powerful lessons learned by going hungry or being fired or evicted. They think starvation is an acceptable consequence of not working a bad job, so long as they themselves have a full stomach. Whether you actually pull yourself up by your bootstraps or you hang yourself with them is of no importance to J. D. Vance. It's a stance against the obligation to care for each other.

One way to break employers' low-wage dependency, and combat individualism, is through a more militant labor movement like the one that appeared alongside the labor shortage in the fall of 2021. The paroxysms of economic disruption are supposed to illustrate capitalism's fundamental flaws and provide the radical lessons that can push workers to take meaningful action. Usually, however, workers are cowed into acquiescence. The 2021 strike wave is an example of what happens when they take those lessons to heart. Eventually, however, the market will adjust. More people will go back to work, and more will be willing to cross picket lines. Working-class power requires organization, not unique labor market conditions.

The common refrain that "nobody wants to work anymore" didn't explain the labor shortage, but it can't be rejected outright either. The bosses proved it. When workers found other jobs or skated by on unemployment for a while, managers set about complaining on social media. They didn't take their place on the burger assembly line. They didn't want to work either—they wanted others to do it for them. Work is a scam, and they know it too.

The labor shortage was, to a great extent, a scam as well. It was a part of the pandemic crisis that capitalist society manufactured, and could have solved relatively quickly by following the basic logic of supply and demand. On the other hand, it also helped generate working-class resistance. Striking is always a risky proposition, but the dangers of the pandemic changed the calculus slightly. "We're out here for better jobs, for a better life," said Randy on the John Deere picket line. "It's a risk, I guess. But it's also a risk to just sit there and get shit on day after day."

We have a lot to learn by hearing from those on the front lines. Nonetheless, it's time to take a step back for a moment, to consider the pandemic from a new angle. When the pandemic hit, why were essential workers in such a vulnerable spot to begin with? How can we conceptualize the mistreatment of those workers who are so central to our own well-being? How did the pandemic exacerbate the long-standing trend that forces workers and their families to endure unacceptable risks? The pandemic requires that we consider not only what transpired in 2020 and after, but what political shifts set us up for such a catastrophic crisis.

CHAPTER 6

RISKY BUSINESS

Mabel Coleman was married for forty-four years to Roy Chester Coleman, a housekeeper at Overton Brooks VA Medical Center in Shreveport, Louisiana. "I've made many mistakes in life," she told me, as a lead-up to one she didn't make. "Best decision I ever made was to say yes to that man."

On March 22, 2020, Louisiana governor John Bel Edwards issued a stay-at-home order, urging all nonessential workers to shelter in place inside their homes. But there was no lockdown for Roy. On March 23, he woke up as on any other day and went to work. On March 24, he was at the emergency room twice with sinus congestion and headaches. On March 27, he was admitted to the hospital again and diagnosed with COVID-19.

Roy, who was Black, was well regarded at work and in his community. "You need someone to do anything," Mabel said, "Roy was your man." Roy was an army veteran and a volunteer EMT. He was a deacon at his church, where he also taught Sunday school. At age sixty-four he had two great-grandchildren. When Roy didn't show up to work one day, "the entire damn hospital took notice immediately," Mabel said.

His union, the American Federation of Government Employees, filed a complaint to the Occupational Safety and Health Administration against the VA on March 31.[1] "The VA has directed federal employees, including those at high risk for COVID-19, to continue reporting to work even when these employees are known to have been in close proximity to individuals and patients exhibiting symptoms of COVID-19 or who have met the testing criteria for COVID-19," read the claim.

"They knew people had it [the virus]," Mabel told me. "They didn't give a damn."

"The VA has not supplied all federal employees with the PPE they desperately need to protect themselves, their peers, and patients from COVID-19 exposure," a report from Roy's union said.[2] He wasn't alone. Data from The Shift Project at the Harvard Kennedy School, which polled tens of thousands of essential workers during the lockdown, showed that fewer than one-fifth of employers had provided masks to their workers by April, and only 7 percent required that they wear them.[3]

"It got better after the union started pushing," said Mabel, who had heard from some of Roy's coworkers that the hospital began issuing more PPE and increased paid sick time for frontline workers. "But it was too late for him."

He died in the same hospital where he worked.

The hospital flew its flag at half-mast for Roy and held a brief ceremony with his coworkers the next morning. Mabel was not invited.

As was the case with so many essential workers who succumbed to COVID-19, Roy's death was not intentional. But it wasn't purely accidental either. Roy was placed at great risk unnecessarily. He should not have been allowed to work without proper PPE. He was aware of some of the hazards he faced but by no means all. "We didn't know who to trust," Mabel told me, explaining that they received conflicting information from the medical community, the Trump administration, their church, his union, and of course the hospital administration. Then she dismissed this confusion as incidental. "Either way Roy had to work, so maybe it didn't matter who we listened to."

In deeply conservative Louisiana, one of the most polluted regions in the country, residents are accustomed to living and working in hazardous conditions. An ethnographic dive into bayou country by sociologist Arlie Russell Hochschild found staunch opponents of the EPA's attempts to clean up the state, which has been ravaged by oil companies and their affiliated industries.[4] People there were hostile to any "government regulation" that sounded like a job killer. Toxic dump sites and putrid rivers were just the unavoidable risks of a vibrant economy. Yet, for workers, it didn't seem like the trade-off was working. Louisiana is one of only five states that has not passed a minimum wage law, choosing to rely on the federal minimum poverty wage instead.

In places where many workers are habitually exposed to dangerous working conditions, including chemical and biological agents, it is easier for others to be exposed too. That's how risk works. Working alongside a deadly pathogen was extraordinarily and uniquely dangerous. Yet it was made so not just by the virus but by a long history of capitalist society exposing workers, and all of us, to unnecessary risks.

◆

NOT LONG AGO we thought it was just the opposite, that economic development heralded the end of the age of infectious disease. In 1971, the Egyptian scholar Abdel Omran proposed the theory of "epidemiological transitions," whereby "degenerative and man-made diseases displace pandemics of infection as the primary causes of morbidity and mortality." In other words, capitalist development would slowly extinguish the threat of infectious diseases in rich countries, which would be plagued instead by noncommunicable diseases, such as heart disease and cancer.

At first blush, the theory makes sense. My own research for a previous book took me from the dilapidated shantytowns surrounding Johannesburg to the favelas of São Paulo and the slums of Mumbai. It's hard to disabuse oneself of the feeling that the disease profile of the impoverished Global South is intimately linked with open sewers, poor wastewater management, and inadequate hygiene, just as it was when cholera microbes found fertile ground in the fetid ghettos of nineteenth-century New York, Paris, and London.

Moreover, throughout the twentieth century, communicable diseases became rarer in places with stronger capitalist economies. The culmination of the 1918 flu in the US inaugurated a period of great optimism about the future of health in rich countries. The conquest of infectious disease seemed close at hand. Rapid advances in virology, microbiology, and other health sciences, the products of increased education and funding for research, were extending our lifetimes and lent credence to Omran's argument. The future would not only be prosperous; it would be healthy and long.

After all, doctors found vaccines for tetanus (1921), yellow fever (1932), and polio (1954), and smallpox was finally eradicated from America by midcentury. Scientists also delivered antibiotics for tuberculosis and venereal disease during this time. Giving voice to this wave of optimism, in 1969, US surgeon general William Stewart declared it was "time to close the book on infectious disease as a major health threat." The Communicable Disease Center became the Center for Disease Control, reflecting a revised mandate. Nixon launched a "war on cancer," which came to be seen as the new and possibly last vexing chronic illness. By 1980, nearly all deaths in the US were from diseases of old age, chronic disease, or suicide.

Then the AIDS crisis punctured the buoyant bubble of optimism about eradicating infectious diseases. Even tuberculosis, which had been presumed dead, exploded in urban centers in the 1990s. Consequently, an inchoate discourse that described "emerging infectious diseases" exhumed an ancient nemesis that appeared, zombie-like, to haunt the future of health. Soon, Ebola and SARS (both of which emerged from the world's manufacturing hub in Guandong), a barrage of avian flus (which got to humans via mass poultry processing), and MRSA were legitimate threats across the developed world. And there was another heinous surprise. The virus that caused the Spanish flu in 1918, H1N1, had gone into abeyance just as quickly as it appeared, hanging out in the filth and mud and eventually migrating from bats to birds to pigs. But in 2009, it made the zoonotic leap back to humans and came alive again as swine flu. About five hundred thousand people died of it across the world, most of whom were under sixty. (By a stroke of bad luck, I was the first person infected with it in South Africa.)

By the outbreak of COVID-19, epidemiologists and climate scientists had seen pandemics in the making for decades. Today a new infectious disease is discovered five times a year, including an estimated 3,200 novel coronavirus strains still waiting to make that zoonotic leap. Capitalist globalization carried these microbes and pathogens across the world at faster speeds and to more places. Between 1980 and 2000 in the United States, deaths by pathogens increased by more than 60 percent. Omran got it wrong. Economic development hadn't eradicated contagious diseases—it spread them.

Rather than increasing our social defense mechanisms in response, capitalist political economy has weakened our immunity to disease outbreaks and even run-of-the-mill contagions. One reason for this is that employers have been slowly abdicating their responsibility to provide healthcare to workers. This quiet shift has had incredible consequences.

✦

THE PANDEMIC DIDN'T create a crisis—it revealed one. A slow but tectonic shift has taken place in our body politic. Families' increasing reliance on double earners means they're more vulnerable when either one gets laid off. The proportion of families without healthcare has risen almost 25 percent since Reagan took office. Pensions have given way to more vulnerable and unpredictable 401(k) plans.[5] Since the 1980s, policy changes in the way that corporations and government administer social welfare have resulted in what political scientist Jacob Hacker called a "risk shift" away from business and the state and toward average workers. This historic rearranging of the burdens of health, wealth, and well-being has created an age of economic insecurity. The pandemic only accelerated this long-standing trend.

The most insidious dimension of the risk shift—especially in the context of a pandemic—is in healthcare. The root of the problem is embedded in the legacy of the Social Security Act and the New Deal. New Deal liberals and unions fought for a system of universal healthcare coverage. They failed to guarantee this ambitious goal largely because of intense pressure from conservatives in government. Then in 1945, President Truman considered the idea, which enjoyed decent public support. But it was staunchly opposed by the Chamber of Commerce, the American Medical Association, and the American Hospital Association. Even some labor unions objected because they'd fought so hard to win employer-sponsored health plans, which were a major way to attract new members. When a universal system was off the table, employers voluntarily stepped into the breach and made a good case for themselves as providers. Jobs, after all, included both sick and healthy workers, which made the idea of pooling social risk through the workplace seem ideal.

Southern lawmakers began to worry when the economic effects of World War II caused pro-labor and union forces to grow in strength. They worked to pass anti-labor legislation that cut down the New Deal system. By midcentury, right-leaning anti–New Dealers and southern conservatives then began to push for tax breaks for employers who sponsored health insurance. This incentivized even more employers to offer coverage. Between 1940 and 1950, enrollment in employer-sponsored healthcare increased fivefold. For the first time, the majority of Americans got their coverage through work. At the time, the relative stability of American workplaces made this bargain look like an attractive alternative to the political fight posed by state-sponsored care.

By the 1970s, those tax breaks for companies amounted to hundreds of billions of dollars. Providing corporate-sponsored healthcare became a business all its own. Every president from Reagan on had a hand in expanding this general shift. Today, the country's single largest tax expenditure is for employer-based coverage, an exemption that costs the federal government hundreds of billions of dollars in lost revenue.[6]

The administration of their employees' healthcare gave corporations excessive leverage. They could raise or lower prices and control access, giving them inordinate power over the health of the working class. This made workers' well-being contingent upon the profitability of their boss. In essence, the risk shift happened in two parts. The first was an attack on the state's attempt to cover workers universally. The second was the tying of workers' health to their employer's wealth, and thereby to their own exploitation.

Today most jobs pay less in real dollars, a reflection of waning union strength, and health insurance coverage costs have increased exponentially. Rising costs have encouraged employers to purge workers from their plans or otherwise cut costs. In the two decades between 1998 and 2018, the overall share of the population covered through workplace plans decreased by 8 percent, a decline driven by lower coverage rates among Americans with lower household incomes.[7] In other words, to cover soaring costs, employers are undermining the very system they helped build.

Costs have risen even higher for workers. From 2008 to 2018, premiums for employer-sponsored health insurance increased 55 percent, twice as fast as workers' earnings. As healthcare costs have gone up, employers have opted to pass increases on to their workforce, often in the form of higher deductibles.[8] Since at least the 1980s, employers have balanced their costs by spreading high-deductible plans that raise out-of-pocket prices for their employees. The proportion of workers with these plans more than quadrupled between 2006 and 2018.[9] High deductibles reduce the likelihood that workers will use healthcare services and, so, reduce employers' share of the costs for those services. In 2003, 40 percent of privately insured adults had no deductible, and only 1 percent had deductibles that exceeded $3,000; in 2016, only 22 percent paid no deductible, and 13 percent had one over $3,000.[10] Not only did deductibles get larger, they also ate up a larger portion of workers' incomes: while only 3 percent of Americans had a deductible of 5 percent or more of their income in 2003, by 2016, 12 percent did.[11] Overall, by 2016 almost a quarter of non-elderly adults with employer-sponsored health insurance fell into the category of "underinsured."[12] Being underinsured means a person technically has insurance but it can't cover enough of the value of their claim. By 2020, almost half of working-age adults were underinsured.[13]

The steepest increase in the underinsured rate after the Affordable Care Act was passed occurred among Americans with employer-sponsored coverage, rising from 17 percent in 2010 to 28 percent in 2018. In other words, even as more Americans got their insurance through work, employers shuffled more and more of the costs back onto workers. We then arrive at our bizarre reality today, in which more people have health insurance but more of them are also underinsured, meaning they have out-of-pocket expenses that make accessing care difficult or impossible. And inadequate coverage is directly linked with forgoing necessary care because it's too expensive. Health insurance is meaningless if people can't use it to visit the doctor.

What employers call "cost-sharing" is really just a clever term for a risk shift. They claim cost-sharing pushes healthcare consumers to choose their plans wisely, keeping healthcare costs low. The problem is that the healthcare market is unlike other markets. The "consumers" in this experiment are sick people in need of care, not *homo economicus*. Parents whose child needs an important surgery won't often second-guess their doctor when they recommend an expensive procedure over a cheaper one.

The relatively tight labor market of 2017–2019 made it harder for employers to off-load risk, generating a mild panic within the business class. Employers "will have trouble continuing to shift medical bills onto employees as they have for several decades," wrote the *Harvard Business Review*.[14] Deductibles had hit a ceiling. Then the pandemic arrived, and the floor fell from under our feet.

How has the pandemic affected health insurance coverage? The Kaiser Family Foundation estimates that about two to three million people lost employer-sponsored health insurance from March to September 2020.[15] This figure, which seems mild, doesn't capture the extent of the crisis. Many of those who lost their jobs didn't have employer coverage to begin with, given that low-wage jobs typically carry fewer benefits. Moreover, a flat uninsured rate still means there were uninsured millions during the worst health crisis in a century.

◆

CAPITALIST SOCIETY IS implicated in a deadly irony: it creates the conditions we need to live longer, healthier lives but keeps us from benefiting from those advances as widely and equitably as is necessary. Over the last few decades—the heyday of neoliberal austerity—for-profit healthcare organizations have reduced our healthcare system's surge capacity.

Decades of profit-driven cutbacks of hospitals' in-patient capacity meant that during the pandemic, when we needed in-patient care more than ever, it was often unavailable. From 2008 to 2016, per capita public health spending fell by almost 10 percent.[16] Data from the CDC and the American Hospital Association show we have over half a million fewer hospital beds than we did in 1975, despite a larger and older population.[17] We have fewer nonprofit hospitals and 60 percent more for-profits than we did then.[18] In the wake of the Great Recession, the explosive growth of for-profit healthcare corporations increased the census of hospitals and nursing homes, delivering more bang for the investor's buck. Even though employment in healthcare steadily rose, public funding for it was reduced in most states, forcing municipalities to cut programs, dial back services, and reduce capacity in hospitals. Staffing shortages became the norm, and workers had fewer resources at their disposal, like supplies and medical equipment. The result is that we were left without adequate capacity in the event of an emergency.

When the pandemic hit, the US had fewer than three hospital beds per thousand people, the same number as Turkey. By contrast, Japan and South Korea had thirteen and twelve, respectively, an advantage that helped them weather the storm with exponentially fewer deaths.[19] *USA Today* noted that only eight states had enough beds to treat their sixty-and-over populations, who were especially vulnerable to COVID. This kind of hospital strain cost lives. The CDC's medical journal estimated that as hospitals exceed 100 percent capacity of intensive-care-unit beds, as they did during at least two waves of the pandemic, eighty thousand excess deaths would be expected two weeks later.[20]

America's reductions in healthcare capacity were matched by a decrease in lifesaving equipment. In May 2020, 87 percent of nurses reported having to reuse a single-use disposable mask or N95 respirator, and almost one-third of nurses said they had been exposed to COVID-19 patients without wearing appropriate PPE.[21] Two months later, in July 2020, almost 350 US healthcare workers had died as a result.[22]

In 2020, the national lack of PPE came as a surprise to most, though knowledgeable parties had seen it coming for years. The National Institute for Occupational Safety and Health found in 2006 that in a national pandemic, whereby 30 percent of the population gets sick, we would need 3.5 billion N95 respirators. When the COVID-19 pandemic hit in February 2020, we had about 30 million.[23] This was the result of several factors.

In 1998, the Clinton administration created a National Pharmaceutical Stockpile of 105 million N95 masks. The stockpile, run by the CDC, was there to help us survive in the event of a pandemic. In 2003, the Bush administration transferred control of the stockpile to Homeland Security. In 2009, the Obama administration used 100 million of the masks to protect against swine flu (H1N1) but, crucially, never replenished the stash. Instead, it tried to strengthen the ability of private manufacturers to produce a supply quickly in the event of an outbreak. In the meantime, in search of cheaper labor, many of the major domestic PPE producers, like 3M and Honeywell, outsourced their production to Asia.

This meant that when we desperately needed PPE, we had to import it. More than any rich country in the world, we were suddenly hyper-reliant on a smooth and functioning global supply chain, which did not exist. China was the largest exporter, but its own stock was rapidly depleting, given that the outbreak happened there first. It also didn't help that the Trump administration had started a trade war with that country not long before, fracturing international relations. The one major PPE producer that remained in the US, Halyard Health, developed technology to make 1.5 million N95s per day, ten times the going rate and seemingly enough to satisfy the predicted surge demand in the event of a US outbreak.[24] But the Trump administration chose not to fund the project.

The cost of PPE is incurred by hospitals, unlike the costs of other medical supplies like catheters and medications, which are billed to patients. Hospitals therefore are incentivized to maintain a low supply. The pandemic demand shock incentivized the federal government to invoke the Defense Production Act, requiring the private sector to start making PPE, but the government failed to act quickly. The lesson here is that we need far greater production, storage, and distribution capacity of free PPE.

Unavailable PPE meant healthcare personnel were more likely to become ill, requiring care and reducing their ability to work. Sick doctors and nurses decreased the supply of healthcare workers and burdened the caregiving system at the same time. We know what happened next.

Nurses and doctors wore the same masks for weeks on end. Nursing home staff routinely used makeshift plastic, garbage bags, or discount raincoats as PPE. Lower-status workers in dietary departments were often told they didn't even need such protections since they weren't doing direct patient care. Yet studies found that line cooks had some of the highest COVID-19 death rates in the country because the virus spread so easily in poorly ventilated and cramped kitchens.[25] Doctors were forced to ration lifesaving materials among those patients they thought had the best chance of survival. (My aunt, Barbara Kisselbach, was one of the unlucky ones who died of COVID-19 in a Pennsylvania hospital where there wasn't enough oxygen to go around.)

✦

EVEN AFTER VACCINES were developed and ready for distribution, the state hampered efforts to make them widely available. About half of American employers did not offer paid leave for workers to get the vaccine and recover from it.[26] Biden's American Rescue Plan offered initial funding for such programs, which were mostly directed at healthcare and other essential workers, but the legislation let the aid expire just as the vaccine window opened for the wider population. Employers' lack of support put Black and Latino workers at a special disadvantage, as they were far more likely than whites to report that they would be vaccinated if they could afford time off to get the shot and recover.[27] Marty Walsh's Labor Department had actually proposed expanding paid leave for vaccinations during the drafting of the American Rescue Plan. Thanks to intense lobbying from business groups, the final program was vastly restricted.

The combination of profit-driven austerity and employer domination of workers' healthcare options, especially in the industries that are deemed essential to human life, undercut our ability to safeguard our collective health, wealth, and well-being during the pandemic. In an attempt to explain vital PPE shortages, a medical journal concluded that "because health is a public good, markets are not suitable mechanisms for rationing the resources necessary for health."[28] Interstate competition for scarce ventilators, N95s, and hospital beds does not just signal a market failure. Those problems are the result of overt policy decisions that neoliberalism tries to normalize and depoliticize. The COVID-19 crisis won't end up subverting neoliberalism, but it certainly unmasked its ideological ruse.

There are myriad systems to administer welfare state provisions, but no other rich capitalist nation relies so heavily on employers to provide healthcare to workers and their families. If American workplaces were stable and safe, or if they were successful at reliably providing quality benefits and care, this wouldn't be a problem. But rather than fulfilling their obligations, employers have been skirting them for decades. And as jobs have gotten worse, so have the welfare state programs that they administer.

The graph below shows the US Private Sector Job Quality Index (JQI) as measured from January 1990 to January 2021. The JQI

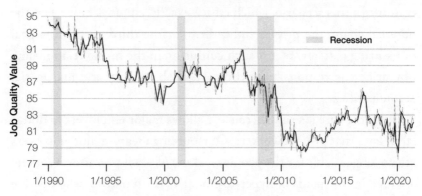

The US Private Sector Job Quality Index

A good job is hard to find. SOURCE: Private Sector Job Quality Index, 1990–2021. Monthly measurements as dots, recessions in gray

measures the amount of high-paying/quality jobs versus low-paying/ quality jobs. A job is considered high- or low-quality depending on whether it pays more or less than the average weighted wage in its industry. A JQI value above one hundred means the economy contains more high-quality jobs than low-quality jobs, whereas a value below one hundred means there are more low-quality jobs than high-quality jobs. This graph shows that there has been a more or less steady trend of more low-quality jobs than high-quality jobs since 1990. The index shows that job quality recovered a bit after the Great Recession but declined again starting in 2017. The first few months of 2020, even before the pandemic hit, mark the lowest JQI measurement to date.[29]

In 1990, we had a roughly equal division between high- and low-quality jobs. Since then, 63 percent of the jobs created have been low-quality. Why?

A major cause of declining job quality, and the risk shift to workers, has been "workplace fissuring," economist David Weil's coinage for the trend in major American business to outsource to independent contractors what are deemed fringe services, like janitorial, food service, and delivery.[30] Consider a dietary worker at a national nursing home chain. The property where she works is owned by a private equity firm. Her day-to-day duties are supervised by a third party, which also supervises dietary staff in colleges, universities, and hotels across the country. In this scenario, which entity, exactly, employs her?[31] Is it the national chain, the private equity firm, or the third party? The goal of fissuring is to create just such confusion in the hiring relationship, obscuring the responsibility to provide job security and managerial accountability.

Fissuring spreads risks because it allows major employers to dodge labor laws that protect workers. Outsourcing means major employers are no longer liable for the people working on their premises. Workers are then in the hands of hyper-exploitative third parties, who operate with a degree of immunity given their low public profile. Weil estimates that in fissured workplaces, the probability that a worker complaint, like an accusation of wage theft or health and safety violations, will result in a government investigation is 0.3 percent.[32] Fissuring enables employers to operate with total impunity. You can think of it as guaranteeing plausible deniability for worker rights. Employers that fissure their workplaces also spread risk through a spillover effect—low wages and a lack of labor protections at some employers in a particular industry drag standards down at other employers in the same industry, a race to the bottom where workers always lose.

The pandemic was workplace fissuring on steroids. In May 2020, NTT's Global Managed Services Report, which analyzes trends in outsourcing, found that 45 percent of global corporations planned "to outsource more of their IT than they insource" within eighteen months—a percentage nearly double the current amount.[33] Within the United States, institutions such as colleges, law firms, and medical practices were eager to use the crisis as an opportunity to outsource jobs.[34] Even employers who received generous federal assistance, such as Boeing and United Airlines, didn't hesitate to contract out IT staff and catering operations.[35] And employers didn't just spread risk through fissuring and spillovers—they tried to enshrine it in law.

Nowhere was this more the case than with gig companies. Fissuring typically starts with companies shedding one or two services, and then, like a crack in a windshield, it spreads exponentially over time.

The entire rideshare economy—where drivers are independent contractors and not employees of Uber, Lyft, etc.—is an example of a fissured industry.

Many gig workers slogged through the pandemic, but most of their services were rendered impossible during the lockdown phase. As they trickled back to work, they found themselves facing a new employment reality.

In November 2020, California voters faced Proposition 22. Drafted by major gig company lawyers, its aim was to escape a 2018 state law that classified gig workers as employees rather than independent contractors. UC Berkeley polling had shown that just a year earlier, a mere 39 percent of Californians supported Prop 22. But on Election Day, the measure passed with a resounding 58 percent support.[36] What happened in between? The most expensive ballot measure campaign in American history: gig companies spent $218 million to promote the legislation, a total that, as the *Los Angeles Times* pointed out, amounts to $630,000 per day.[37] It is no wonder, then, that the gig companies' campaign could flood advertising venues and ultimately crush its opponents, whose funds totaled a comparatively paltry $15 million.[38] This endless stream of cash allowed gig companies to monopolize the public conversation and successfully co-opt the message of their opposition.

This vote came with serious consequences for gig workers, but it also created the potential to ripple across the entire economy. The law created a new employment category: "the contract gig worker."[39] Even if other businesses don't start their own fight at the ballot box, they can still take full advantage of this new labor category. In January 2021, for example, grocery chains Vons, Pavilions, and Albertsons came to an agreement with DoorDash to fire their delivery staff—which had previously worked full-time with benefits—and replace them with an army of subcontracted "Dashers."[40]

However, just months after the vote, a superior court in California struck down Prop 22 as unconstitutional, which its opponents had long argued. Why did voters have the chance to consider an unconstitutional law? Because that's how powerful gig companies are. And, indeed, they haven't given up their fight; they're moving forward with plans to introduce similar legislation in other states.[41]

◆

JOB QUALITY HAS also been declining in other ways. In my last book, I examined the breakdown of the old industry standard through the lens of work time. While everyone is working more hours today—about five weeks more per year than in 1975—low-wage, precariously employed workers lead the trend. That group, disproportionately women and people of color, has increased its hours by about 24 percent compared to just 4 percent among the highest earners.[42] Dual-earner households have become the norm, effectively doubling working families' exposure to precarious work.

Long hours are bad for our health. One extensive multicountry study found that long hours are "the largest of any occupational risk factor calculated to date."[43] Overwork is associated with drug and alcohol abuse, depression, weight gain, illness, and death.[44]

Hours didn't become just longer—they became more volatile as well. Many service sector employers have become less willing to absorb the economic risk that comes with providing stable schedules to workers when the level of customer demand fluctuates. Instead of assuming this risk, employers off-load it onto workers in the form of inconsistent schedules that make it next to impossible to plan a life. A survey done by the Shift Project at the Harvard Kennedy School found that two-thirds of service sector employees knew their schedule less than two weeks in advance, and 70 percent were subject to last-minute changes.[45]

When workers' income varies from week to week, their ability to pay bills or remain eligible for Medicaid is at risk. An unstable schedule limits the ability to access formal childcare, forcing workers to rely on a patchwork of short-notice informal arrangements. And erratic schedules can lead to a dizzying array of health problems brought about by sleep disruption. Not surprisingly, research has shown that workers with variable schedules are twice as likely to report psychological distress.[46]

COVID-19 has helped shift this instability onto labor's back. Some cities, such as Chicago and San Francisco, as well as the state of Oregon, have predictive scheduling laws that classify COVID-19 under an exemption built in for emergencies.[47] In other words, just when workers need more dependable hours and schedules to get through a public health crisis, that same crisis is the rationale for why companies don't have to provide them.

In general, workplace safety enforcement seemed laxer than ever during the pandemic: in July 2020, only 27 percent of workplace fatality cases ended in citations, a sharp decrease from the previous year's 65 percent.[48]

This cavalier approach to workers' health was often politically motivated. Trump's administration tried to indemnify corporations against any lawsuits from their employees who contracted COVID on the job—a move that would have dramatically shifted risk to the most vulnerable. The former president failed to generate enough support nationally for such a law. But conservative state legislatures succeeded, issuing executive orders that granted immunity to employers whose workforce retaliated for unsafe environments. Illinois, for example, changed its workplace compensation law so that when an essential worker acquired COVID, the state, by default, presumed she contracted it at work. This made it far simpler for workers to get medical coverage for bills or unemployment insurance for lost wages, or even death benefits for their families. Business groups concerned about the cost of the claims sued and successfully forced the state to return to its pre-pandemic law, which required workers to prove they contracted the disease at work. Given the highly transmissible nature of the virus, it became easy for companies to sow doubt about where and how exactly workers became ill.

Employers also began making their own rules. In the summer of 2020, as the economy accelerated its reopening phase, company liability became an important issue, as many feared lawsuits from workers who might allege that they acquired the coronavirus on company time. Conservative groups warned of a flood of frivolous "predatory, self-serving lawsuits" based on claims from workers who had "plotted to line their pockets with Covid-19 related lawsuits."[49] In the first year of the pandemic, of the lawsuits tracked by the law firm Hunton Andrews Kurth, about 20 percent of the ten thousand coronavirus-related lawsuits were about labor and employment issues. Only a small fraction of that number were about workplace exposure to COVID-19. Given the high volume of OSHA workplace complaints, however, this signals the opposite of what conservatives feared. The barriers to filing a lawsuit are so large that likely many thousands of aggrieved workers simply didn't follow through. Nevertheless, many salons, restaurants, gyms, offices, schools, and even Hollywood movie sets secured waivers that would limit the legal recourse of workers if they got sick at work because they agreed not to sue.[50] Even Trump's own 2020 presidential campaign made event attendees sign a waiver indemnifying it against allegations that they acquired the virus while at the event venue.

The pandemic risk shift went gangbusters in the most dangerous jobs of the crisis. At nursing homes, the epicenter of the virus outbreak, companies secured liability waivers that not only shielded them from lawsuits but also suppressed knowledge and data about patient care, working conditions, and responsibilities to families.[51] "Granting broad immunity to nursing facilities under these circumstances increases the enormous risks that residents are already facing," a report by the Center for Medicare Advocacy concluded. It also "fulfills the nursing home industry's longstanding efforts to avoid accountability by preventing litigation."[52] Likewise, Trump's injunction of the Defense Production Act in meatpacking plants both forced workers back onto the kill floor and limited their legal recourse: work completed under the DPA directive included some gray-area indemnity against worker and general public lawsuits, since the work was, in a sense, forced.[53]

It used to be the opposite. High liability costs once convinced employers to accept the nation's first social insurance system.[54] It was preferable to the alternative: by the 1920s, every state had workers' compensation laws on the books, and it was easy and common for workers to use them.

Today, the US is an outlier among its peer nations in its dearth of federal legislation providing paid sick leave—overall, nearly 30 percent of American workers lack access to it. The pandemic did, at least temporarily, partially relieve this burden for some workers. Although the March 2020 Families First Coronavirus Response Act (FFCRA) instituted emergency pandemic paid sick leave, it only applied to businesses with fewer than five hundred employees.[55] Those who were lucky enough to receive coverage saw concrete benefits: states that gained access to paid sick leave through the FFCRA saw about four hundred fewer confirmed COVID-19 cases per state per day.[56] Some employers also implemented their own paid leave policies in the face of public scrutiny; Olive Garden, for example, increased access to paid sick leave by 49 percent, significantly diminishing instances of employees working while sick.[57] In the end, however, paid sick leave was unavailable to two-thirds of low-wage workers, exactly those most vulnerable to exposure in the first place.

For those who lost their job, earlier risk shifts ensured that things were even more difficult. At one time, the sole lifeline for most US workers who lost their job was unemployment insurance, a system that is now broken. At midcentury, almost all workers were eligible for unemployment insurance, but in 2019, just over one-quarter of unemployed workers received any benefit at all. And the assistance they receive was only a fraction of what the same benefits paid out in the New Deal era.[58] The problem, as explained in Chapter 1, is that the architecture of the system links state taxes to the number of workers who file for benefits, thereby incentivizing employers to challenge claims or find ways to deny them outright. As a result of the fractured condition of unemployment insurance, many thousands of workers waited weeks and months to receive their benefits during the pandemic, and countless others never got them at all. That being said, the March 2020 Pandemic Unemployment Assistance program doubled the reach of preexisting UI programs and advanced racial and gender equity by including all kinds of workers who are excluded from the typical program.[59] In under a year, however, as the pandemic still raged and kept people from working, the improved programs ended.

As the safety net has frayed or disappeared, employees and their families have lived through dramatic tides of financial and occupational instability. The once-dominant idea of a shared fate between employer and employee stands in stark contrast to the naked and unmitigated exploitation we have today.

Even in good times, our peculiarly American work-based safety net provides no comprehensive support for the kinds of programs workers and families need. Practically alone in the world, we offer no significant family, sick, or medical leave programs. During the pandemic, these policy vacuums pushed people back to work sooner than was necessary or safe and led to later waves of the virus. These failures help explain the unmitigated disasters faced by both essential workers and the unemployed.

◆

THE RISK SHIFT thesis does not argue that our society became riskier, just that workers and families were increasingly exposed to hazards that had always been around. The pandemic was different because society suddenly became objectively more dangerous. In this context, the history of off-loading risks onto essential workers had even more dire consequences, which may signify a shift into a new era of society suffused with risk.

To illuminate this next shift, I'd like to pivot toward conceiving of risk even more broadly, by examining how it has increasingly permeated our everyday lives. And so we move to a place where the word "risk" does not suffice: the poison-drenched air of Pripyat, Ukraine, ground zero of the Chernobyl disaster.

The event is still the deadliest nuclear meltdown in history. Over one hundred people died in the fallout, and children of mothers pregnant at the time of the explosion had inflated rates of cancers and other abnormalities. For years prior, Ulrich Beck, a sociologist from the University of Munich, had been writing a book he called *Risk Society*. It was published just after the horrible event of Chernobyl, in April 1986, a happenstance that catapulted his argument into the national dialogue. Beck's book argued that modern industrial society had become overshadowed by a defining preoccupation: managing and containing risk that it itself had produced. Chernobyl was a useful way to tell that story not only because of the risks of radiation but also because the Soviet regime lied to cover it up, and was then found out. Suddenly, other disasters of the recent past (and some still to come) all seemed to confirm Beck's hypothesis; he became known as a "Zeitgeist sociologist."

More than a response to a particular past event, Beck's theory spoke to a pervasive uncertainty about the future. "A fate of endangerment has arisen in modernity, a sort of counter-modernity, which transcends all our concepts of space, time, and social differentiation," he wrote. "What yesterday was still far away will be found today and in the future at the front door."

Had Beck lived to see the COVID-19 pandemic, he certainly would have said it was the result not just of a biological event but of a society that had gambled for a long time with its collective safety—and the house was winning.

This lack of collective care poses new kinds of risks. The cult of individualism, so often attributed to ancestral Protestants in our civic gene pool, came under intense scrutiny during the pandemic. It seemed clear that our health was highly contingent upon what other people were doing. Individually, we could mask up and hunker down, get vaccinated and encourage others to as well. But our odds of getting sick were substantially lowered when fewer of those around us were sick. That also meant that less-responsible people around us imperiled our health, despite prudent action on our part.

When I interviewed workers for this project, they commonly mentioned the ways that the general public exposed them to unnecessary risks. There was Tessa Johnson, the nurse and union leader from Bismarck, North Dakota, surrounded by conservative patients who refused professional medical advice under the mistaken impression that COVID was a hoax. "I'd see them around town," Johnson told me, "unmasked, not a care in the world. And I knew eventually I'd see them in the hospital." When I spoke to her in the winter of 2021, North Dakota had the highest rate of COVID-19 infections of anywhere in the world.

Chicago teacher Kenzo Shibata noted that parents, especially white parents, were urging in-person classes to commence before schools were adequately prepared. "I get it, working from home sucks and you want your kid out of the house," he said. "But that doesn't mean I have to die." Retail and grocery clerks routinely reported feeling anxious at work because customers constantly violated social distancing guidelines. Servers at restaurants reported increased harassment by patrons during the pandemic too.

The risk society poses a collective problem, not an individual one. During a pandemic there is simply a larger amount of risk that cannot be mitigated at the individual level. Counting on everyone to be thoughtful and diligent about mask wearing is no substitute for a legally enforceable mask mandate. Beck understood this better than anyone. He argued that widespread risk generated a "boomerang effect" whereby those responsible for producing or off-loading risks will inevitably be exposed to them as well. The poison in the wells of the poor will eventually reach the wells of the rich. An interconnected world means no amount of bottled water can permanently secure the health of those in power. That's all the more reason risk shifts are so maddening—in the long run they're self-defeating. An injury to one really is an injury to all.

"Chernobyl made conscious what has already been true for a long time," Beck wrote, conjuring allusions to a famous turn of phrase by Marx: "Private control of the means of perception has been overthrown."[60] During the pandemic it became more difficult for individuals to make accurate risk assessments, illuminating a shift that may characterize a new stage of a risk society. The pandemic workplace was a more extreme version of Beck's vision. And the risk shifts were seismic, beyond the slow erosion of rights and regulations described by Hacker. This warrants a different way to conceptualize the pandemic.

Imagine you're going to walk across a rickety suspension bridge. Decades of benign neglect has meant that the bridge has fallen into disrepair. Do you risk it? That calculation depends on several factors—your need to cross the bridge in the first place, the actual degree of ricketiness, and your own ability to navigate the potential pitfalls if you decide to risk a crossing. In this thought experiment, you have what you need at your disposal to make an informed judgment. The dangers associated with this bridge are how Beck imagines the world before the risk society.

Now imagine another bridge. This one looks better, but it's hard to tell. You're unfamiliar with the complex architectural designs that were used to build it. You must consult bridge experts to help you decide whether a crossing is reasonably safe. They can help you manage the risks, the calculated probability that you will fare well to the other side, though there are no guarantees. This is the bridge in Beck's risk society.

Now there's a third bridge in town. This one looks stable and new, with even a few fresh flourishes to give it the appearance of safety and reliability. There are no warning signs anywhere. But the bottom boards are rotten at the core and the suspenders are ever so slightly frayed, imperfections invisible to the untrained eye. To be on the safe side, you consult the bridge experts again. Unbeknownst to you, this time the bridge experts are mostly in the pocket of the Big Bridge Lobby. Some aren't even bridge experts at all but profit off bridge construction and enjoy an expansive public platform with millions of followers. You don't have the information you need to make a rational calculation, and you are unprepared when the bridge collapses under your feet. Welcome to the hazard society.

The idea of a "hazard society" best describes the nature of the pandemic workplace. In a hazard society, the risks come quick and sometimes invisibly. They aren't merely the result of decades of policy failures and irresponsible mission drift but of deliberate decisions by employers to earn short-term profits. Workers believed the scientists and doctors who explained the risks of in-person work. They watched their coworkers die. Yet at times the risks were unclear, in some part thanks to the authorities themselves. The CDC didn't even collect data on workplace exposure outside of a few industries. For most workers, the foremost authority on the safety of their workplace was their boss, who was typically no authority at all, and had a clear conflict of interest.

For most essential workers, the pandemic removed the capacity to make a real risk assessment. When I interviewed essential workers, I often asked them about their "decision" to go to work. These questions were routinely met with confusion. They just went. The rent was due, the kids were hungry, the car needed gas. As Marx once put it, the "dull compulsion of economic circumstances" tends to eclipse other social forces. Roy Chester Coleman, the hospital janitor from Louisiana we met at the chapter's opening, just went because that's what he always did.

The hazard society was more of a problem for essential workers than it was for society writ large. In that sense, the concept is inherently narrow in scope and less generally applicable in practice. It has the benefit, however, of appreciating the real depth of the hazards essential workers faced during the pandemic.

Simply going to work was a huge risk; the legacy of historical risk shifts made pandemic work downright hazardous. And this had the further effect of undermining our ability to care for each other even outside of paid work. Risking that arena of our lives has even more dire consequences. The pandemic worsened the country's long-standing "crisis of care": it deepened preexisting social problems and reproduced conditions that led to deficient care systems. That's our next topic: how social reproduction came under the knife like never before in 2020, and why we can't afford any more cuts.

CHAPTER 7

THE CRUCIBLE OF CARE WORK

THE CRISIS OF BAD JOBS AND UNSAFE WORKPLACES DURING THE COVID-19 outbreak boiled over now and again into open confrontations between management and workers. Sometimes those fights ended with safety improvements, more paid leave, or a union. Too often they ended in sickness or worse. When essential workers became ill, they fell into the care of their peers in the healthcare industry. "Workers literally took care of each other," Tre Kwon, a nurse and labor activist, told me. "I wish it hadn't happened that way, but I am glad we were there when they needed us."

The spotlight placed on healthcare workers during the pandemic illuminated a peculiar triple paradox. First, though healthcare workers are clearly essential, they themselves are often excluded from the provision of care that they administer. This is especially true among the growing ranks of low-wage caregivers who lack adequate access to healthcare plans or can't afford the time off to see a doctor. Second, the explosive numerical rise of the care work industry has taken place alongside a crisis of care, a condition in which our very capacities to care for each other are both undervalued and overused. Overcrowded hospitals, overworked caregivers, decrepit nursing homes, and unaffordable healthcare all contribute to a society that's unable to provide basic human dignity for the sick, aged, and disabled.[1] No matter how many workers we employ to care for our fragile and frail society, they can't be as effective as we need them to be unless they have safe, stable, well-paying jobs. Third, while healthcare is a growing field, workers are leaving it in record numbers. A growing nursing shortage, for example, has already undermined the standard of hospital care across the country.

In the previous chapter, I conceptualized the pandemic as a new kind of hazard society, made worse by decades of political and economic risk shifts onto the backs of workers and their families. The very act of caring for each other became more necessary than ever before but involved incalculable risk. Building on that analysis, here I view the pandemic—and especially the relationship between healthcare and work—as a crisis of social reproduction. Social reproduction happens where the demands of the home and workplace overlap. It's the term used among scholars and feminist activists to describe the work necessary for the regeneration of the paid and unpaid labor force on which capitalist profitability depends. Caring for the sick, elderly, and frail; rearing and educating children; growing, producing, and distributing food and drink; developing medicines and treatments for disease; cleaning and organizing homes and communities; and providing emotional and therapeutic support for those in need are all forms of socially reproductive labor. To say the pandemic was a crisis of social reproduction means it undermined our ability to reliably carry out these duties, a capacity that was already strained. Even in good times, without continual acts of care, paid or not, society collapses. Workers performing socially reproductive labor might be the most essential of all.

I examine the concept of social reproduction in detail below, mostly through the lens of paid care work, which took on special significance during the pandemic. To start, I'd like to take a vignette from my own life to explore how home care work has changed and, even though workers are fighting back, how it hasn't.

✦

MY FIRST JOB out of college was working as a home care aide just outside Seattle in 1999. Robert had suffered a stroke as a complication of a routine surgery. It left him immobile from the waist down, with slurred speech and the appearance of having suffered a stroke. I cooked and cleaned, took him to the bathroom, dressed and undressed him, and administered some basic medications. I went shopping for him and did simple upkeep around the home and yard. Sometimes I stayed late and we watched buddy comedies together before he fell asleep.

It was rewarding for both of us. Robert got the benefit of living an independent life outside of an institution. I was able to connect with a person I deeply admired, both for who he had been—a Chinese medical doctor and herbalist—and for who he had become, a gentle and kind man who relied on a small crew of round-the-clock helpers for his daily dignity and survival. The pay was ten dollars per hour. It wasn't Robert's fault. He was given a set amount from Medicaid to pay wages for his caregivers. He always apologized profusely about the paltry sum he provided, but we both assumed there was nothing we could do. After a year, I left to work at a bakery, which paid less but involved no commute, so I could save on gas.

Robert and I had it wrong. During the exact time I worked for him, unbeknownst to us, home care workers in California were organizing a union. There were no unions in the industry at that time. The work itself was often done informally, for disabled or elderly friends and relatives. When it was more of a traditional job, home care aides—a largely female immigrant workforce—were dispatched to clients via hiring services. The work was long and arduous, with low pay and few regulations. Both workers and clients reported widespread abuse.

Starting in 1986, for twelve years an extraordinary coalition of workers, clients, union organizers, and community advocates fought for a better system. They wanted to find a way to raise patient care standards and job quality in the home care industry. In the late eighties, home care workers made the state minimum wage of $3.75, a sum low enough to put full-time workers below the federal poverty line. They were disqualified from medical insurance, sick leave, pension, or holiday pay. Their jobs were among the most grueling and worst paid in the country.

Winning was always going to be hard. Workers were dispersed over a huge sprawling area of Los Angeles County and spoke over one hundred languages, and the industry averaged about 40 percent turnover, making regular contacts with potential leaders and veteran activists difficult. There was no single employer of record; it was a fissured work environment before the term was even coined. Many home care recipients as well as the general public opposed the workers' union, assuming it would drive up costs in an industry already underresourced. The challenges, however, posed a huge opportunity. Organizing home care workers held the potential to define an entirely new workforce, a class in itself, and to transform it into a class for itself, with the ability to upgrade a vital part of the care economy.

The healthcare workers' union, SEIU, was at that time engaged in new kinds of social movement unionism through its campaigns to win "justice for janitors" in a few major cities across the country. New leadership, some of whom were recruited from left-leaning social justice groups, brought new vitality to the union that was useful during the home care campaign.

Throughout the eighties and nineties, the union mobilized tens of thousands of disparate workers into a grassroots movement—they wanted better wages, better care for patients, and more stable jobs, like other professional healthcare workers. The organizing was less focused on workplace concerns and more on legislative goals. Home care workers joined with others across California to pressure the government to twice lift the minimum wage, first to $4.25 in 1996 and then to $5.75 in 1998.

Then the union sued the state to force it to bargain with workers. In a sense, this was an example of unfissuring the workplace.[2] The result of that lawsuit and organizing effort was the creation of In-Home Supportive Service (IHSS), a public entity that became the caregivers' employer of record as well as the authority that offered job training, skills development, and safety standards. The union also won $800 million more in funds for Medicaid to fund home care work, winning allegiance from workers, public health advocates, and allies in government.[3]

In 1999, the union finally agreed to a contract with the state. It was a stunning victory. About seventy-four thousand workers joined SEIU Local 434B that year, some of whom had for years been working informally, caring for friends and family for free. Now they were eligible for pay and benefits. At that time, it was the largest organizing victory for the US labor movement since the United Auto Workers unionized Ford's River Rouge plant in 1941, an early sign that healthcare labor would replace industrial labor as the new vanguard of working-class struggle.[4] It was also an especially creative display of collective action in the "care economy."

Winning a public employer and bargaining rights for people who were previously unrecognized as workers practically invented an entirely new labor relations environment for caregivers. Their turnover declined, wages rose, benefits appeared, and the job became semiprofessional. By 2000, San Francisco home care workers earned $9.75, the highest in the state, and enjoyed comparably generous benefits. Over the past thirty years, SEIU has replicated the strategy in copycat movements, creating a public employer for caregivers in thirteen states where none had existed previously.

The more I learned about this campaign in the industry, the more I felt compelled to be part of it. I eventually moved to California and became a union organizer with SEIU, an experience that changed my life and, hopefully, the lives of a few California caregivers.

Still, even with a union, many home care aides are worked over and overworked.

+

FOR THE LAST sixteen years, Edith Guttierez has regularly worked twenty-four-hour shifts as a home care worker in New York City—but she's only paid for half of that time. And she's not alone. About 8 percent of New York State's 240,000 home care workers are assigned twenty-four-hour shifts, many of them consecutive back-to-back shifts. Rest is intermittent, and real sleep is nearly impossible.[5] The workers, almost all women of color and immigrants, are responsible for the health and safety of those needing round-the-clock care. Many home care attendants have historically been paid for thirteen hours of a twenty-four-hour shift, in accordance with a New York Department of Labor guidance dating back to the 1990s.[6] The frequency of twenty-four- and even forty-eight-hour shifts increased during the pandemic because patients requested that caregivers reduce their travel to and from work as much as possible. As Edith commuted over an hour by bus and subway to and from work, she was at greater risk of contracting the virus and spreading it to her patients.

When she and her coworkers complained to their employment agencies, they were told to ignore their patients during sleeping hours. If they chose to care for their patients, it was their own decision. Rather than accept this callous advice, Edith and other home care attendants organized with the Ain't I a Woman?! campaign to demand the end of twenty-four-hour work shifts. Ain't I a Woman?! was founded by women garment workers in US sweatshops to fight against eighty-hour workweeks and low pay, but it has since taken up the cause of caregivers, who face perhaps even more abusive conditions.

Their efforts have led to the introduction of state legislation mandating that people in need of twenty-four hours of assistance receive it from workers in two nonsequential twelve-hour shifts.[7] If passed, caregivers would finally be paid for the time they work rather than being forced to toil twelve hours for free.

The twenty-four-hour workday is enshrined in New York State labor law, and the state has shown no interest in changing it. More surprisingly, the caregiver's union, 1199SEIU, hasn't made it a priority either. Unionization has hardly been a panacea. Historically, unions were the primary means by which workers chipped away at the length of the working day. Yet as organized labor's power plummeted, so did their ability to moderate the metronome of American capitalism. The result:

the slow return of a long-hours economy that has barely registered as a complaint among the largest official labor organizations.[8] This is unfortunate, since the long-hours economy has hit low-income workers the hardest. Stagnating wages, declining union density, and rising social precarity have meant that low-wage workers simply can't afford to work less. Moreover, the jobs are still pretty bad, and caregiving organizations still compete with fast-food franchises to retain their workforce.

In New York City, the Ain't I a Woman?! campaign has repeatedly tried to engage with 1199SEIU, the caregivers' union. But the union has not yet taken up ending time and wage theft in earnest, and they are not a sponsor of the legislation. In March 2022, 1199SEIU announced a "historic" $30 million wage fund to pay back 120,000 home care workers who had more than $6 billion of wages stolen while working twenty-four-hour workdays. After seven years of delay, this settlement will award workers 0.5 percent of the back pay they're actually owed. The legality of the twenty-four-hour workday, and wage theft, remained in place.

At a rally to challenge the meager outcomes of the union's efforts, fuming workers spoke out. "With this settlement, the union is trampling upon my right and dignity," said Mei Kum Chu, a retired home attendant and former member of 1199SEIU. "Is this the union's response to my suffering from 24-hour workdays all these years?" "With this agreement, 1199 is stomping on us like cockroaches," said Epifania Hichez, also a former caregiver who said she suffered from hand pain and sleeplessness. One caregiver, Lai Yee Chan, approached me with her hands up to display disfigured fingers and a crooked wrist, the result of decades of grueling twenty-four-hour shifts.[9]

The work caregivers like Edith, Mei Kum, Epifania, and Lai Yee perform is invaluable, and so we simply do not value it at all. And herein lies one of our most important social fault lines exposed by the pandemic. Caregiving is indispensable to society, yet we routinely deny caregivers the ability to do the job with dignity, good pay, and quality working conditions, thus driving down the level of care they're able to administer. Shortchanging workers in home care, nursing, day care, and childcare might seem like a bargain, but it's really a gamble.

◆

WHY ARE THERE so many care jobs, and why are they so low-quality? The crisis of care has transpired over the last five decades as healthcare has become increasingly privatized, as middle-wage union jobs have disappeared, and as labor hours have steadily increased, thus limiting our time for care. We've added historic numbers of caregivers to the economy at the exact same time. This bitter irony—of the increasing human potential to care for each other cancelled out by profit imperatives—leaves us stuck in a historic position.

Over the last decades, as the graph below shows, healthcare jobs have risen steadily, growing at a faster rate than all other jobs after 2000. This sector generated 56 percent of growth in low-wage jobs

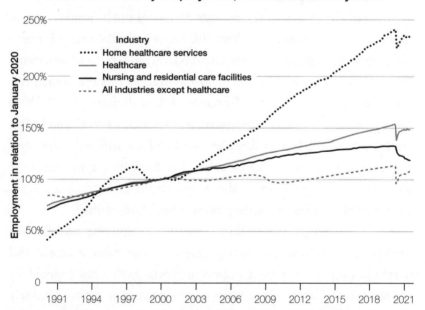

Healthcare Industry Employment, Indexed to January 2020

Healthcare jobs declined during the pandemic but bounced back—except in nursing and nursing homes. SOURCE: Bureau of Labor Statistics, Current Employment Statistics

in the 1980s, 63 percent in the 1990s, and 74 percent in the 2000s.[10] Much of this low-wage growth can be attributed to the shocking rise in home health services, the fastest-growing job in America. This raw data is the empirical foundation for any discussion of a care economy.[11]

The graying of the country partly explains the increase in health-care jobs. Older insured Americans are the primary consumers of healthcare services, and their health problems don't disappear during economic downturns. Given that so many are insured and have high levels of Medicaid access, they can visit the doctor even during hard times. Moreover, healthcare jobs are hard to automate—especially the low-wage jobs—and are basically place bound, making them resistant to globalization or regional relocation schemes. We all need our dental hygienist to be physically present to get a cleaning.

As the graph reveals, the pandemic recession momentarily paused this historic expansion, which has been recession-proof in the past. As the elderly were at greatest risk of contracting COVID, they were disincentivized to go to the doctor unless it was absolutely necessary, and healthcare employment crashed abruptly. Though there was a post-2020 rebound in most sectors, it's important to note that employment in nursing and residential care facilities continued to decline, reflecting the persistent nationwide nurse shortage.

Debates about the new pandemic-induced labor shortage mostly ignored nurses, who have been in short supply for decades. The US Bureau of Labor Statistics projects that eleven million additional nurses are needed to solve the shortage, which is about four times the number of nurses who are currently employed.[12]

Hospitals intentionally understaff nurses to maximize profits. As labor costs account for about half of hospitals' budgets, they make money by cutting lifesaving medical professionals from the payroll. The result is an epidemic of overwork, abuse, low pay, and record-high nurse-to-patient staffing ratios. This problem affects all of us. Understaffing means nurses are in short supply when we need them most. It means they make more mistakes because they're pushed beyond their limits. Understaffing means worse patient outcomes, including higher rates of death.[13]

Moreover, there's not actually a nursing shortage. We have four million licensed nurses in America, about one-seventh of all nurses in the world.[14] The problem is that nursing jobs are horrible, and nurses have been quitting them. The dangerous and stressful conditions they're expected to work under have been driving nurses from the bedside for years.

The pandemic didn't cause this crisis, but it made it more acute. Some nurses, like Kim, whom we met in the Introduction, left their hospitals for traveling jobs. Traveler contracts paid as much as $5,000 per week in early 2022, double their pre-pandemic rate and far above the pay of regular nurses. Other nurses left the field for good. And low pay wasn't the only reason. Citing the stress and dangers of the job, today an astonishing 66 percent of nurses report they are considering leaving the industry and switching careers.[15]

Others stayed and fought. Marlena, whom we met in Chapter 3, went on strike with thousands of other nurses across the country to protest unsafe staffing levels during the pandemic. Because nurses are so necessary, and their replacements so expensive, they often enjoyed enough leverage to win. But in Marlena's case, it was especially difficult. She walked a picket line with hundreds of others at a Tenet-owned hospital in Massachusetts for over three hundred days from 2020 to 2021. During that time, Tenet received more than $1 billion in CARES Act stimulus funds, a $1.5-billion Medicare advance, about $67 million returned from Medicare, $60 million in Medicaid grants, and $250 million in this year's Social Security payroll tax match.[16]

Rather than use this influx of cash to pay its nurses and settle the strike, Tenet furloughed more than 10 percent of its workforce and suspended a retirement benefit for its employees.[17] Ultimately, Marlena and her coworkers finally won safe staffing levels, but it took almost a year of struggle without a paycheck. Most nurses, even those with a union, simply aren't prepared to fight that hard.

A short documentary by the *New York Times* chalked the problem up to greedy hospital corporations.[18] Greed is a compelling explanation because it is simple, and it carries a moral judgment of wrongdoing, which is in high supply.

But the systemic nature of the problem means something more serious is going on that we can't attribute just to bad people in charge. Greed is a personality defect. The pervasive nature of pandemic profiteering in healthcare suggests a more structural problem that requires a radical solution. Nurses regularly push for legally mandated safe staffing levels. In 2004, a union-won nurse-to-patient staffing law went into effect in California that has been shown to improve both jobs and patient outcomes. Attempts to copy the legislation elsewhere have always been defeated by powerful private hospital lobbies.

National Nurses United was one of the first unions to officially endorse a national single-payer healthcare system. Such a system, embodied in the Medicare for All legislation introduced by Representative Pramila Jayapal and Senator Bernie Sanders in 2021, seeks, among many things, to establish safe staffing levels for healthcare workers across the country. No one knows better than nurses what they need to adequately staff hospitals, so the union has also pressured lawmakers to ensure that any political reform includes training, education, and collective bargaining rights for nurses. The real long-term solution is to abolish privatized healthcare altogether, an even higher bar than Medicare for All. But until national reforms of this kind make it out of Congress, a main way for nurses to get safe staffing is to strike for it.

Critics of healthcare reform argue that if a system eliminates private companies' ability to profit off the sick, they will be disincentivized to hire, and jobs will dry up. But that actually describes the situation we have now. More than anywhere else in the economy, we need people working in healthcare. We need to make sure those jobs are good enough to attract talented personnel.

The nursing shortage notwithstanding, today more Americans work in healthcare than any other single field. The Bureau of Labor Statistics predicts healthcare jobs will grow about twice as fast as any other category in the next decade. Job openings for nurses are projected to grow at a faster rate than all other occupations from 2020 through 2026.[19] We will also add 1,152,500 home health aides. Of the top fifteen occupations predicted to add the most jobs in the next decade, six are in healthcare: home health aides, nurses, medical assistants, health services, nursing assistants, and nurse practitioners.[20] When you picture the future of work, picture a woman of color—in scrubs.

When you picture the future of caregiving, picture the 3.4 million home care workers and the 1.6 million certified nursing assistants in long-term care homes. Picture them comforting our loved ones, singing them to sleep, saving their lives, and holding their hands as they die. Picture them feeding our pets and taking out our trash. Picture them opening their checks every other week and seeing that they still make, on average, less than fifteen dollars an hour, far below a living wage, often not enough to exist above the federal poverty line. Picture them dying in the process of saving lives, as they did in droves during the pandemic. Now picture this: the Families First Coronavirus Response Act and the Emergency Family and Medical Leave Expansion Act, which mandated that businesses grant eighty hours of paid sick leave to workers through the end of 2020, excluded home care aides.[21]

◆

THE CARE ECONOMY'S rise is rooted in the seventies, in the long shadow of a dismantled New Deal. I grew up in Bethlehem, Pennsylvania, a town once dominated both economically and culturally by basic steel. Bethlehem Steel built one ship per day during World War II, as the combination of military Keynesianism and strong unions ensured high wages for workers. Its bosses weren't starving either. Bethlehem Steel built its headquarters, Martin Tower, in the shape of a cruciform just to meet the demand among executives for corner offices. Years later, we all gathered to watch as it was detonated, crumbling in on itself when the bottom supports were dynamited. It was both a spectacle and a specter. The town's signature identity, aside from the Moravian religion, had just been blown up in our faces, and we were haunted by what might come next. What did come next, the ghosts of steel, had been well under way for decades: hospitals.

Bethlehem, and the Lehigh Valley in general, quietly became a region of healthcare jobs. Today the area's two largest employers—Lehigh

Valley Health Network and St. Luke's University Health Network—
are both huge, consolidated hospital systems that employ more workers than "the Steel" did at its peak.[22] This doesn't even include the
droves of new nursing facilities and armies of immigrant care aides
spread out across the valley. Rarely, however, did we see those two
things—deindustrialization and healthcare jobs—as related. Historian Gabriel Winant's research on Pittsburgh, our rival steel town,
sheds light on this steel-work-to-care-work transformation.

Winant shows that the story of the caring class is interwoven with
the demise of America's industrial working class. When industrial
jobs disappeared, the bodies left in its wake were battered, bruised,
hunched, addicted, poisoned, mangled, and sick. Since 2000, life expectancy among the white working class has actually declined in the
US, a pattern seen almost nowhere else on earth.

The decline is largely explained by an increase in suicides, opioid
overdoses, and alcohol-related illnesses, the so-called deaths of despair
studied by economist Anne Case and Nobel Prize winner Angus Deaton. If the life expectancy of these people had continued to rise as it
had throughout the early part of the century, about six hundred thousand more Americans would still be alive, Case and Deaton found.

"Destroy work and, in the end, working-class life cannot survive,"
they argue. "It is the loss of meaning, of dignity, of pride, and of self-
respect…that brings on despair, not just or even primarily the loss of
money."[23]

Some of the erosion of well-paying blue-collar jobs can be attributed to automation, which reveals another curious way in which
the rise of low-wage healthcare work and the decline of comparably
better-paying factory labor are related: automating the middle of the
labor market helped grow the bottom of it.

The progressive automation of well-paid blue-collar production
jobs allowed us to produce more for less and lower costs for consumer
durable goods. As consumers spent less money on these goods, they
were able to spend more on personal services, like personal healthcare
aides. Robot-enabled savings on manufactured goods triggered more

consumption of services, spurring growth of service jobs.[24] The low wages workers earn in these jobs, in turn, are a safeguard against their automation. Why invest the huge sums necessary to innovate when you can increase productivity by cheaply extending workers' hours instead?

Most of the expanding low-wage healthcare jobs aren't easy to automate anyway, despite their ironic designation as "low-skilled labor." In the midcentury, "unskilled labor" described the routine manual tasks associated with industrial production and large-scale manufacturing. Today it's different. Unskilled labor mostly describes jobs requiring intuitive tasks that often appear "natural" or "innate": cooking and serving food, caring for people, etc. It's not coincidental these skills are traditionally coded as women's work. They are seen as having been cultivated in the home rather than through education or training. Performing them doesn't even register as work most of the time.

A computer science postulate called Moravec's paradox argues that robots tend to be avid learners when it comes to difficult computational tasks but are comparably bad at the nonroutine tasks humans perform through intuition. This is why we can increasingly automate tasks that involve high-level cognition or complex data processing, but after years of trying, we still can't build a robot that can change a diaper.

The shifting definition of unskilled labor suggests that while it seems to measure an objective capacity, it's really more of a status marker. Who holds the power to decide what kinds of labor are designated as skilled or unskilled is an important social question. (It's tempting to imagine a glorious future when being a landlord or owning stocks is diminished as unskilled labor.)

As the seventies became the eighties, workers, skilled or not, relied on an increasingly tattered safety net and weaker institutions like unions to govern their postwork life. The postwar working class had built the closest thing America ever had to shared prosperity, and though they were compensated comparably well, they paid a steep price down the line. As Winant puts it, "the collapse of the industrial core of the economy created social problems that became translated, through the mediation of the welfare state, into the form of health problems."[25]

The new working class in healthcare professions is basically dedicated to the task of caring for their forebears from the factories, though it would be incorrect to suggest some kind of symmetry beyond that relationship. Whereas the old working class at least enjoyed decent standards and a voice on the job through unions, the newer one does not. The victories I describe above notwithstanding, it's almost entirely nonunion.

With a union, the job I had taking care of Robert would be a better job today—but nowhere near good enough. The present state of home care became clearer to me when I interviewed a few pairs of caregivers and their clients. Tyler Tunison and Keith Gurgui have a special bond that illustrates the interdependent nature of giving and receiving care.

"The way he works is important to the way I live," Keith told me. "I will do whatever I can to make sure he gets what he deserves. That's what he does for me."

In 2012, ten days before he was to start his freshman year of college, Keith was on a vacation in Delaware. A swimming accident left him paralyzed from the neck down; in an instant, everything changed and his future was far from certain. Tyler, a home care aide for the last six years, was at Keith's side for the entire pandemic. He bathes, feeds, and dresses Keith to ensure he's comfortable. "Without personal care aides, I would not be living at home independently, be able to work, have gone to school. I'd be in a nursing home, miserable, depressed," Gurgui said.

Tyler bounced around low-wage jobs in retail before joining what seems like a family business—his brother, girlfriend, and sister-in-law are all care aides as well. Tyler is the kind of person you want caring for you or your loved ones. He's committed, careful, and laughs easily, never seeming to take himself too seriously. "This work is really good for me," he says. "There's nothing more important than helping people." In all the years he has been doing this work, he's taken only one vacation, since he receives no paid leave. What did he do with that free time? He spent all of it as an unpaid caretaker for his indigent grandparents, who needed the kind of care he could provide.

Home care workers like Tyler earn a median income of $21,000 per year, just above a poverty rate. Tyler has two children, ages two and seven, and says that with his girlfriend's wages they can pay for rent and groceries. But there's no future in it. "It's not something I can do forever, unfortunately," he says. "I can't grow old and retire on this." Nor can he rely on it for a dependable schedule. "Every day I go to work I always expect to be there longer than I'm scheduled," Tyler said.

More healthcare jobs can be seen as an obvious good, especially in a post-pandemic context. If we have to work, we might as well do so in the service of our collective health. The problem is that caregiving jobs are so bad that they result in poor quality of life for workers. In turn, a job without paid sick leave, vacation days, or a livable wage undermines their labor, and the quality of care with it. By shortchanging nurses, we are undermining our own care. The crisis of work has become, in other words, a larger crisis of social reproduction.

◆

SOCIAL REPRODUCTION, AS mentioned above, describes the processes necessary to regenerate the workforce. There is a narrow view of the concept that looks specifically at the role of unpaid, often female-dominated and home-based care work. This social reproduction is typically hidden from plain sight. It lies, as the philosopher Nancy Fraser says, "behind the hidden abode" of capitalist exploitation. Fraser draws on Marx, who fretted a good chunk of his own life in the hidden abode of the British Museum writing about capitalist exploitation. Marx understood that class society wasn't the result of market relations or the unfair *distribution* of rewards and resources. Rather, class inequality resulted from a process tucked neatly into the "hidden abode" of the capitalist production process itself. And behind that process, in a sense, lies the invisible labor of social reproduction that allows all other work to be possible. The benefit of this view is that it's clearly focused on an otherwise ignored segment of the working population, and it illuminates the home as a productive space that's central to markets and capital accumulation.[26]

The broader view of social reproduction expands the concept to paid work as well. It also includes a greater diversity of jobs that "count" as social reproduction. When you care for your own children, there's no impact on GDP. The narrower view of social reproduction sees this work, accurately, as nonetheless necessary to capitalist political economy. If you get too busy and decide to put your kids in day care, GDP will go up. The broader view, which I endorse, allows us to see the caregiver's work as equally important in either case.

There is a defining contradiction of economic life in capitalist society. On the one hand, social reproduction is a necessary condition for the stability of the capitalist system—making sure that workers are regularly housed, clothed, rested, and fed, and their children cared for, is essential before any of them can go to work, even if they work from home. On the other hand, the capitalist drive to unlimited profits and accumulated wealth tends to destabilize the process of social reproduction on which it relies.[27] It drives wages down and hours up. Housing costs and prices rise as the minimum wage stagnates. States reduce social services, and the resulting increased demand for care gets punted to monetized care companies. Eventually, something has to give.

What if we can't do it? What if the minimum wage is so low that it forces us to work two or more jobs, as do almost 10 percent of Americans, leaving no time for housework and childcare?[28] What if health insurance costs scare us away from getting basic care when we need it, as they do for one in three Americans, leading to more serious and expensive medical needs down the line?[29] What if our workfare programs push millions of poor people into the labor market just so they can collect benefits, even when they have competing obligations to children or elders in their home? What if we pay home care workers such shoddy wages that they leave their industry for fast-food jobs that pay slightly more, creating a massive care worker deficit just when we need them more than ever? What if—stick with me here— a deadly global pandemic throws the economy into free fall and costs us our healthcare and our job, and we're sick with a virus that no one knows how to cure?

The pandemic put us face-to-face with these impossible questions. It profoundly disrupted our ability to work for a wage while performing the usual amount of home-based labor. During the pandemic, then, wage workers became our caregivers more than ever before. Social media was aflutter with posts describing the deep emotional connections that citizens, especially nonessential workers, felt for grocery clerks, gas station attendees, delivery drivers, and healthcare workers. This increased reliance, however, deepened the distinction between waged and unwaged care work in stark ways. After all, we weren't banging on pots and pans for unemployed family members caring for each other. We were saluting the employees taking care of all of us.

At the same time, shelter-in-place orders redirected our attention to the home, turning the public-private division inside out. One way that "women's work" has been historically undervalued is through its containment in the privatized domestic sphere. Suddenly, however, our homes were also workspaces, which tended to advertise the role of housework in making capitalism tick. By dragging the domestic sphere into the sunlight, the pandemic rendered it less a hidden abode and more a public battleground.

The amount of work we did for social reproduction increased during the pandemic, exacerbating a preexisting crisis. As hospitals exceeded their capacity and healthcare workers became overextended, the vital work of physical caretaking sometimes fell on friends and family of the unwell. Overall healthcare coverage declined only slightly, but the underinsured rate increased significantly. People either ignored certain medical problems, treated themselves, or had friends and family come to their aid. As families took their loved ones out of nursing homes, elder care fell more on untrained professionals who were already strained with other work and caregiving responsibilities. Parents were forced to play a more active role in caring for and educating their children from home.

The home, which has traditionally been characterized as a haven of sorts from a heartless world, was suddenly at the heart of the capitalist economy. As the radical geographer Ruthie Wilson Gilmore has shown, "edges are also interfaces."[30] In other words, the borders between nations and the boundaries between communities or social institutions belie a close relationship, not a hard-and-fast divide. Paradoxically, this shift toward more home-based reproductive labor increased its public visibility and endowed it with a special recognition it rarely gets otherwise. This shift also heightened the need for parents, legislators, and employers to discuss reproductive work like never before, admitting, to a degree, that it must be prioritized. In effect, the pandemic exposed the fragile state of social reproduction by blurring the boundary demarcating the productive work many tended to think occurred outside the home and the reproductive work happening within it.

This blurring boundary was brought into sharp relief when essential workers staged walkouts, protests, slowdowns, sick-outs, or strikes. Far from abandoning their duties, these workers staged disruptions in an effort to increase their capacity to perform their vital functions. When nurses in California, Pennsylvania, and Massachusetts struck for better staffing ratios, they underscored a major impediment to our ability to care for each other. When Chicago and Philadelphia and Los Angeles teachers refused to teach in-person classes until they, their students, and their students' families could be vaccinated, they pressured local authorities to prioritize these groups' health needs.

When workers disrupted their work routines, they also made it clear that the work they're paid to do is only a portion of their social value. After all, nursing home workers don't simply spoon-feed the elderly and change their bedpans. They comfort them, and they comfort their families after they're gone. Doctors don't just keep people alive but make tough calls about who deserves a ventilator. Nurses don't show up only at the bedside but at the bargaining table, demanding better conditions for their patients. Grocery store clerks don't merely stock shelves, they help keep order during panic-buying pandemonium. The pandemic spotlighted the multidimensional nature of essential workers' labor and helped us understand the importance and, by extension, the potential power, of these workers.

In essence, strikes and other disruptions among socially reproductive workers have a double character because they occur at both the point of production (because they take place in a workplace) *and* the point of social reproduction (because they're enmeshed in the critical care infrastructure that scaffolds our entire society). These actions are voicing complaints that concrete changes by management can typically solve—more money, improved benefits, better hours. At the same time, socially reproductive strikes seek to improve social conditions more broadly, beyond the scope of the workers' job itself.

This is why socially reproductive workers often bargain for "common good demands," changes that transcend the workplace and aim to directly improve the communities to which these workers are so intimately connected. Before the pandemic, it was teachers who led the way in this arena, striking for things like rent subsidies and immigration protections for their students' families. Over the course of the pandemic, thousands of workers took a page from the teachers' playbook. Detroit bus drivers struck to cancel rider fees, Oakland nurses struck to reinstate public control of their hospital, GE factory workers demanded that their plants produce ventilators, and Chicago teachers protested for police-free schools.[31] In March 2020, the Communications Workers of America alongside the International Brotherhood of Electrical Workers reached an agreement with Verizon that won unionized workers additional paid sick and family leave, including an astounding twenty-six weeks of paid leave for workers diagnosed with COVID-19 and eight weeks of paid leave (plus eighteen weeks at 60 percent pay) for workers who had to care for someone diagnosed with the virus or a child whose school or day care was closed because of the pandemic.[32] A year later, Columbia graduate school workers commenced a strike for a fair contract, demanding, among other things, increased childcare benefits.[33]

These workers are and always have been essential. That this is most visible when they're not doing their jobs—on the picket line, for example—is a consequence of how profoundly underappreciated and unrecognized their labor is. Strikes or disruptive protests in these sectors simultaneously expose the exploitation that is central to capitalism *and* force us to recognize that we all benefit when care workers have better jobs.

All of this activity focused a shocking amount of public attention on the role of caregiving in capitalist society. It was matched by a historic demand for public provisioning. The CARES Act and the American Rescue Plan saved lives and temporarily tamped down the poverty level. Today nearly 25 percent of US GDP comes from the caregiving work key to social reproduction, the most of any of the G7 countries. As a percentage of overall employment, social reproduction is performed by 23–28 percent of all paid workers.[34] That's close to the number we once employed in better-paying manufacturing jobs.

A social reproduction lens allows us to both zoom out, to conceptualize the pandemic as a larger crisis of labor endemic to capitalist society, and zoom in, to focus on specific kinds of labor, like home care, that the pandemic highlighted. The care sector is booming with low-wage jobs, making it harder for workers to deliver the kind of care we all need. A crisis of social reproduction, however, is even broader. It frays the fabric of our social bonds but also insists that we look for new ways of maintaining a cohesive society.

◆

THE PANDEMIC RIPPED us apart. Historian Jill Lepore spent time reading what she called "plague novels" in 2020, devouring works by Giovanni Boccaccio, Daniel Defoe, Albert Camus, José Saramago, and Mary Shelley. She found they collectively told a story of the descent of humanity. First, the characters in the stories lost their minds. "They consulted astrologers, quacks, the Bible," she wrote. "They searched their bodies for signs, tokens of the disease: lumps, blisters, black spots. They begged for prophecies; they paid for predictions; they prayed; they yowled. They closed their eyes; they covered their ears."[35]

The pandemic drove us mad too. Americans worshipped false prophets, refused the advice of medical experts, willingly put their loved ones in harm's way, protested outside nail salons, and spread misinformation like it was the cure for what ails them. "The plague novel is the place where all human beings abandon all other human beings," Lepore wrote.[36]

Yet her summary of the fictional accounts didn't tell the whole story. During the pandemic, it seemed far more common that people came together to take care of each other. In her masterful investigation into the communities that form in the wake of disaster, *A Paradise Built in Hell*, author and activist Rebecca Solnit documented such outpourings of collective care after the Loma Prieta and Mexico City earthquakes, September 11, and Hurricane Katrina. Her book found second life during the early parts of the pandemic because its analysis was perfectly suited for the moment. In fact, I assigned it to my college students after our class went remote because it so usefully summarizes trends that were already emerging during the lockdown phase of the pandemic.

Caring for each other, as Solnit's book documents, either through formal employment, friendly assistance, or family obligation, is as much a reaction to catastrophe as division is. Indeed, it is an antidote, the very essence of social reproduction. That spirit was on full display during the early days of the pandemic through the creation of mutual aid networks.

College students banded together to share resources as they quickly shipped home from school. A Minnesota group called COVIDsitters matched willing volunteers with the children of essential workers and was replicated across the country. A group called Invisible Hands formed a network in New York City to provide groceries to at-risk people who couldn't shop in person, and many such networks popped up elsewhere. Others offered free routers to expand Wi-Fi access, peer-to-peer mental health support, and homemade hand sanitizer and face coverings. I helped form a group in my little corner of Vermont. We offered grocery shopping and delivery, childcare, some home repair, transportation, even gardening assistance—by the fifth day we had hundreds of volunteers and only a handful of people who needed our services. When it fizzled out, I became a volunteer firefighter instead. Across the country, the desire to pitch in was epic. One survey in late May 2020 found that 37 percent of Americans had donated time, money, or resources to support their community.[37] The pandemic, lo and behold, also brought us together.

Some reports suggest there were over one thousand such mutual aid groups around the country during the height of the lockdown period. Whatever else these groups accomplished, they inspired a whole genre of fawning pandemic media coverage, heartwarming stories that illuminated the kind actions of neighbors and strangers pulling together. Employees combined their paychecks to erase the medical debt of a coworker. Strangers chipped in online to find a home for an evicted single mother. All these human-interest stories came on top of a barrage of uplifting stories about collective resistance to poverty, hunger, and destitution. This emotional blackmail allowed us to imagine that what sociologist Mark Granovetter once called "the strength of weak ties" was enough to save us. And also to conveniently forget that the problems these groups were attending to should not have existed in the first place.

From a social reproduction perspective, mutual aid cannot be the horizon of our caring capacity. Voluntarism is no substitute for government action, just as GoFundMe is not health insurance. We should instead develop a robust social system from the very principle of mutual aid. It is, after all, as Kropotkin argued, "the necessary foundation of everyday life."

A society built on a foundation of real mutual aid—all for one and one for all—cannot rely on goodwill. More than an ethic of care or a neighborly spirit, we need real "care infrastructure."

Care infrastructure describes the social organization of solidarity, a web of policies, resources, and services that can meet or exceed our collective needs. It describes free, high-quality childcare, free universal healthcare, paid family and medical leave, and reliable access to care in our homes and communities. It means our economic system is focused on providing health, longevity, and security to everyone, above all else. I was pleasantly surprised when the first draft of Biden's infrastructure legislation included $400 billion for the care economy. I was unpleasantly unsurprised when it was carved out a few months later.

The caring workforce is slowly rebounding from their pandemic job losses. This is lucky, because we need them more than ever. If the pandemic has taught us anything, it's that a crisis for low-income workers is a crisis for all of us. This care crisis was exacerbated by decades of privatized healthcare policy and austerity measures that sapped the health sector's vitality and left us vulnerable to the virus during the pandemic. We should understand this care crisis as something more—it's embedded in the preexisting tendency in capitalist society to undermine social reproduction.

Any system that ignores or degrades our ability to perform indispensable socially reproductive tasks is doomed. The bad and good news is that capitalism is just such a system.

Our society, as currently organized, cannot provide adequate care infrastructure. Therefore, while we should push for the reforms we need now, we should do so with the understanding that a truly caring society will require a deeper social transformation. The pandemic exposed us as frail and fragile, deeply vulnerable economically, politically, and biologically. Rebuilding after this crisis requires that we not return to normal.

In the next chapter, I review a few political goals that push the horizon of change further into the future. I do this not to delay our arrival at a safer and fairer society but to encourage us not to settle for dead-end reforms that offer only tweaks to our current way of life. There's a danger that we'll never get there, of course, but also that we'll take our eyes off the real prize: revolutionary transformation. The primary lesson from this crisis is that the best way to protect ourselves from biological threats is to reorganize our society so that common people have more power and resources. Right-wing pundits call that socialism, and for once they're right.

CHAPTER 8

THE PANDEMIC PENDULUM

As the epigraph for this book suggests, the crisis we're in now is an interregnum of sorts. The way our society is organized is dangerous and nonsensical, and it put a great number unnecessarily in harm's way during the pandemic. Yet the prospects for deep transformation are bleak. We're stuck.

The workers on whom we depend to deliver our high standard of living, to procure our essential goods and services and quality care, are the ones we treat the worst. We prioritize work, not workers. And when workers try to improve their conditions, which would benefit all of us, our society stands in their way.

The solutions to bad jobs are clear and widely acknowledged—fewer hours, higher wages, unions, broad social benefits, worker ownership, labor-friendly schedules, more paid leaves, creative and challenging job tasks. We just lack the political will to implement them.

Before the magnetic attraction of a complete "return to normal" has pulled us too far from our brightest dreams, we can glimpse an alternate future and make headway toward its fruition. Our best chance is that the Left's ideas and politics become salient in a way that allows us to redesign the economy to the benefit of all. A real recovery from the COVID-19 crisis can't be measured in the return of jobs or the status of the virus; it can only be measured in the extent to which we have moved away from the ruthless capitalism of the last century and toward a more egalitarian society.

This chapter examines some of those ideas in detail and describes lessons we should learn from the crisis. It's not a road map to freedom or a recipe for justice. I evaluate some popular and not-so-popular proposals for social change after the pandemic. I consider modest strategies and decidedly revolutionary goals, all of which offer a vision of a future where workers have more money, more voice, more power, and more security. As luck would have it, were these policies to be realized, we'd all have more democracy too. The pandemic offered a glimpse into a dystopian future but also cracked open a utopian window. It's our job to peer through.

The Left is stereotypically composed of dreamers, stargazers brimming with lots of big ideas but no way to solve real problems. They're ideologues, not architects. But crises can transform dreamers into

Trends in US Public Opinion Toward Big Business and Labor Unions

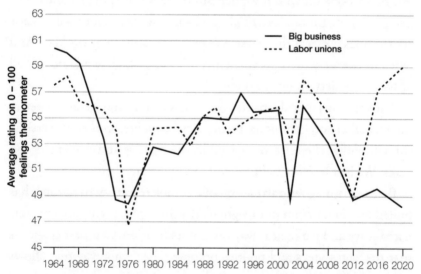

SOURCE: Emily DiVito and Aaron Sojourner, "Americans Are More Pro-Union—and Anti–Big Business—Than at Any Time in Decades," *Guardian*, May 13, 2021; American National Election Surveys, 1964–2016 cumulative data file and 2020. Graph by Aaron Sojourner

pragmatists. Today's left flank is committed to union organizing, racial justice, healthcare reform, and sane climate policy. And their ideas are more popular than ever.

Using polling data from the American National Election Studies, economists Aaron Sojourner and Emily DiVito show how the recorded gap in popular feeling toward labor unions and big business is larger than it's been in a long time. For the five decades this data was collected, these opinions trended in tandem, until 2012, when they began to thoroughly diverge. This probably reflects rising awareness of wealth inequality and corporate power, and popular support for the 2018–2019 strike wave. In 2020, national sentiment toward labor unions was more positive than in any year on record, while public feeling toward big business was the most negative on record, dating back to 1964.[1] These trends were true for almost all political groups and age cohorts. Among Republicans, the difference in sentiment for unions and against business hit a record high in 2020. Compare this to the late 1930s, a high-water mark for labor militancy, when 60 percent of Americans opposed the sit-down strikes in the industrial heartland and half said they would call in militias to forcibly end them.[2] Today, 68 percent of Americans approve of trade unions and half say they'd join one if they could. But only 10 percent are actually members.

Sways in popular public opinion toward more worker-friendly policies are one mechanism by which workplace activism could advance up the political ladder. For example, a majority of voters, including 40 percent of Republican voters, support the Protecting the Right to Organize (PRO) Act, an early centerpiece of Biden's jobs plan. The sweeping legislation would be a much-needed upgrade to modern labor law and would advantage workers when they unionize.

Throughout this book I've shown that unions do more than advance their members' interests. During the pandemic, they saved lives in nursing homes, won public health protections in schools, and pushed for other benefits that rippled out beyond their workplaces. These findings have important implications for policymakers, employers, and workers, who share the goal of increasing public health.

Ensuring that workers have the most advantageous legal environment in which to organize should be a primary goal of all Americans. Indeed, stronger unions are a necessary condition for the feasibility of every reform considered in this chapter.

Still, the PRO Act passed in the House but not the Senate, where Democrats Kyrsten Sinema of Arizona and Joe Manchin of West Virginia refused to override the filibuster, which would have allowed Democrats to pass it without Republican support. Republican voters report 54 percent support for the right of public sector workers to form unions. That's less than the 82 percent of Democrats, but it's still significant. Republican leaders have, after all, led the movement over the last decade to vastly expand the right-to-work landscape of the country, which greatly limits unions' ability to represent workers. Leaders in both parties are simply stopping workers from getting what they want.

Other popular policies are denied us too. Biden's Build Back Better agenda came close to winning historic investments in childcare, universal prekindergarten, and twelve weeks of paid sick and parental leave for all. This was far less than most countries offer, but it was still a step forward, offering twenty million workers some paid time off who currently have none. The vast majority of Democrats and half of Republicans support the proposal. It also has business support because state subsidies make it cheaper for businesses than paying their employees' benefits directly. But the leave provision was pared down to four weeks through conservative attacks and then scrapped altogether through partisan ratfucking by Manchin and Sinema, whose votes were needed to pass it. What does the US have in common with the Marshall Islands, Micronesia, Nauru, Palau, Papua New Guinea, and Tonga? They're the only countries in the world that do not offer national paid leave.[3]

Paid family and sick leave had never been a real goal for American policymakers, but some hoped the pandemic would change that. Low-income essential workers were forced to work through bouts of

COVID, inadvertently spreading the virus far and wide, because they had no financial cushion to take time off from work. Counties where workers had more paid sick leave were able to flatten the curve faster, keeping workers and the general public safer.[4]

Had Biden's original agenda passed, the US would still offer a paltry amount of paid leave compared to the rest of the world's rich countries. The fact that Democrats couldn't even convince their own leaders to support these modest reforms doesn't mean they can't happen, just that workers and unions will need to create a crisis so that paid leave—and any other progressive demand—is preferable to widespread unrest. Change will have to come from below.

◆

IN *THE GREAT TRANSFORMATION*, the economic historian Karl Polanyi outlines a process he calls the "double movement."[5] Dialectical in nature, it describes the push and pull, or the pendulum swing, of opposing forms of social organization. At one extreme, laissez-faire capitalism tends to "dis-embed" the economic dimensions of society from the political realm, leading to wide commodification of everything, including labor itself. As a reaction to the problems this causes, liberal reformers begin a countermovement to "re-embed" the economy in the social sphere, submitting it to democratic oversight. These changes are cyclical. Think of the New Deal after the Great Depression and then the neoliberal countermovement against the legacy of the New Deal.

After decades of rising inequality, stagnating wages, longer hours, austerity, growing indebtedness, and weaker social protections from risk shifts, popular sentiment during the pandemic suggested reason for cautious optimism. The electoral refutation of Trump and support for social spending meant that against all odds the pendulum had reached its apex and was beginning to swing back.

When I began writing this book in earnest in the summer of 2021, Bernie Sanders was floating a $6.5 trillion spending bill that would expand Medicare, improve infrastructure, lower prescription drug prices, reform immigration law, and support the rights of workers to organize. It passed in the House. During negotiations with Biden's administration, however, it was cut in half, to $3.4 trillion. By the time I was done writing in early 2022, Biden's Build Back Better agenda had been whittled down to $1.7 trillion. And there was still much room for compromise. They were nickel-and-diming the American people on policies that would limit the transmission of COVID-19 at the exact time the Omicron variant was burning through the country, overwhelming emergency rooms—again. In the single largest policy failure of the pandemic era, Build Back Better went bust.

What does this mean for workers? What workers needed during the pandemic, and whenever it recedes, is only a more urgent version of what they've needed for decades.

Three related goals could improve the power that workers have on and off the job: healthcare reform, a Green New Deal for labor, and reducing our overall dependence on paid work. These goals will only be won if workers can increase their power through unions and create a major crisis for corporations. In other words, we should support unions not only for the benefits they bring their members but also as vehicles for larger political change.

In the long term, the real solution to capitalist domination of our lives is socialism. The ideas that underscore that paradigm shift have gotten surprising mainstream exposure. The Democratic Socialists of America count nearly one hundred thousand members in their ranks, spread out over two hundred chapters across the country, the vast majority of which formed during Bernie Sanders's campaign for president in 2016. Sanders's defeat in his second presidential bid may have pushed him out of the national spotlight, but 2020 confirmed that both his diagnosis of the problem and his proposed fixes were fundamentally correct. To start the paradigm shift, workers will need to win major healthcare reforms, one of the Left's signature policy goals.

Medicare for All

The tension between pragmatism and utopia, reform and revolution, is a dusty debate on the Left. It also takes us nowhere because most radicals carry both impulses simultaneously. They're not opposites, but rather alternatives that are always context specific. No one expresses this dual character better than Ady Barkan, a thirty-two-year-old socialist lawyer turned healthcare activist.

In early December 2017, Ady was boarding a flight from Phoenix to Washington with fellow activist Liz Jaff when he noticed conservative Arizona senator Jeff Flake on board. Ady decided to confront him about how the GOP's massive tax bill would wildly expand the deficit and undercut Americans' ability to pay for important healthcare programs. Ady didn't speak in the abstract; he spoke his truth. "A year ago I was healthy," he began. "I was running on the beach." Then he told Flake about his surprise amyotrophic lateral sclerosis (ALS) diagnosis, for which there is a life expectancy four to five years. Ady had a four-month-old son, Carl, when he received his diagnosis. "What should I tell my son, what should *you* tell my son," he asked Flake, "if you pass this bill and it cuts funding for disability and I can't get a ventilator?"

Ady, by then in a wheelchair, spoke to the senator for twelve minutes, with Flake rebuffing every point. Toward the end, Ady made his pitch. By voting against the bill, he told Flake, "You can be an American hero. Think about the legacy that you will have left for my son and your grandchildren if you take your principles and turn them into votes. You can save my life."

The exchange was filmed by Jaff and went viral. By the time the flight touched down, #flakesonaplane was trending, and Barkan and Jaff had an even bigger plan. Soon after, they launched Be a Hero, a national grassroots campaign to confront congressional leaders on healthcare issues, a bid to win Medicare for All in Ady's shortened lifetime. (Flake, predictably, voted for the bill anyway; facing low approval ratings in his own state, he decided in 2019 not to run to retain his seat.)

Ady's story would be poignant in any circumstances, but in today's America, where even comparatively well-off people like Ady and his family struggle to pay for care, it speaks for millions of insured, uninsured, and underinsured people strangled by the rigged healthcare system. Pretty soon, Ady couldn't walk and could barely speak. But as his voice became weaker, his message was amplified. He used it to enlist a citizens' army in the fight for healthcare justice.

"The way that I have tried to make meaning out of my A.L.S. is to turn it into a weapon for struggle, so that it becomes more than merely tragedy," he said. "More than merely loss."[6]

Through bottom-up organizing and a solid PR strategy, the Be a Hero campaign quickly became a ubiquitous presence in the DC halls of power, and Ady became the most visible healthcare activist in the country, a true nonpareil. In 2018, I was arrested outside Flake's office during a civil disobedience action against the Senate's confirmation of Brett Kavanaugh, the accused sexual predator who eventually became a judge, to the Supreme Court. Ady was there too, and I introduced myself briefly to communicate my respect. Moments later we were all handcuffed and hauled off to jail, Ady in a high-tech wheelchair.

It is easy to admire Ady's commitment and spirit, which make him an effective organizer, but in 2020 I began to see his struggle in a new light. During the presidential election, he grilled the Democratic candidates on their healthcare plans and eventually endorsed Elizabeth Warren. He is an effective strategist, with his eyes set on nuts-and-bolts reforms, but it is his grand vision that is most compelling. Though his anecdotes are usually personal, and though he knows his life will be short no matter what medical advances are made, his policy demands and movement-building strategy are based on the fact of social interdependence.

Ady depends on round-the-clock care from nurse's aides, which most families can't afford, and which during the pandemic was more difficult to secure. He depends on the Be a Hero staff to get his message out. And he depends on a political movement to overturn our decrepit healthcare system and finally win universal coverage, which might depend on people like Jeff Flake to eventually do the right thing.

But what does a Medicare activist have to do with the broad spectrum of labor issues this book has addressed so far?

As a young lawyer, Ady started out working with the community group Make the Road, where he represented low-wage workers against wage theft. He drafted policy papers to enhance the working conditions of low-wage New Yorkers, advocating for paid sick days and unionization efforts. Ady recognized the relationship between healthcare activism and labor organizing. In a society where millions get their healthcare and livelihood through work, good jobs are essential to quality health.

By the time I caught up with him again while doing research for this book, he was adamant that class struggle was at the heart of the campaign for healthcare reform. He couldn't speak but communicated through a technology called Eyegaze, which uses lasers to track his eye movements on a screen, converting them into audio files of his voice. "We need to get everyone rowing together," he said, meaning a coalition of political actors led by unions and healthcare advocates.

In light of all the social vulnerabilities the pandemic exposed, we should prioritize the fight for universal healthcare. Even in good times, our healthcare provisions are uneven, posing serious risks to public safety. The privatized nature of our welfare state makes a coordinated response to public health threats exceedingly difficult. Job-based healthcare coverage unnecessarily mixes economic and physical security. How can a labor movement change that?

As elaborated on in Chapter 6, the current system of employer-based healthcare was a result of class struggle. In the 1940s, when labor power was surging through mass strikes, the movement pushed for a publicly funded national health insurance program, encapsulated in the 1945 Wagner-Murray-Dingell bill. The bill was defeated, and the passage of the 1947 Taft-Hartley Act greatly limited unions' powers to strike, halting their momentum. Unions were forced to settle for the "second-best solution" of employer-based coverage.

The COVID welfare state staved off the worst outcomes, but we have learned no lessons from the pandemic. Instead, we allowed our decrepit government support programs to reassert themselves. After two years of workers suffering in dangerous conditions, more than 40 percent of essential workers still have no paid sick leave.

Unions have often fought to keep healthcare attached to jobs in order to attract members, but it's a self-defeating strategy. Every time a new contract is on the table, union healthcare plans are on the chopping block. Workers are routinely forced to trade money for healthcare benefits, a major driver of wage stagnation. The system also dampens workplace militancy. Since their healthcare is tied to their jobs, workers have one more reason to avoid the sort of risky workplace action that could win them better working conditions. When workers *are* able to win good coverage, those wins are much easier to roll back than national programs like Social Security or Medicare. Companies can make modifications discreetly, outside of the national spotlight and without much opposition. A Medicare for All system would cost employers the powerful leverage that controlling access to healthcare gives them over workers, providing workers the opportunity to bargain for better hours, wages, and safety. Unions are slowly coming around to this reality. Today, the National Nurses United, National Education Association, United Steelworkers, United Auto Workers, and public sector federations in the AFL-CIO have joined over six hundred other union organizations to endorse a single-payer system.[7]

A nationalized program like Medicare for All would move from a multi- to a single-payer model, streamlining the system. By reducing administrative overhead and expelling profit-driven insurance companies, it would lower costs for services and prescription drugs. A joint study conducted by Yale, the University of Florida, and the University of Maryland found that transitioning to a single-payer system would save $450 billion each year, $2,400 in annual savings for the average American household.[8] Other studies predict even higher savings, up to $600 billion in administrative costs and $200–$300 billion in savings on prescription drugs.[9] While the savings estimates vary, a 2020 survey of twenty-two individual studies found a trend: they all predicted savings over the first several years of implementation—yes, even the study done by the Koch brothers.[10]

Other alternatives, like a public option or a Medicare buy-in, would leave an estimated one hundred million people at the whim of private companies, who would still be able to profit off the sick.[11] GoFundMe is not an insurance policy, and we need a system that doesn't force Americans to beg from friends and family to pay for routine care. In addition to money, a single-payer system would save something more valuable. Among peer nations, the US currently has the highest rate of preventable deaths.[12] And a 2021 study by a nonpartisan consumer health advocacy organization found that a staggering one in three COVID-19 deaths, and 40 percent of infections, were attributable to gaps in health insurance.[13] Research shows that by ensuring quality universal coverage, we could prevent an estimated sixty-eight thousand deaths a year.[14]

We need to tax the rich and spend the revenues on the public good. The federal budget is, after all, our money. In the March 2021 American Jobs Plan, the Biden administration proposed that $400 billion be spent to bolster Medicaid's home- and community-based services (HCBS). This would be great news for people like Ady. Yet his organization has insisted that this funding be contingent upon protecting the rights of care workers to unionize. These workers assist with eating, bathing, dressing, and other household activities. They're in high demand these days due to the explosion of COVID cases at congregate living settings, the aging population, and the general unmet need for home-based care that predated the pandemic.[15]

Care work is done predominantly by women and people of color for poverty wages. Ady's campaign to attach organizing rights to such funding increases would not merely improve the lives of caregivers or perhaps the quality of the care received. It would also overturn a discriminatory policy that has plagued even progressive reformers for almost a century.

A Green New Deal for Labor

The New Deal was a real attempt to reconcile the carnage of the Great Depression with the long-term promise of shared prosperity. It became an obvious historical flashpoint during the pandemic, provoking comparisons between Biden and Roosevelt. Both inherited a crisis, both showed surprisingly liberal policy stances early in their tenure, and both spoke up on behalf of workers. The similarities stop there unless—and I couldn't be happier for history to prove me wrong here—Biden can convince even his own party to make lasting changes that will benefit workers.

The New Deal, once the vital center of American liberalism, offered working people guarantees of a minimum wage, unemployment compensation, and Social Security, as well as the right to organize unions and bargain collectively. A lesser-known fact is that domestic and agricultural workers, who were predominantly Black and female, were excluded from New Deal protections. The 1938 Fair Labor Standards Act (FLSA), which set the first maximum-hour limits and established the minimum wage, and the 1935 National Labor Relations Act (a.k.a. the Wagner Act), which guaranteed collective bargaining rights, did not extend to most low-wage care workers.

Home-based caregivers' exclusion from the National Labor Relations Act meant they were not allowed the collective bargaining rights that would confer the power to fight for better conditions. A few decades later, the passage of the 1964 Civil Rights Act had little relevance for most domestic workers because its antidiscrimination and anti–sexual harassment clauses didn't apply to workplaces that employed fewer than fifteen people.[16] The 1970 Occupational Health and Safety Act was similarly irrelevant since it didn't apply to homeowners who employ workers for "domestic household tasks" in their homes. And when the FLSA was revised in the 1970s, the Department of Labor continued to exclude home-based caregivers from basic labor rights. It was only when the FLSA was revised a second time, in 2015, that home care aides were finally included. But in the twenty states where the minimum wage doesn't exceed the federal minimum, those workers are only guaranteed a poverty wage of $7.25 an hour.

This legacy of legal exclusion has had dramatic consequences. The industry's median hourly wage is just over $12 an hour, or $16,200 per year.[17] Domestic workers are three times as likely as other workers to live in poverty, and almost none of them have paid sick leave or belong to a union.[18] The historical bellwether of progressive ideals actually reinforced the racialized and gendered hierarchy of the labor market.

The Green New Deal (GND)—the Left's most ambitious answer to our dire social crisis—would rectify this historic injustice. By bringing all workers, regardless of race, gender, occupation, or citizenship status, into the fold of social protections, it would guarantee that those working on the foundation of our economy have the protections they need to support the rest of us.

The GND is a congressional resolution that describes a wide-ranging framework for addressing climate change and other social ills. In many ways, it is mainly a jobs program. *Scientific American* estimates that a carbon tax would create as many as two million jobs across the country by 2030, and over four million by 2050.[19] These projected jobs, modest in comparison to figures put forth by the program's political backers, will be focused in labor-intensive industries like construction, heating, ventilation, air-conditioning, and refrigeration.

Discussions of the GND have too often focused on training coal miners to install solar panels. But green jobs are crucial to combatting the effects of climate change, which have already begun to manifest across many different kinds of workplaces. In recent years, record-breaking heat waves have threatened workers in sweltering construction sites, wildfire smoke has filled agricultural fields, and workers have become sick in overheated packing warehouses.[20] Teachers and fast-food workers in cities across the country quit, walked out, or struck over furnace-like conditions in the summer of 2021.

The pandemic, however, reminded us that we need to consider growing another kind of green job—care work.[21] Care work is perennially underdiscussed in this light. It is not only inherently low-carbon, but socially necessary. The pandemic clearly demonstrated that the country's crisis of care is a preexisting condition of sorts, one that makes society all the more susceptible to collapse when acute crises hit, pandemics or otherwise.

The increasing population of people who need care combined with the increasing frequency of climatic disasters demands a strengthening of the country's crumbling care infrastructure. As sea levels rise, hurricanes strengthen, heat waves worsen, and wildfires spread, care workers will be on the front lines of the crisis, making sure that the most vulnerable among us survive these unnatural disasters. In fact, they are already performing this work. Home healthcare aides in Paradise, California, for instance, served as first responders when the historic Camp Fire hit, wheeling their patients' beds away from the encroaching flames.[22] During Hurricane Harvey, nursing home workers in Texas sent out a call for help and rescued their elderly clients from historic levels of flooding.[23] As the so-called invisible hand of the market attempts to push us off an ecological cliff, it's the invisible hands of the behind-the-scenes care workers that are propping up our care infrastructure.

Unions and labor rights organizations like the National Domestic Workers Alliance, Caring Across Generations, and the SEIU have been advocating for the rights of home care workers for years.[24] Creating better jobs in this sector would benefit the elderly and disabled too because it would allow them to age and recover in their own homes. Deinstitutionalizing the elderly and disabled has long been a demand of the disability rights movement, and the growing demand for home care workers reflects the need for people to age with dignity.

A Green New Deal for labor should put Medicare for All at the center of building our care infrastructure. It should remedy care workers' historic exclusion from the benefits of social citizenship, ensuring the right to paid overtime, workplace safety, meal and rest breaks, fair scheduling, freedom from discrimination and sexual harassment, and immediate citizenship status for undocumented domestic workers. Further, care workers must have the legal right to collectively bargain so that they have the confidence to speak up or even strike when they're neglected. These would be game changers for Tyler, who takes care of Keith, and Edith, who works twenty-four-hour shifts, all of whom we met in Chapter 7. The GND might also afford them greater control of that most precious commodity, so elusive during the heart of the pandemic: time.

Time for What We Will

The labor movement of the nineteenth century was committed to fighting for their rightful share of free time. Eight hours for work, eight hours for rest, eight hours for what we will: the rallying cry of the movement for shorter hours that eventually won the eight-hour day and the weekend. Dignity, they argued, meant free time to explore the world and enjoy the people in it. The pandemic in many ways gave second life to this old slogan.

Most people I interviewed said they felt a distinct change in their time-spending priorities during the pandemic. Even those who needed the work hours the most for economic reasons resented their workplace for taking them away from their families and friends. Likewise, opinion polls reflected a general soul-searching about life's purpose in 2020. They showed a shift away from career-oriented goals to more time-rich experiences with plentiful leisure. Though we were assaulted with articles urging us to use the pandemic productively, as if COVID-19 was a sabbatical, there seemed to be a greater recognition that the amount of time people spend at dead-end jobs simply isn't worth it.

Even in good times we need a robust antiwork policy framework. Social reproduction can't happen if we're all in full-time jobs. The nine-to-five grind is simply incompatible with a future that makes life worth living—and with getting all the dishes done. We must first separate healthcare from work, and then we must reduce work time to a minimum.

During the pandemic I published a book arguing for a return to a movement for shorter hours, what I called "labor's forgotten fight." For over a century, the average hours of labor steadily declined. Then in the 1970s, we reversed course. I found that the average American now works about five more weeks per year than in 1975. During that same time period, wages have all but stagnated for the vast majority of us, while income and wealth inequality have soared.[25]

But those statistics hide a more important story. Though high-earning men tend to work the longest, the hours of low-income workers have increased the most. This latter category, composed disproportionately of women and people of color, also has the most volatile and unpredictable schedules. Week to week, even day to day, these workers' hours fluctuate at the whim of employers, making it impossible for them to plan their days or earn dependable income. Moreover, low wages mean that even as their hours have jumped ahead, this group has fallen behind financially. Consequently, they're the most likely to struggle for more hours, access to second or third jobs, and anything else that can gain them greater control over their working lives.[26]

My research for that book had started years earlier, and I was worried that releasing the book in the midst of a historic slump in employment would make demanding we all work less appear silly or, worse, insulting. As it turns out, the pandemic only magnified trends I had analyzed.

According to the Bureau of Labor Statistics American Time Use Survey, the most significant temporal shift during the pandemic was a decline in the time we spent commuting to work.[27] What did we do with that additional free time? Data shows we worked. Our primary job soaked up about 35 percent of our extra hours.[28] Early in the pandemic, home-working employees added two and a half hours to their workday, according to NordVPN Teams, which tracks virtual private network (VPN) usage at more than ten thousand companies across the world. Some countries, such as Denmark, Spain, and Belgium, saw an initial spike, then a return to pre-pandemic hours. Americans registered a three-hour spike and then a plateau, signaling perhaps a new normal. VPN usage not only recorded longer days but more erratic schedules, weekend and holiday work, and a surprising number of hours logged after midnight.[29] The shift to remote work further disrupted the already elusive nine-to-five job, replacing it with an asynchronous work-life imbalance.

As if simply missing out on life weren't enough, long hours (more than fifty-five per week) are the single greatest cause of occupational disease across the world, according to a study conducted by the World Health Organization and the International Labour Organization, released in 2021.[30] Their shocking study, the latest research on the topic, shows that three-quarters of a million people died from ischemic heart disease and stroke due to excessive working hours in 2016. Ischemic heart disease involves narrowed arteries from chronic stress, lack of rest, and lack of exercise. That means that across the world, more people are dying from overwork than from malaria.[31]

It wasn't just white-collar workers who were overworked during the pandemic. Thousands of essential workers were pushed to strike against mandatory overtime. In the fall of 2021, Kellogg's workers in Omaha walked picket lines against forced overtime and low pay. In Topeka, Frito-Lay workers struck against eighty-hour weeks and back-to-back twelve-hour schedules they dubbed "suicide shifts." Meanwhile, low-income workers, who are disproportionately represented among the essential labor force, often struggled to get *enough* hours. As businesses fought to remain consistently open, many workers fell further into debt, working inconsistent, lower-paying shifts through those dangerous days. The pandemic deepened the crisis of time among both the overworked and the underemployed, while widening the gap between them.

We should pursue policies that bring our time economy in line with our international peers by instituting generous time-off policies. Before the pandemic, we worked about six hours per week more than the French and eight hours per week more than the Germans. We even logged more work time than the perceived workaholics in Japan, who even have a word, *karoshi*, that means "death by overwork." The

United States has fewer paid holidays than our peers have and is the only wealthy nation without a legal right to paid sick leave, vacation time, or maternity leave.

Partly for these reasons, the popularity of a four-day workweek, without a corresponding reduction in pay, gained momentum in the US and around the world during the pandemic. In May 2020, New Zealand prime minister Jacinda Ardern promoted the idea that a pandemic recovery would mean a shorter workweek. In June 2021, the Japanese government recommended experimenting with it to help meet its economic priorities.[32] At the same time, Iceland had a successful trial program and Spain began working on a plan of its own.[33] A handful of tech companies, start-ups, and other web-based employers in the US gave it a whirl too. Thirty companies in the United Kingdom started a six-month trial program in January 2020. Typically, these experiments, which were going on long before the pandemic, end positively, showing that workers can produce virtually the same amount of work in less time.

As compelling as that simple formula is, looking for ways to be more productive is the wrong rationale for shorter hours. Why, we should be asking, are we doing any nonessential work at all?

The industries and job classifications deemed essential during the pandemic were ostensibly designed to ensure our physical safety, health, and economic stability. Clearly, we can't survive without workers to secure our health, supply food, deliver essential goods, or provide the smooth delivery of energy, fuels, and computing power. Yet, as described in Chapter 2, many employers exploited the essential designations and stayed open when they should have shut down. This controversy highlights abusive employers but also raises the question: What actually is essential work?

Does art count? The New Dealers thought artistic expression was essential for American culture to thrive. Therefore, they funded the arts through a public works program. Without that program, we'd have no documentary history left by photographers Dorothea Lange and Walker Evans. We'd be without the murals of Diego Rivera, whose mural assistant, Louise Nevelson, worked through the Works Progress Administration. There'd be fewer abstract expressionists like Jackson Pollock, Willem de Kooning, and Mark Rothko, who all painted with funding from the Treasury Relief Art Project, even though the latter two weren't American citizens. What would the Harlem Renaissance have been without Aaron Douglas, just one of the thousands of African American artists funded through the Federal Art Project?[34]

Where's the Pandemic Sculpture Park Foundation Grant? Even if we did have one, who has time to enjoy viewing art when they're working fifty- or sixty-hour weeks or juggling childcare with two precarious jobs? An outcome of the pandemic should be a national reckoning with excessive work, with the explicit intention of shortening the workday, workweek, and work year. To the greatest extent possible, let's stop doing nonessential work.

Time deficits are not just anti-leisure; they're a barrier to social change. "You can't just give these big ideas and not give people the road map to get there," said Sara Nelson, the flight attendants' union president we met in Chapter 3. "Part of giving people the road map to get there is giving them wins, and then putting money in their pockets, and giving them time off so they can actually be activists," she said. Excessive work hours that sap the energy and hope necessary to fight a boss or a work rule are a major impediment to workplace organizing. The ability to work less will increase the time available to fight for deeper social change.

Unions were once the main force fighting for shorter hours. As their power has eroded, the shorter hours movement has ground to a halt. To reinvigorate it at all will require unions to stage a comeback. Throughout this book, I have shown that when essential workers are unionized, they make significant differences that save lives. "In the psyche of the American labor movement, we've been taught to believe that we're the sideshow," said Nelson, noting that in trade agreements, bankruptcy laws, workplace safety, and healthcare proposals, accommodating provisions for workers are always an afterthought. "We're not the sideshow, we're the main event. We're the economy. We gotta start acting like it."

The Importance of Being Unruly

As usual, Nelson is correct. During the pandemic, workers were indeed at the center of the national debate over how to contain the virus and what a capitalist economy owes its laborers. In 2020, union activity seemed to bubble up here and there, but there was no national strategy to take advantage of the crisis. In 2021, there was an uptick in strikes and organizing. Yet major union leaders by and large seemed to be waiting on Biden to produce pro-labor conditions. Biden, in the meantime, seemed to walk away from his professed pro-labor stance, turning his back on striking workers even as they asked for his support. He may well be the most pro-union president in recent history, but that's a low bar.

Still, as I write in early 2022, the bargaining power of workers is higher than it has been in decades. Some basic ideas on the Left seem widely sensible, and Democrats control the House and Senate, at least until the midterms in November 2022. Action by and for workers is the only hope for Democrats to retain any of their current political position. Will unions capitalize on that opportunity in the near future?

If a Green New Deal is a goal for workers, it's worth remembering how labor helped win proworker legislation during the New Deal in the first place. Roosevelt had been in office about the same amount of time as Biden has when workers launched a surge of militant strikes. The country faced a barrage of interwoven crises: mass unemployment, homelessness, extraordinary poverty, and widespread public lynchings by racist mobs. Police and private guards were routinely called to attack peaceful demonstrators, and many workers still lacked the legal right to collectively bargain with their employer. In other words, workers had it pretty bad back then too. And still they managed to fight hard and win big.

As employment picked up after the doldrums of the Great Depression, workers went on the offensive. They struck across the Upper Midwest, in actions led by Communist Party members. These smaller strikes laid the foundation for the 1936–1937 militant sit-down strikes in Flint, Michigan, where workers occupied their factories for over forty days, making it impossible to hire replacement workers. Their struggles inspired similar actions in plants across the Midwest for the rest of the decade. The strikers' wives formed flying squads that acted as human shields to defend the plants from police. Eventually Roosevelt and the National Guard intervened, and the workers' settlement laid the foundation for the power of the autoworkers' union.

Action also leaped to the West Coast, where longshoremen, meatpacking workers, and truck drivers struck in the midthirties. In 1933, Alabama coal miners led successful union organizing drives at their own jobsites and then proceeded to organize entire towns.

Labor insurgency led to proworker legislation like the National Industrial Recovery Act of 1933, which regulated wages and granted collective bargaining rights. Two years later, the Wagner Act extended collective bargaining rights and eliminated company-sponsored unions. Initially challenged as unconstitutional, the Wagner Act's full legal force didn't take effect until it was upheld by the Supreme Court in 1937, again following a wave of strikes and disruptive protests.[35]

Lessons for today could not be clearer: labor law reform won't facilitate mass organizing; it will result from it. It is currently impossible— and effectively illegal—for significant union growth to occur through the antiquated process administered by the National Labor Relations Board. Current board rules allow employers to curtail the rights of workers to organize and vote for a union, an undemocratic anachronism that needs to change.

Still, in 2022, the Amazon Labor Union victory demonstrated that, even under poor legal conditions, workers can win big. In Chapter 3, we met Chris Smalls, who had stationed himself outside Jeff Bezos's mansion with a personalized guillotine after being fired by Amazon for organizing a protest over COVID safety concerns. Though no longer an employee, he vowed to get unions at the company and give Bezos the ultimate comeuppance. Two years later, Smalls helped lead workers at his former Staten Island facility to a historic—almost unprecedented—victory, and became president of the fiercely independent Amazon Labor Union. The union's grassroots multiracial movement, relying solely on organic experts inside the warehouse, contrasted sharply with the previous union attempt at an Amazon warehouse in Alabama, which had been led by established professionals at the country's main retail workers' union.

As I write this in the immediate wake of ALU's March 2022 vote, most of the lessons have yet to be unlocked, the manifestations of such a shocking win yet to reveal themselves. But this they showed us: there's no trick to forming strong unions. Warehouse workers there pored over the classic texts from communist labor leaders that are usually reserved for academic syllabi. Drawing lessons from labor history, they followed the classic playbook—build a movement and fight like hell. And perhaps, also, pack a sense of humor. "We want to thank Jeff Bezos for going to space," said Chris, popping a bottle of champagne and savoring a celebratory gulp at the union's victory press conference, "because while he was up there, we was signing people up."

Still, a real reversal of the half-century decline in union density will likely only happen through large strikes for union recognition, beyond the legal channels designed to depoliticize workers' demands and delay their right to a free and fair election. In other words, militant worker-led movements are simply the most pragmatic approach to mass union organizing.

The labor organizer and writer Jane McAlevey has noted the thousands of union contracts that will expire in 2022, granting a strategic window for workers to coordinate strike activity. "If more than 1 million US workers—or even fewer in key labor markets—take collective action toward common demands to radically improve their quality of life on and off the job…the working class could radically lift the floor on what is considered acceptable corporate and shareholder behavior," she wrote.[36]

Labor's strategy must prioritize expanding the kinds of militant workplace activism that have galvanized small groups of workers across the pandemic. "They didn't listen to us when we asked nicely," said Marlena Pellegrino, whom we met in Chapter 3 on the nurses' picket line in Worcester, the pandemic era's longest strike. "They only listened to us 'cause we forced them to listen. It's the same with the president, you know," she told me.

Hope in Dark Times

The prospects for a move in a socialist direction are indeed dim when the American Right holds so much sway. The monstrous forces of radical conservatism suffered a blow toward the end of 2020, but the wound wasn't fatal. What came to be called the "politics of resentment" in the post-Obama years is really a "politics of retrenchment." It is dedicated to turning back the clock on social progress while pursuing a future of austerity and material deprivation. Should progressives fail to build a viable alternative to business as usual, a regrouped right wing could easily fill that void. This threat, always lurking, imperils us all.

Trump's administration and capitalist society left us unnecessarily vulnerable to the pandemic. Interstate bidding wars for ventilators and PPE, understaffed hospitals, and the staggeringly unequal impact of the virus in rich and poor neighborhoods showcased that the free market's fundamental design produces widespread inequality. The effect was disastrous, leading many to decry that we must make a choice between prioritizing public health and the economy, between our lives and our livelihoods. It's worth considering alternatives to this barbarism.

The increased government spending during the pandemic led some pundits to declare that during a crisis, everyone's a socialist. If only!

As the private sector hemorrhaged, the Fed flexed its magical money machine and the national budget seemed bottomless. If we could, after all, erase significant poverty with the stroke of a pen in the CARES Act, what else could we do? We could fund a Green New Deal, erase more poverty, delete debt, and cancel college tuition. That we didn't do that, and instead spoon-fed money to billionaires, says more about our system's priorities than its possibilities. The simple secret about wealth in capitalist societies—it is shared only among those who control it—got leaked in 2020. Spread the word, dear readers: capitalism constrains economic freedom.

We should see this moment as a failure of capitalism to provide equitable access to its riches, a perfect portrait of its outdated and irrational nature. That realization, I hope, is a harbinger of life beyond capitalism. What we need instead is a democratically planned economy that provides material comfort for everyone at the same time it protects our collective public health.

A society where we collectively decide how to produce and distribute goods and services will not spring up overnight. There are nonetheless encouraging signs of incremental change. Members of both major political parties favor expanding coverage of, or completely covering, the healthcare needs of the American people, regardless of their ability to pay. In the 2020 elections, Jamaal Bowman and Cori Bush, members of the Democratic Socialists of America, were elected to the House. They joined Bernie Sanders, Squad members Alexandria Ocasio-Cortez, Ilhan Omar, Ayanna Pressley, Rashida Tlaib, and more than sixty other DSA members who have won office since 2016, garnering millions of votes and pushing the Democratic Party further left than it has been in decades.

The Left's guiding maxim—that an injury to one is an injury to all—has never been more obvious. If those around you are sick, your health is endangered. If they're healthier, you enjoy more freedoms. This simple formula has radical implications. Lawmakers and employers should be subject to the decisions they make for others. Want the federal minimum wage kept at $7.25 for over a decade? Then you should have to live on it yourself. Want your families to receive the best possible care? Then make sure all caregivers receive the same. By tying our fates together, we ensure that we act in the collective interest as often as possible. There's a truly pragmatic argument for universal access to basic rights like healthcare, housing, and good jobs.

Such a system would have handled the pandemic better. A nationalized healthcare industry, freed from the vexing inequities of free market fundamentalism, would be less likely to create the shortages that just-in-time production forced on us. Worker-owned restaurants and bars would be more likely to institute better safety measures for their worker-owners and, by extension, for their customers. We should heed the advice of New York assemblyman Ron Kim, one of the bigger thorns in Cuomo's side after it was discovered he'd hidden nursing home deaths in his state. Nursing home chains are run by a cabal of healthcare moguls who prey on families with no alternative but to institutionalize their elderly members. Kim argues for a worker-led cooperative structure for nursing homes to decrease corruption and improve safety and quality of care. "We should take them over, make them public," he told me. "We need to empower workers there so all the money doesn't end up with profiteers."

This vision isn't all that far-fetched—nationalized healthcare exists in the UK in the form of the National Health Service, state-owned banks exist in various countries throughout the world, and hundreds of worker-cooperatives already operate here in the United States, including extremely popular nationalized energy companies. Achieving these attainable reforms in the medium term would help build support for a transition to a more equitable, just, and safe society in the long term.[37]

An April 2021 report from the Pew Research Center unearthed a general appetite for political and economic change in many large capitalist countries. The study, which polled thousands of adults across Germany, France, the UK, and the US in late 2020, found that a majority of French respondents and approximately half of respondents in the other three countries were in favor of major changes to or a complete overhaul of the economic system.[38] In all the countries polled, a majority of respondents supported left-leaning, redistributive government policies like job training programs, public housing, higher taxes on the wealthy, and increased government benefits for the poor.

Ady Barkan, whom we met earlier in this chapter, would certainly benefit from these kinds of wholesale changes. As a socialist organizer, he understands that "only a truly ambitious, radical departure from the status quo that replaces the exploitative for-profit model with one that guarantees healthcare as a right for all" will be enough.[39]

But appetites for political change may not always lean left. Neoliberal pundits and politicians have already returned to their run-of-the-mill austerity talking points: national debt hysteria, fear of higher interest rates, inflation paranoia. Under immense pressure from the financial sector, Democratic politicians may repeat the same mistake they made after the 2008 crisis, when they bailed out Wall Street and offered working people nothing but the leftovers.

Early in the pandemic, the Left mistakenly assumed that the crisis laid bare capitalism's systemic weaknesses in ways that were widely visible. With unjustified conviction, we presumed the problems of the pandemic would be attributed to systemic causes and would make people more receptive to systemic alternatives. In a sense, we overestimated the pandemic's political gravity and underestimated the resilience of capitalist society to swallow up any alternatives.

Why should we believe that we will learn from this crisis when we haven't from others? After all, we've virtually normalized mass deaths from gun violence, police shootings, poverty, and lack of medical insurance. It's quite possible that the hit the economy took from COVID-19 will undermine labor's power and steal its confidence for action. It may diminish our aspirations and squash our hopes for a better world. Indeed, rather than experiment with an uncertain future, many people will go groveling back to some semblance of normal, looking for stability that, in comparison, is undesirable but acceptable.

The pandemic built up pressure for political change. But Biden's administration proved incapable of moving past the obstructionists in its own party and unwilling to take executive action before the midterms. While there was still a sizable aid package on the table, its greatly diminished scope seemed to reflect the twilight of his optimistic campaign promises. His polling numbers did a nose-dive. The energy from #Striketober fizzled out, and the rising wages spurred on by the labor shortage were wiped out by inflation.

But then, suddenly, there came the seismic union victory at Amazon and the almost daily roll call of new unions at Starbucks, hopeful signs that seemingly reenergized labor's left flank. Could it be? Was labor outrunning its recent past by reinventing its most tried-and-true strategies of worker-led organizing? Or was this reckoning with labor's too-big-to-fall institutions just another reminder of how far workers' fortunes had actually fallen? After all, to reverse decades of union decline, it would take unprecedented thousands of successful organizing drives. Moreover, the Left's inability to overcome the malignant forces inside the Democratic Party meant that the political winds only blew us closer and closer to the ultimate dead end: the return to normal.

"We can't go back there," Melanie said. "'Normal' is what brought us here in the first place."

In Chapter 2, we met Melanie Brown, the salmon fisherwoman who refused to fish in 2020, one of many locals who deferred to local health concerns about another wave of disease coming from the outside to Bristol Bay, Alaska. Melanie's great-grandparents, also salmon fishers, were killed by the Spanish flu, carried by fishermen from the Lower 48. She sacrificed her livelihood that year for what she thought was the greater good.

In 2021, Melanie, freshly vaccinated, and more confident about the industry, was back on the water.

"How does it feel to get the chance to fish again?" I asked her over the phone in late spring. She took a deep breath and a long pause.

"I don't think I'll know until I'm out on the water. I have to be there to know," she told me.

I decided that if I really cared about the answer to that question, I would have to be there to know as well. Which is how I ended up waist-deep in the brackish waters of the Naknek River, at the mouth of Bristol Bay, in the summer of 2021, attending to a twisted gill net. I went to meet Melanie and her fishing family in person and to get a sense of what it was like for them to be back at work.

On the Fourth of July, we took toward the ocean in her twenty-five-foot skiff, to the same spot on the Naknek that her great-grandfather had purchased generations ago. We pulled the nets in and let them back out over a few hours. It was rainy and cold, and the soggy tundra surrounding the inlet attracted flocks of migratory birds. During lulls in the action, we rocked on the undulating tides and talked about the fishing industry. The unions had been busted decades ago. The processors on the "slop line," who are mainly migrant workers, were housed in work camps surrounded by barbed wire. Fisherfolk aren't paid until the end of the six-week season, at which point they find out the price per pound that the major fisheries are willing to pay. It's a rigged system, planned to offer the least amount of transparency and democracy, and produced a good deal of confusion and shoulder shrugging when I asked about it. It was so simple, it defied explanation. The process was opaque because one group had more power than the other. After a year of disruption, everything, in other words, was pretty much back to normal.

For all the tumult of 2020, the interlocking crises of the pandemic, labor, racism, climate change, and challenged election results, perhaps what's most shocking of all is how little the pandemic fundamentally changed the way we live and work. I began thinking about this book under lockdown. By the time I finished writing it, the idea of flattening the curve, a collective action for the common good, seemed like a quaint memory. The economy had rebounded, our social lives had slowly drifted back to normal. At the peak of the Omicron variant wave, even Dr. Fauci was emphasizing the singular importance of getting as many people back to work as possible.

Yet there was no great optimism about our health or wealth like the national ebullience that came in the wake of the 1918 flu pandemic. Indeed, if anything, there was a palpable dread that this was only the beginning. This is because we have failed to change our society's underlying structure in a way that would prevent a similar catastrophe when the next pandemic comes. In fact, we have failed to make even minor adjustments to basic social programs that would allow workers to fare better through the next crisis, or to pass labor law reforms that make it easier for workers to form unions. As the pandemic waned, a staggering 77 percent of private sector workers had no access to paid parental leave and 24 percent had no paid sick leave.[40] It's not that we forgot these programs saved lives during the pandemic, it's that we didn't care. It is the capitalist system's deep resistance to change—not its dynamism—that makes it so critical that we replace it. Our lives depend on it.

"I think that if we prove that people power can overcome entrenched corporate healthcare interests," Ady told me, "it will inspire people to know that we can also defeat the fossil fuel industry and Wall Street too." Ady can find optimism in this mess not because he's happy-go-lucky but because he knows how to fight. A real recovery from the pandemic will mean large-scale social transformation, which will only happen through a fight.

As I've shown in this book, poor conditions for essential workers imperil us all. They increase our exposure to risk and decrease our capacity for social reproduction. These conditions are only ameliorated and mitigated through labor movement battles. Situating these movements in the long struggle for worker justice, it becomes clear that we're at a historic inflection point. The pandemic exposed the morbid symptoms of capitalism under extreme stress. It also illuminated the power of workers to defend the common good. Will we learn the right lessons from these dark days? Can labor take advantage of the current crisis and generate a parallel one for capital? The story of the pandemic is incomplete without centering the actual engine of history—class struggle. So is the future.

CONCLUSION

MORBID SYMPTOMS

SOMETHING IS PROFOUNDLY WRONG WITH THE WAY WE WORK today. The employment bargain that once underwrote shared prosperity is in tatters. For half a century, we've made a virtue out of a system that gives us longer hours and lower wages. We've learned to focus on what workers cost, not what they're worth. We've run roughshod over unions and continually passed "labor laws" that limit workers' power and freedom. Our electoral system all but eliminates the possibility of a labor party, whether one by that name or not, and workers have continually been left to choose between candidates who endorse different levels of exploitation.[1]

The "labor question"—how should we, as a society, treat ordinary workers?—was once at the heart of the American experiment. Along with free elections, it formed a core concern in a fledgling democracy. Though it is far from answered, today the question is rarely posed. In fact, as jobs have gotten worse, there's been a corresponding rise in the cultural expectation to love those jobs unconditionally.

The pandemic provided a moment of reckoning, a chance to grapple with a reality we've refused to face with sober senses. This book evolved from that moment, to interject an analysis of the current crisis and offer a few ways forward that might lead to deeper understanding and social transformation.

The pandemic illuminated a world where our collective well-being is tied to the well-being of essential workers. Their working conditions are our living conditions. This will be true long after the pandemic recedes, and when the next one arrives. With that in mind, we all have a stake in improving the lives of those who took care of us during our darkest days.

In the opening chapter, Kenia Madrigal, the mother who moved her four children into her SUV after losing her job and being evicted during the pandemic, introduced us to some of the effects of the unemployment crash. I examined ways that the recession, the most unequal economic crisis in American history, was experienced along race, gender, and age lines. And in the wake of that came a stunning and unprecedented government response. Unemployment insurance is broken, but from Trump's CARES Act to Biden's American Rescue Plan, the state provided a historic influx of cash that staved off broad social collapse. Of course, it happened in the most American way possible, without any lasting structural changes to our welfare state. The policy experiments we tested in 2020—expanded unemployment insurance, a child tax credit, increased paid sick leave—should become permanent features of our economy. They functioned better than the ones we have now, and they decreased poverty. Plus, the increasing likelihood of future pandemics demands that we be more prepared now than we were in 2019.

Chapter 2 moved on to an analysis of "the lucky ones," who kept their paychecks but were forced to endure dangerous jobs during the chaos of the pandemic. The hardships and struggles of essential workers, and mostly their disproportionate exposure to risk, helped them form a kind of essential worker class, or "imagined community." Essential workers in certain places and moments pursued such a communal identity. Though it was imperfect and incomplete, an essential worker class consciousness at times seemed poised to overcome the status, racial, and occupational hierarchies that so often impede working-class power. Alas, that power proved not to be durable. It was undercut by conflicts with the unemployed and by political schisms within the working class.

Strikes, walkouts, acts of solidarity, and other labor protests sprung up sporadically early in the pandemic. Through these different forms of protests, essential workers demanded better pay and better safety gear, and their fights occasionally led to important short-term victories.

Worker safety became a central concern throughout the American economy as the pandemic progressed. With the backing of unions, workers often won lifesaving concessions from management, including greater amounts of PPE and safety protections on the job. These victories improved workers' welfare and had a ripple effect through communities, ultimately making everyone safer.

Unions saved lives during the pandemic. The cases of nursing home workers in Chapter 4 showed that unions decreased mortality and infection rates not only among elderly residents but among their own ranks as well. Nursing home workers are a largely Black, female workforce whose jobs are consistently derided as low-skilled labor. I don't know what it took to keep a high-risk person alive during the pandemic, especially when they were essentially living in a COVID-19 petri dish, but it sure as hell involved skill. In some cases, it also involved fighting back, as workplace disruptions were one way nurses and aides pressed management for more PPE and other safety protections.

Strangely, just as essential worker class consciousness waned, worker militancy seemed to gain momentum. In the late fall of 2021, workers threw picket lines up across the country in a wave of shutdowns that journalists dubbed #Striketober. This activity exploded alongside a persistent labor shortage that affected many essential industries.

The labor shortage continued beyond the end of the economic cushion workers had amassed from COVID supports, invalidating the prevailing logic that a return to austerity would herald a return of a low-wage labor force. It didn't. As Chapter 5 argues, we should see the labor shortage as a crisis of capitalism's ability to provide high enough wages or good enough jobs to staff the actual number of essential workers we need to thrive.

In Chapters 6 and 7, the book took a step back to reconceptualize the pandemic first as a "hazard society" and then as a "crisis of social reproduction." Drawing on social and political theory, I pivoted from an analysis of why the pandemic transformed work and workers to how we can think about those changes more broadly. The pandemic exacerbated a decades-long risk shift by employers and government, who through policy and program changes incrementally dumped their healthcare and other obligations onto the backs of American workers and their families. This ever more hazardous environment also contributed to an ongoing care crisis in the home and increased our reliance on paid essential workers for our basic care and necessities. By recasting these ideas as especially relevant to the COVID crisis, I hope I have generated a fuller understanding of what the pandemic workplace means for all of us in the long run.

Chapter 8 examined what I believe are important political aspirations for labor—universal healthcare, reduced dependence on paid work, and political transformation that allows workers more control over our failing democracy. But labor can't wait. History shows that only by creating a crisis for employers and the state can labor win the kinds of policy reforms we all need. Biden and Harris took over in 2021 with a degree of fanfare and hope, bringing with them a platform that seemed designed to actually change things. Then in short order, paid family leave, expanded access to Medicare that would include dental and vision, limits on prescription drug prices, taxes on billionaires, virtually any climate action, and labor law reforms fell like dominoes. Biden managed to disappoint by perfectly embodying his only selling point from the beginning—that he wasn't Trump—and by keeping his most ardent promise, that he wasn't Bernie Sanders either. As much as we desperately need large-scale political reforms from above, it seems likely they will only come from below in the immediate future. For that we will need a rejuvenated labor movement.

The weakness of organized labor forestalled the possibility of significant labor reforms during the pandemic. There should have been, and still can be, a national mobilization for better working conditions—a March on Washington by and for the frontline class. That such a march or protest was never close to materializing does indicate a lack of enthusiasm or creativity on the part of large unions, which certainly have the resources to make it happen. Many low-wage workers in essential industries are clearly eager to protest. In massive waves, they joined the Black Lives Matter protests in the summer of 2020, during which, I can't help but mention, the AFL-CIO building was literally burned and trashed. The building was probably not purposefully targeted, but seeing its entranceway charred was a reminder that the federation had not acted decisively to drive explicitly racist police unions from its ranks.

Today only 6 percent of the private sector is unionized, and workers outside of education and some other public services were starkly disadvantaged during the pandemic by the fact that their unions were simply too impotent to pose a credible threat to management's dictates. In some industries, low union density also meant labor leaders didn't even try. They received word of poor working conditions as if it were a fait accompli and took no action. This weakness isn't endemic to unions themselves but rather the product of a long attack on their freedoms and powers. Rebuilding labor's strength is absolutely a necessary precondition for a healthier and safer society.

Capitalism can't be reformed in ways that provide the level of economic stability and quality of jobs that Americans require to live a dignified life. The kinds of social democratic reforms I explored in Chapter 8 are good starting points. However, we ultimately can't settle for tweaks to our current system. In the long run, which, given the urgency of climate change, has to happen in the short run, we will be far better prepared for the next pandemic if we reorganize our society to give average workers the political, economic, and cultural power to make decisions that benefit all of us.

Forming a union should be easy, devoid of management interference. All private businesses should be worker-owned cooperatives. We should use our great wealth to reduce the amount of time we each need to work to generate a livable income. Healthcare and other industries that are vital to our physical and mental well-being should be free and universally accessible. Other related policies can address the racial and gender wage and wealth gaps. As the pandemic's persistent labor shortage showed, capitalist society isn't competent enough to provide the wages necessary to generate and support employment in life-sustaining healthcare, childcare, eldercare, education, and food distribution jobs. We saw what happens when private businesses make public health rules. It's time to consider real alternatives to capitalism.

The combined value of all the various COVID relief packages exceeded $5 trillion. Over the end of one presidency and the beginning of another, the federal government paid for eviction moratoriums, mortgage and student debt relief, and forgivable loans to small businesses, and vastly expanded its coverage for emergency relief services. As economist Ben Casselman noted in the *New York Times*, a middle-class family of four received over $11,000 of COVID aid, not counting the expanded child tax credit, valued at about $3,600.[2]

All of this injected cash did more than lift millions out of poverty. Hiring grew each month after April 2020, especially for low-income workers, who also saw their wages rise. But these recent trends don't make up for decades of wage stagnation and job degradation. Instead, we should see the extraordinary largesse of the pandemic welfare state as compelling evidence that there is money for the kinds of supports workers need, like Medicare for All, free higher education, a debt jubilee, and a Green New Deal. The difference between what the pandemic relief packages funded and these more ambitious programs is that the former require no structural transformation of American capitalism, while the latter challenge its fundamental basis. Nonetheless, knowing that the state can pony up in a crisis is useful.

◆

I'M WRITING IN the early days of 2022, with the future quite uncertain. The Omicron variant recently swept across the world in yet another pandemic wave, forcing widespread shutdowns of schools, day care centers, childcare programs, and some other workplaces.[3] As it receded, and we scrapped masks in public schools, the hybrid Delta-cron variant emerged in Europe. Yet, by and large, there was almost no discussion about shutting nonessential industries, no pleading demands to flatten the curve, and no pots-and-pans orchestra cheering on our essential heroes.

The polish on the value of essential workers has lost its sheen. Though they once possessed the talismanic quality of our caretakers, the handmaidens of a safer public sphere, it has begun to seem the general public has no use for them anymore. Workers' pandemic savings were depleted, and they were forced back to work in the midst of record COVID caseloads. In interviews I conducted during the fall of 2021, some of which were follow-ups with people I'd spoken to earlier, service workers routinely lamented their fall from high social status during the pandemic, "when people actually gave a shit about us," as Kim, the traveling nurse we met in the Introduction, put it. "Patients come in now and all they wanna know is why there's not more staff to wait on them hand and foot," she said. "It's like everyone forgot there was a pandemic." When the Michigan Nurses Association picketed Sparrow Hospital in late 2021, demanding safer staffing levels, one nurse carried a sign that said, "Last year's heroes, this year's zeros."[4]

Collective amnesia is a powerful stumbling block to righting historical wrongs. But the long struggle for worker justice provides lessons we can't afford to forget. The essential working class endured the cruelest blows of the pandemic. They were infected with COVID-19, and died of it, at higher rates than all but the elderly, and their sacrifices were met with only brief moments of collective sympathy instead of enduring government support, which is what was warranted. True, in some ways, the pandemic resulted in more favorable bargaining conditions for the working class. But without strong organizations to capitalize, opportunities were squandered and real policy changes fluttered into the ether, like beach sand through a child's fingers.

Still, it is impossible to deny that pandemic-era strikes, walkouts, and protests earned an enduring place in the long history of labor struggle. Those actions demonstrated that we all win when workers have more power and justice, when their jobs are safer and more secure, when their voices are heard and respected, when their unions overcome reactionary management interference. There are myriad lessons from the pandemic, but let this be one of the most significant—that a collective good can emerge from the blood, sweat, and sacrifice of a thousand small battles the public at large didn't even know were being waged.

Recognizing our shared fate—that an injury to one is an injury to all—means doing all we can now to make sure that in the future, or at least when the next pandemic arrives, essential workers have the power, freedom, and security to safeguard our health and wealth. To get the kinds of sweeping changes we need and deserve, the kinds that would constitute a true recovery from this crisis, is a major challenge. One that dares us all to fight one day longer.

ACKNOWLEDGMENTS

I've seen the best minds of my generation become union organizers. Over many years I've learned more from them than anyone else, lessons and wisdom that have informed everything I write, including this book. Their rebel hearts guided me through page after page.

I'm grateful to the essential workers who shared their stories during the most tumultuous times of their lives. Not all of them made it into this book by name—and not all of them survived to see this book in print—but I learned so much from every conversation. They offered me an intimate portrait of a group of people I otherwise encountered only behind masks, scrubs, foggy glasses, face shields, and plexiglass sneeze guards. This book, like so much else over the last two years, would have been impossible without them.

Soon after the pandemic began, I conceived this book with Ashley Lopez, my agent at Waxman Literary Agency, and Brian Distelberg of Basic Books. Despite the circuitous route I took to write it, the book is remarkably close to the vision they helped me sketch out. I also thank Michael Kaler for his thoughtful editing of the manuscript, shaping it into a more coherent whole, and the rest of Basic's editing and production team.

I benefited greatly from a dedicated group of student research assistants: Kufre Nkereuwem Udoh, Finn Lester-Niles, Cooper Kelley, Elaine Zhang, Madeleine Joinnides, and especially Caitlin Barr, who worked with me for years. As well, I assembled a small network of Chinese workers, translators, research assistants, and others who made my interviews there possible. For facilitating my meetings with essential workers on the other side of the world, I thank Alex Beth, Mingjing Yin, Nevin Domer, Elliot O'Donnell, Liu Wane Xuewei, Sabina Jiang, and Lulu Zhou.

I racked up my usual debt to people helping me to manipulate and interpret quantitative data. Carmen Sanchez Cumming, Thomas Wentworth, my colleague Matthew Lawrence, and Dr. Rachel Swaner all tested their patience with me. Andrew Fieldhouse taught me a thing or two about interpreting public tax codes.

If you're writing a book, it helps to have someone who will walk through the woods with you for hours, and talk about it. I had Adam Dean, who more than any other person helped me realize the various goals of this project. His unwavering support, cheery disposition, and attention to both the polemical scope and the data-driven research of the book were crucial. I also weaseled my way onto the research team he led with Sim Kimmel and Atheen Venkataramani, who shaped my approach to studying labor and public health.

Greta Morgan's lessons on songwriting helped me figure out what nonfiction storytelling is all about. Aaron Jaffe read a very rough draft of Chapter 7 and steered me toward a more thoughtful consideration of social reproduction theory. Ginger Adams offered some wordsmithing editorial suggestions on a few chapters too. I'm grateful to Emily Rose, who taught me that the most profound insights one can come to about life and labor have already been said—but they bear repeating. As an organizer and a "good art friend," Margaret Lee sharpened my thinking about unions and the politics of labor time. Finally, when I had no time to reread the classics of Western Marxism, Max Ward convinced me to spend months doing it with him anyway, which ultimately informed my thoughts on class formation among essential workers.

During the heart of the pandemic, my comrades in the AAUP— Laurie Essig, Dima Ayoub, Genie Giamo, David Miranda Hardy,

Peter Matthews, and half of the economics department—built the foundation of a movement for workers at Middlebury that influenced how I thought about labor struggles in higher education. Likewise, my sisters and brothers on the Weybridge Volunteer Fire Department reminded me to write about the value of mutual aid.

Amid the harrowing changes brought by the pandemic, my mom kept our family together. My dad, my steadfast editor, read every word of this manuscript—twice. My brother, Chris, a legal advocate for workers, reminded me to look at collisions between labor law and migrant workers.

I'm lucky to live with my most ardent supporters. There we were, stitching a life together, while the world tried to unravel the threads. Erin, who hates all the same things I do—including work—nonetheless made time and room for me to write when there wasn't any time or room. It's an ineffable debt that will take a lifetime to repay, for which I'm so grateful. (Someone should tell her I said this because I'm sure she'll never make it this far in the book.) Asa, a fierce work abolitionist in his own right, inspired me to make time and room for play. Our days spent adventuring outdoors in Vermont were bursts of joy during the doldrums of the pandemic quarantine. And then there's sweet Tessa, who arrived in the middle of a whirlwind. This book dedication belongs to her, for reminding me to engage the world slowly, one step at a time, in a state of wonder.

NOTES

Introduction: An Injury to All

1. "Ebola Virus Disease," World Health Organization, September 2014, https://web
.archive.org/web/20141214011751/https://www.who.int/mediacentre/factsheets/fs103
/en/.

2. Jane Spencer and Christina Jewett, "12 Months of Trauma: More Than 3,600 US
Health Workers Died in Covid's First Year," *Kaiser Health News*, April 8, 2021, https://
khn.org/news/article/us-health-workers-deaths-covid-lost-on-the-frontline/.

3. Myra Blanco et al., "The Impact of Driving, Non-Driving Work, and Rest Breaks on
Driving Performance in Commercial Vehicle Operations," US Department of Transportation, May 2011, https://vtechworks.lib.vt.edu/handle/10919/55114.

4. Alexander Hertel-Fernandez et al., *Understanding the COVID-19 Workplace: A
View from the Essential Workforce*, Roosevelt Institute, 2020.

5. Paul Frymer and Jacob M. Grumbach, "Labor Unions and White Racial Politics,"
American Journal of Political Science 65, no. 1 (January 2021): 225–240, https://scholar
.princeton.edu/sites/default/files/pfrymer/files/ajps12537_rev.pdf.

6. Celine McNicholas et al., "Why Unions Are Good for Workers—Especially in
a Crisis Like COVID-19: 12 Policies That Would Boost Worker Rights, Safety, and
Wages," Economic Policy Institute, August 25, 2020, www.epi.org/publication/why
-unions-are-good-for-workers-especially-in-a-crisis-like-covid-19-12-policies-that-would
-boost-worker-rights-safety-and-wages/.

7. Carl Campanile and Bernadette Hogan, "Hospitals Must Provide Medical Workers
N95 Masks Daily Under Cuomo Edict," *New York Post*, April 13, 2020, https://nypost
.com/2020/04/13/hospitals-must-provide-workers-n95-masks-daily-under-cuomo-edict/.

8. Adam Dean, Atheendar Venkataramani, and Simeon Kimmel, "Mortality Rates
from COVID-19 Are Lower in Unionized Nursing Homes," *Health Affairs* 39, no. 11
(September 10, 2020): 1993–2001, https://doi.org/10.1377/hlthaff.2020.01011.

9. Benedict Anderson, *Imagined Communities: Reflections on the Origin and Spread of
Nationalism* (New York and London: Verso, 2016).

10. Annabel X. Tan et al., "Association Between Income Inequality and County-Level COVID-19 Cases and Deaths in the US," *JAMA Network Open* 4, no. 5 (May 3, 2021): e218799, https://doi.org/10.1001/jamanetworkopen.2021.8799.

11. "Chart Book: The Legacy of the Great Recession," Center on Budget and Policy Priorities, June 6, 2019, www.cbpp.org/research/economy/the-legacy-of-the-great-recession.

12. Hye Jin Rho, Shawn Fremstad, and Hayley Brown, "A Basic Demographic Profile of Workers in Frontline Industries," Center for Economic and Policy Research, April 7, 2020, www.cepr.net/a-basic-demographic-profile-of-workers-in-frontline-industries/.

13. Adie Tomer and Joseph W. Kane, *To Protect Frontline Workers During and After COVID-19, We Must Define Who They Are*, Brookings, June 10, 2020, www.brookings .edu/research/to-protect-frontline-workers-during-and-after-covid-19-we-must-define -who-they-are/.

14. Julia Raifman, Alexandra Skinner, and Aaron Sojourner, "The Unequal Toll of COVID-19 on Workers," *Working Economics Blog*, Economic Policy Institute, February 7, 2022, www.epi.org/blog/the-unequal-toll-of-covid-19-on-workers/.

15. Matthew Haag, "Virus Rules Let Construction Workers Keep Building Luxury Towers," *New York Times*, March 25, 2020, www.nytimes.com/2020/03/25/nyregion /coronavirus-nyc-construction.html.

16. "Last Year of Private Union Elections," Union Election Data, accessed February 3, 2022, https://unionelections.org/data/union/.

17. Steven Greenhouse, "Biden Stakes Claim to Being America's Most Pro-Union President Ever," *Guardian*, May 2, 2021, US news, www.theguardian.com/us-news/2021 /may/02/joe-biden-unions.

18. Kim Moody, "How 'Just-in-Time' Capitalism Spread COVID-19," *Spectre Journal*, April 8, 2020, https://spectrejournal.com/how-just-in-time-capitalism-spread-covid-19/.

19. Nicholas A. Christakis, *Apollo's Arrow: The Profound and Enduring Impact of Coronavirus on the Way We Live* (New York: Little, Brown Spark, 2020).

20. Benjamin Mueller and Eleanor Lutz, "U.S. Has Far Higher Death Rates Than Other Wealthy Countries," *New York Times*, February 1, 2022, www.nytimes.com /interactive/2022/02/01/science/covid-deaths-united-states.html; Bernd Debusmann Jr., "Why Is Canada's Death Rate So Much Lower Than US," *BBC News*, February 15, 2022.

21. Felicia Keesing et al., "Impacts of Biodiversity on the Emergence and Transmission of Infectious Diseases," *Nature* 468, no. 7324 (December 2010): 647–652, https://doi .org/10.1038/nature09575.

Chapter 1: The Dispossessed

1. "How the Great Recession Impacted American Workers," *Knowledge@Wharton*, September 10, 2018, https://knowledge.wharton.upenn.edu/article/great-recession-american -dream/.

2. Austin Clemens, "New Wealth Data Show That the Economic Expansion After the Great Recession Was a Wealthless Recovery for Many U.S. Households," Washington Center for Equitable Growth, October 5, 2020, https://equitablegrowth.org/new-wealth

-data-show-that-the-economic-expansion-after-the-great-recession-was-a-wealthless
-recovery-for-many-u-s-households/.

3. Congressional Budget Office, *Report on the Troubled Asset Relief Program—October 2012*, October 11, 2012, www.cbo.gov/publication/43662.

4. Renae Merle, "After Helping a Fraction of Homeowners Expected, Obama's Foreclosure Prevention Program Is Finally Ending," *Washington Post*, December 30, 2016, www.washingtonpost.com/news/business/wp/2016/12/30/after-helping-a-fraction-of-homeowners-expected-obamas-foreclosure-prevention-program-is-finally-ending.

5. National Employment Law Project, *The Low-Wage Recovery: Industry Employment and Wages Four Years into the Recovery*, April 2014, www.nelp.org/wp-content/uploads/2015/03/Low-Wage-Recovery-Industry-Employment-Wages-2014-Report.pdf.

6. Brad Plumer, "How the Recession Turned Middle-Class Jobs into Low-Wage Jobs," *Washington Post*, February 28, 2013, www.washingtonpost.com/news/wonk/wp/2013/02/28/how-the-recession-turned-middle-class-jobs-into-low-wage-jobs/.

7. Congressional Research Service, *Labor Market Patterns Since 2007*, October 3, 2018, https://sgp.fas.org/crs/misc/R45330.pdf.

8. Rosenblat quoted in Bloomberg: "It was dire economic straits that gave birth to the gig economy in the first place. Uber and Lyft sprang from the 2008 financial crisis—a time when many people were willing to accept that any work was better than none at all. Americans rallied around the concept of a 'side hustle,' and governments effectively endorsed the practice by declining to get involved in the smartphone-based labor markets taking shape." Joshua Brustein, "The Gig Economy Was Built to Thrive in a Downturn—Just Not This One," *Bloomberg*, May 5, 2020, www.bloomberg.com/news/newsletters/2020-05-06/the-gig-economy-was-built-to-thrive-in-a-downturn-just-not-this-one.

9. Ruth Milkman and Stephanie Luce, "Labor Unions and the Great Recession," *RSF: The Russell Sage Foundation Journal of the Social Sciences* 3, no. 3 (2017): 145–165.

10. Chris Bertram, Corey Robin, and Alex Gourevitch, "Let It Bleed: Libertarianism and the Workplace," *Crooked Timber*, July 1, 2012, https://crookedtimber.org/2012/07/01/let-it-bleed-libertarianism-and-the-workplace/; Corey Robin, "Lavatory and Liberty: The Secret History of the Bathroom Break," *Corey Robin* (blog), March 8, 2012, https://coreyrobin.com/2012/03/08/lavatory-and-liberty-the-secret-history-of-the-bathroom-break/; Corey Robin, "What Happens to a Bathroom Break Deferred," *Corey Robin* (blog), March 24, 2012, https://coreyrobin.com/2012/03/24/what-happens-to-a-bathroom-break-deferred/; Lewis Maltby, *Can They Do That?: Retaking Our Fundamental Rights in the Workplace* (New York: Portfolio Penguin, 2009).

11. Bertram, Robin, and Gourevitch, "Let It Bleed: Libertarianism and the Workplace"; Maltby, *Can They Do That?*; Corey Robin, "Fancy Dress at Fancy Law Firms? You're Fired!" *Corey Robin* (blog), April 4, 2012, https://coreyrobin.com/2012/04/04/fancy-dress-at-fancy-law-firms-youre-fired/; Corey Robin, "When Fear Is a Joint Venture," *Washington Post*, October 24, 2004, www.washingtonpost.com/wp-dyn/articles/A56449-2004Oct23.html.

12. Bertram, Robin, and Gourevitch, "Let It Bleed: Libertarianism and the Workplace"; Corey Robin, "Boss to Worker: Thanks for Your Kidney. And, Oh, You're Fired!," *Corey Robin* (blog), April 23, 2012, https://coreyrobin.com/2012/04/23/boss-to-worker-thanks-for-your-kidney-and-oh-youre-fired/.

13. Bertram, Robin, and Gourevitch, "Let It Bleed: Libertarianism and the Workplace."

14. Heather Long, Andrew Van Dam, Alyssa Flowers, and Leslie Shapiro, "The Covid-19 Recession Is the Most Unequal in Modern U.S. History," *Washington Post*, September 30, 2020, www.washingtonpost.com/graphics/2020/business/coronavirus-recession-equality/.

15. Christopher Rugaber, "Richer US Households Fueling a Hot Job Sector: 'Wealth Work,'" Associated Press, July 30, 2019, https://apnews.com/article/4fb9e698a6d94f1d 8269b5dd032b1333.

16. Austin Clemens, "New Great Recession Data Suggest Congress Should Go Big to Spur a Broad-Based, Sustained U.S. Economic Recovery," Washington Center for Equitable Growth, March 4, 2021, https://equitablegrowth.org/new-great-recession -data-suggest-congress-should-go-big-to-spur-a-broad-based-sustained-u-s-economic -recovery/.

17. Nicole Bateman and Martha Ross, "Low-Wage Work Is More Pervasive Than You Think, and There Aren't Enough 'Good Jobs' to Go Around," *The Avenue* (blog), Brookings, November 21, 2019, www.brookings.edu/blog/the-avenue/2019/11/21/low-wage-work -is-more-pervasive-than-you-think-and-there-arent-enough-good-jobs-to-go-around/.

18. Nicole Bateman and Martha Ross, *The Pandemic Hurt Low-Wage Workers the Most—and So Far, the Recovery Has Helped Them the Least*, Brookings, July 28, 2021, www .brookings.edu/research/the-pandemic-hurt-low-wage-workers-the-most-and-so-far-the -recovery-has-helped-them-the-least/.

19. Eli Okun, "Kudlow Breaks with CDC on Coronavirus: 'We Have Contained This,'" *POLITICO*, February 25, 2020, www.politico.com/news/2020/02/25/kudlow -white-house-coronavirus-117402.

20. International Labour Organization, *ILO Monitor: COVID-19 and the World of Work*, 6th ed., September 23, 2020, www.ilo.org/wcmsp5/groups/public/---dgreports /---dcomm/documents/briefingnote/wcms_755910.pdf.

21. International Labour Organization, *Impact of the COVID-19 Crisis on Loss of Jobs and Hours Among Domestic Workers*, June 15, 2020, www.ilo.org/wcmsp5/groups /public/---ed_protect/---protrav/---travail/documents/publication/wcms_747961.pdf.

22. Maximiliano Dvorkin, "Which Jobs Have Been Hit Hardest During COVID-19?" Federal Reserve Bank of St. Louis, August 17, 2020, www.stlouisfed.org/publications /regional-economist/third-quarter-2020/jobs-hit-hardest-covid-19.

23. Jed Kolko (@JedKolko), "This recession really is different. All other downturns in the past 50 years have been…." Twitter, October 1, 2020, 7:06 a.m., https://twitter.com /jedkolko/status/1311668918428205069.

24. Alyssa Davis, "The Leisure and Hospitality Sector Has the Largest Gap Between CEO and Worker Pay," *Working Economics Blog*, Economic Policy Institute, September 9, 2014, www.epi.org/blog/leisure-hospitality-sector-largest-gap-ceo/.

25. Bureau of Labor Statistics, "The Employment Situation—March 2020," news release, April 3, 2020, 41, www.bls.gov/news.release/archives/empsit_04032020.pdf.

26. Bureau of Labor Statistics, "The Employment Situation—April 2020," news release, May 8, 2020, 42, www.bls.gov/news.release/archives/empsit_05082020.pdf.

27. Bureau of Labor Statistics, "The Employment Situation—March 2020," 41; Bureau of Labor Statistics, "The Employment Situation—April 2020," 42.

28. Cornell Law School, *The U.S. Private Sector Job Quality Index (JQI) March 2020*, April 3, 2020, https://d3n8a8pro7vhmx.cloudfront.net/prosperousamerica/pages/5527/attachments /original/1585924362/200403_JQI_Report_-March_2020_Release.pdf?1585924362.

29. Elise Gould and Jori Kandra, *Wages Grew in 2020 Because the Bottom Fell Out of the Low-Wage Labor Market: The State of Working America 2020 Wages Report*, Economic Policy Institute, February 24, 2021, www.epi.org/publication/state-of-working -america-wages-in-2020/.

30. Louis Uchitelle, *The Disposable American: Layoffs and Their Consequences* (New York: Knopf, 2006).

31. Gould and Kandra, *Wages Grew in 2020*.

32. Long, Van Dam, Flowers, and Shapiro, "The Covid-19 Recession Is the Most Unequal."

33. Bureau of Labor Statistics, "Unemployment Rate Rises to Record High 14.7 Percent in April 2020," *Economics Daily*, May 13, 2020, www.bls.gov/opub/ted/2020 /unemployment-rate-rises-to-record-high-14-point-7-percent-in-april-2020.htm?view_full.

34. Scott W. Stern et al., "A Rust Belt City's New Working Class," *New Republic*, March 31, 2021, https://newrepublic.com/article/161867/rust-belt-citys-new-working-class -pittsburgh-review.

35. Kamala D. Harris, "Kamala Harris: The Exodus of Women from the Workforce Is a National Emergency," *Washington Post*, February 12, 2021, www.washingtonpost.com /opinions/kamala-harris-women-workforce-pandemic/2021/02/12/b8cd1cb6-6d6f-11eb -9f80-3d7646ce1bc0_story.html.

36. Joan Entmacher et al., *Underpaid & Overloaded: Women in Low-Wage Jobs*, National Women's Center, 2014, https://nwlc.org/wp-content/uploads/2015/08/final_nwlc _lowwagereport2014.pdf.

37. Kate Bahn and Carmen Sanchez Cumming, *Factsheet: U.S. Occupational Segregation by Race, Ethnicity, and Gender*, Washington Center for Equitable Growth, July 1, 2020, www .equitablegrowth.org/factsheet-u-s-occupational-segregation-by-race-ethnicity-and-gender/.

38. Bahn and Cumming, "Factsheet: U.S. Occupational Segregation"; Emiko Usui, "Occupational Gender Segregation in an Equilibrium Search Model," *IZA Journal of Labor Economics* 4, no. 1 (July 10, 2015): 13, https://doi.org/10.1186/s40172-015-0028-2.

39. Jed Kolko, "Why Blue Places Have Been Hit Harder Economically Than Red Ones," *New York Times*, October 30, 2020, The Upshot, www.nytimes.com/2020/10/30 /upshot/red-blue-economic-recovery.html.

40. Kolko, "Why Blue Places Have Been Hit Harder."

41. Center on Budget and Policy Priorities, *Tracking the COVID-19 Economy's Effects on Food, Housing, and Employment Hardships*, August 9, 2021, www.cbpp.org/research /poverty-and-inequality/tracking-the-covid-19-recessions-effects-on-food-housing-and.

42. Mathieu Despard et al., "COVID-19 Job and Income Loss Leading to More Hunger and Financial Hardship," *Up Front* (blog), Brookings, July 13, 2020, www.brookings .edu/blog/up-front/2020/07/13/covid-19-job-and-income-loss-leading-to-more-hunger -and-financial-hardship/.

43. Stefani Milovanska-Farrington, *Job Loss and Food Insecurity During the COVID-19 Pandemic*, IZA Institute of Labor Economics, April 2021, www.iza.org/publications/dp /14273/job-loss-and-food-insecurity-during-the-covid-19-pandemic.

44. Don J. Q. Chen and Vivien K. G. Lim, "Strength in Adversity: The Influence of Psychological Capital on Job Search," *Journal of Organizational Behavior* 33, no. 6 (August 2012): 811–839, https://doi.org/10.1002/job.1814.

45. Rebecca J. Guerin et al., "Investigating the Impact of Job Loss and Decreased Work Hours on Physical and Mental Health Outcomes Among US Adults During the COVID-19 Pandemic," *Journal of Occupational and Environmental Medicine* 63, no. 9 (September 2021): e571–e579, https://doi.org/10.1097/jom.0000000000002288.

46. Di Fang, Michael R. Thomsen, and Rodolfo M. Nayga, "The Association Between Food Insecurity and Mental Health During the COVID-19 Pandemic," *BMC Public Health* 21, no. 1 (March 29, 2021): 607, https://doi.org/10.1186/s12889-021-10631-0; Leah R. Abrams, Jessica M. Finlay, and Lindsay C. Kobayashi, "Job Transitions and Mental Health Outcomes Among U.S. Adults Aged 55 and Older During the COVID-19 Pandemic," *Journals of Gerontology: Series B*, no. gbab060 (April 10, 2021), https://doi.org/10.1093/geronb/gbab060.

47. Eric B. Elbogen et al., "Suicidal Ideation and Thoughts of Self-Harm During the COVID-19 Pandemic: The Role of COVID-19-Related Stress, Social Isolation, and Financial Strain," *Depression and Anxiety* 38, no. 7 (2021): 739–748, https://doi.org/10.1002/da.23162.

48. Monica Lawson, Megan H. Piel, and Michaela Simon, "Child Maltreatment During the COVID-19 Pandemic: Consequences of Parental Job Loss on Psychological and Physical Abuse Towards Children," *Child Abuse & Neglect* 110, no. 2 (December 2020): 104709, https://doi.org/10.1016/j.chiabu.2020.104709.

49. "Primer: How the Unemployment Insurance System Operates," Economic Policy Institute, accessed September 10, 2021, www.epi.org/publication/primer-how-the-unemployment-insurance-system-operates/.

50. Sharon Parrott et al., *CARES Act Includes Essential Measures to Respond to Public Health, Economic Crises, but More Will Be Needed*, Center on Budget and Policy Priorities, March 27, 2020, www.cbpp.org/sites/default/files/atoms/files/3-27-20econ.pdf.

51. Associated Press, "Florida Governor Orders Investigation of Unemployment System," *WPBF*, May 4, 2020, www.wpbf.com/article/florida-governor-orders-investigation-of-unemployment-system/32371584; Eduardo Porter and Karl Russell, "How the American Unemployment System Failed," *New York Times*, January 21, 2021, Business, www.nytimes.com/2021/01/21/business/economy/unemployment-insurance.html; Rebecca Vallas, "Republicans Wrapped the Safety Net in Red Tape. Now We're All Suffering," *Washington Post*, April 15, 2020, www.washingtonpost.com/outlook/2020/04/15/republicans-harder-access-safety-net/.

52. Adam Tooze, *Shutdown: How Covid Shook the World's Economy* (New York: Viking, 2021).

53. Charlotte Houghton and Mariette Aborn, "As the Economy Continues to Struggle, Can Short-Time Compensation Offer Relief?," Bipartisan Policy Center, January 29, 2021, https://bipartisanpolicy.org/blog/as-the-economy-continues-to-struggle-can-short-time-compensation-offer-relief/; Patricia Cohen, "This Plan Pays to Avoid Layoffs. Why Don't More Employers Use It?," *New York Times*, August 20, 2020, Business, www.nytimes.com/2020/08/20/business/economy/jobs-work-sharing-unemployment.html.

54. Jeanna Smialek, "How the Fed's Magic Money Machine Will Turn $454 Billion into $4 Trillion," *New York Times*, updated March 27, 2020, www.nytimes.com/2020/03/26/business/economy/fed-coronavirus-stimulus.html.

55. "Statement of the Problem: Why Unemployment Insurance Reform Is Needed," Economic Policy Institute, accessed September 10, 2021, www.epi.org/publication/statement -of-the-problem-why-unemployment-insurance-reform-is-needed/.

56. "Executive Summary: Reforming Unemployment Insurance," Economic Policy Institute, accessed September 10, 2021, www.epi.org/publication/executive-summary -reforming-unemployment-insurance/.

57. David Dayen, "Your Coronavirus Check Is Coming. Your Bank Can Grab It," *American Prospect*, April 14, 2020, https://prospect.org/api/content/93c1a092-7e58-11ea -9b6f-1244d5f7c7c6/.

58. Laura Wheaton, Linda Giannarelli, and Ilham Dehry, *2021 Poverty Projections: Assessing the Impact of Benefits and Stimulus Measures*, Urban Institute, July 27, 2021, www.urban.org/research/publication/2021-poverty-projections-assessing-impact-benefits -and-stimulus-measures.

59. "TRANSCRIPT: On CNN, Sen. Schumer Calls for a Marshall Plan for Hospitals, Health Care System to Test and Treat All Who Need It Due to Coronavirus Outbreak," *Newsroom*, Senate Democrats, March 18. 2020, www.democrats.senate.gov /newsroom/press-releases/transcript-on-cnn-sen-schumer-calls-for-a-marshall-plan -for-hospitals-health-care-system-to-test-and-treat-all-who-need-it-due-to-coronavirus -outbreak.

60. Allan Sloan, "The CARES Act Sent You a $1,200 Check but Gave Millionaires and Billionaires Far More," *ProPublica*, June 8, 2020, www.propublica.org/article /the-cares-act-sent-you-a-1-200-check-but-gave-millionaires-and-billionaires-far-more.

61. Sloan, "The CARES Act Sent You a $1,200 Check."

62. Josh Hawley (@HawleyMO), "And here comes the lists of corporate & government giveaways—but remember, negotiators said we couldn't give working people a single penny more," Twitter, December 21, 2020, 12:03 p.m., https://twitter.com/HawleyMO /status/1341112078258614275.

63. Lydia DePillis, "The Government Gave Free PPP Money to Public Companies Despite Warning Them Not to Apply," *ProPublica*, September 23, 2021, www.propublica .org/article/the-government-gave-free-ppp-money-to-public-companies-despite-warning -them-not-to-apply.

64. Jack Gillum and Paul Kiel, "Different Names, Same Address: How Big Businesses Got Government Loans Meant for Small Businesses," *ProPublica*, July 14, 2020, www .propublica.org/article/different-names-same-address-how-big-businesses-got-government -loans-meant-for-small-businesses?token=Q6-lFWuVx1tj_TbkyElNHUdjE_9EDa1_.

65. Robert Brenner, "Agrarian Class Structure and Economic Development in Pre-Industrial Europe," *Past & Present*, no. 70 (February 1976): 8.

66. Jen Kirby, "Trump's Purge of Inspectors General, Explained," *Vox*, updated May 28, 2020, www.vox.com/2020/5/28/21265799/inspectors-general-trump-linick-atkinson; Donald Trump, "Statement by the President—The White House," White House, March 27, 2020, https://trumpwhitehouse.archives.gov/briefings-statements/statement-by-the -president-38/.

67. Lulu Garcia-Navarro and Tim Mak, "Who Is Watching Over Coronavirus Bailout Spending?," Economy, NPR, April 19, 2020, www.npr.org/2020/04/19/838073166/who -is-watching-over-coronavirus-bailout-spending-1st-panel-appointee-talks-over.

68. Cheyenne Haslett, "3 Months in, Commission Overseeing $500 Billion of Taxpayer Dollars Remains Leaderless," *ABC News*, June 20, 2020, https://abcnews.go .com/Politics/months-commission-overseeing-500-billion-taxpayer-dollars-remains /story?id=71334236.

69. David Dayen, "Unsanitized: Donna Shalala Selection Makes a Mockery of Bailout Oversight Panel," *American Prospect*, April 18, 2020, https://prospect.org/api /content/34810e64-818d-11ea-a19d-1244d5f7c7c6/.

70. "Getting to the Point with Congressman Richard Neal," Edward M. Kennedy Institute for the United States Senate, April 13, 2020, YouTube video, www.youtube.com /watch?v=ZtL6QGw0NVs.

71. Brenner, "Agrarian Class Structure," 9.

72. Thea Lee, "EPI Applauds Passage of the American Rescue Plan," *News from EPI* (blog), Economic Policy Institute, March 10, 2021, www.epi.org/press/epi-applauds -passage-of-the-american-rescue-plan/.

73. David Sirota, Julia Rock, and Andrew Perez, "The New COVID-19 Relief Bill Is Good, but Not Good Enough," *Jacobin*, March 11, 2021, https://jacobinmag .com/2021/03/covid-relief-stimulus-minimum-wage-biden-american-rescue-plan.

74. Tax Policy Center, "T21-0041—All Major Provisions in H.R. 1319, the American Rescue Plan Act of 2021, as Passed by the Senate and House, by Expanded Cash Income Percentile, 2021," March 11, 2021, www.taxpolicycenter.org/model-estimates /american-rescue-plan-act-2021-final-version-passed-senate-and-house-march-2021/t21-0.

75. Tax Policy Center, "T09-0117—'The American Recovery and Reinvestment Tax Act of 2009' Conference Report: Major Individual and Corporate Tax Provisions Baseline: Current Law Plus AMT Patch Distribution of Federal Tax Change by Cash Income Percentile, 2009," February 22, 2009, www.taxpolicycenter.org/model -estimates/american-recovery-and-reinvestment-tax-act-2009-conference-agreement /american-14.

76. Anton Jäger and Daniel Zamora, "'Welfare Without the Welfare State': The Death of the Postwar Welfarist Consensus," *New Statesman*, February 9, 2021, www .newstatesman.com/international/2021/02/welfare-without-welfare-state-death-postwar -welfarist-consensus.

77. Sirota, Rock, and Perez, "The New COVID-19 Relief Bill Is Good."

78. Lee, "EPI Applauds Passage of the American Rescue Plan."

79. Chuck Collins, "Updates: Billionaire Wealth, U.S. Job Losses and Pandemic Profiteers," *Blogging Our Great Divide*, Inequality.Org, July 14, 2021, https://inequality.org /great-divide/updates-billionaire-pandemic/.

80. Todd Frankel and Douglas MacMillan, "IRS Records Show Wealthiest Americans, Including Bezos and Musk, Paid Little in Income Taxes as Share of Wealth, Report Says," *Washington Post*, June 8, 2021, www.washingtonpost.com/business/2021/06/08 /wealthy-irs-taxes/.

81. Emily Badger and Alicia Parlapiano, "The Rich Cut Their Spending. That Has Hurt All the Workers Who Count on It," *New York Times*, June 17, 2020, The Upshot, www.nytimes.com/2020/06/17/upshot/coronavirus-spending-rich-poor.html.

82. Kim Parker, Rachel Minkin, and Jesse Bennett, "Economic Fallout from COVID-19 Continues to Hit Lower-Income Americans the Hardest," *Social Trends* (blog), Pew

Research Center, September 24, 2020, www.pewresearch.org/social-trends/2020/09/24 /economic-fallout-from-covid-19-continues-to-hit-lower-income-americans-the-hardest/; Heather Long, "Millions of Americans Are Heading into the Holidays Unemployed and over $5,000 Behind on Rent," *Washington Post*, December 7, 2020, www.washingtonpost .com/business/2020/12/07/unemployed-debt-rent-utilities/.

83. Kathryn M. Leifheit et al., "Expiring Eviction Moratoriums and COVID-19 Incidence and Mortality," *American Journal of Epidemiology* 190, no. 12 (December 2021): 2503–2510, https://doi.org/10.1093/aje/kwab196.

84. Eviction Lab, "The Eviction Tracking System," accessed August 14, 2021, https:// evictionlab.org/eviction-tracking/.

85. Nicholas Fandos, "With Capitol Sit-In, Cori Bush Galvanized a Progressive Revolt over Evictions," *New York Times*, August 4, 2021, US, www.nytimes.com/2021/08/04 /us/politics/cori-bush-eviction-moratorium.html.

86. Paul E. Williams, "Protected from Eviction, Not from Delta," *Social Housing Chronicle*, July 23, 2021, https://housingchronicle.substack.com/p/protected-from-eviction -not-from.

87. "Week 35 Household Pulse Survey: August 4–August 16," US Census Bureau, August 25, 2021, www.census.gov/data/tables/2021/demo/hhp/hhp35.html.

88. Hye Jin Rho, Hayley Brown, Shawn Fremstad, "A Basic Demographic Profile of Workers in Frontline Industries," Center for Economic and Policy Research, April 7, 2020, https://cepr.net/a-basic-demographic-profile-of-workers-in-frontline-industries/.

Chapter 2: Awakenings

1. *Dying for Work*, MassCOSH and Massachusetts AFL-CIO, September 2020, http://masscosh.org/sites/default/files/Dying%20for%20Work%20-%20Pandemic %27s%20Deadly%20Toll%20Sep%202020.pdf.

2. Nicole Dungca et al., "On the Front Lines of the Pandemic, Grocery Workers Are in the Dark About Risks," *Washington Post*, May 24, 2020, www.washingtonpost.com /investigations/2020/05/24/grocery-workers-coronavirus-risks/.

3. Alexander Hertel-Fernandez et al., *Understanding the COVID-19 Workplace: A View from the Essential Workforce*, Roosevelt Institute, June 2020, https://rooseveltinstitute.org /wp-content/uploads/2020/07/RI_SurveyofEssentialWorkers_IssueBrief_202006-1 .pdf.

4. Friedrich Engels, *Condition of the Working Class in England* (Panther Edition, 1969).

5. Fan-Yun Lan et al., "Association Between SARS-CoV-2 Infection, Exposure Risk and Mental Health Among a Cohort of Essential Retail Workers in the USA," *Occupational and Environmental Medicine* 78, no. 4 (April 1, 2021): 237–243, https://doi .org/10.1136/oemed-2020-106774.

6. Kara Manke, "California Farmworkers Hit Hard by COVID-19, Study Finds," *Berkeley News*, December 2, 2020, https://news.berkeley.edu/2020/12/02/california -farmworkers-hit-hard-by-covid-19-study-finds/; Remy F. Pasco et al., "Estimated Association of Construction Work with Risks of COVID-19 Infection and Hospitalization

in Texas," *JAMA Network Open* 3, no. 10 (October 29, 2020): e2026373, https://doi
.org/10.1001/jamanetworkopen.2020.26373.

7. Helen Ho, Daniel Schneider, and Kristen Harknett, *COVID-19 Safety Measures
Update,* The Shift Project, December 17, 2020, https://shift.hks.harvard.edu/COVID-19
-safety-measures-update/.

8. Daniel Schneider and Kristen Harknett, *Estimates of Workers Who Lack Access to
Paid Sick Leave at 91 Large Service Sector Employers,* The Shift Project, March 20, 2020,
https://shift.hks.harvard.edu/paid-sick-leave-brief/.

9. David P. Bui et al., "Racial and Ethnic Disparities Among COVID-19 Cases in
Workplace Outbreaks by Industry Sector, Utah, March 6–June 5, 2020," *Morbidity and
Mortality Weekly Report* 69, no. 33 (August 21, 2020): 1133–1138, http://dx.doi.org
/10.15585/mmwr.mm6933e3.

10. Yea-Hung Chen et al., "Excess Mortality Associated with the COVID-19 Pandemic Among Californians 18–65 Years of Age, by Occupational Sector and Occupation:
March Through October 2020," medRxiv, January 1, 2021, https://doi.org/10.1101/202
1.01.21.21250266.

11. Justin Feldman, "Coronavirus Is an Occupational Disease that Spreads at Work,"
Jacobin, January 19, 2021, https://jacobinmag.com/2021/01/COVID-19-business-work
-public-health.

12. Shuchi Anand et al., "Prevalence of SARS-CoV-2 Antibodies in a Large Nationwide
Sample of Patients on Dialysis in the USA: A Cross-Sectional Study," *The Lancet* 396, no.
10259 (October 24, 2020): 1335–1344, https://doi.org/10.1016/S0140-6736(20)32009-2.

13. David P. Bui et al., "Racial and Ethnic Disparities Among COVID-19 Cases in
Workplace Outbreaks by Industry Sector—Utah, March 6–June 5, 2020," *Morbidity
and Mortality Weekly Report* 69, no. 33 (August 21, 2020): 1133–1138, https://doi.org
/10.15585/mmwr.mm6933e3.

14. Chen et al., "Excess Mortality Associated with the COVID-19 Pandemic."

15. "Bus Drivers," Data USA, https://datausa.io/profile/soc/bus-drivers; Kelemwork
Cook et al., "The Future of Work in Black America," McKinsey & Company, October 4, 2019,
www.mckinsey.com/featured-insights/future-of-work/the-future-of-work-in-black-america.

16. Shawn Fremstad, Hye Jin Rho, and Hayley Brown, "Meatpacking Workers Are
a Diverse Group Who Need Better Protections," Center for Economic and Policy Research, April 29, 2020, https://cepr.net/meatpacking-workers-are-a-diverse-group-who
-need-better-protections/.

17. Charles A. Taylor, Christopher Boulos, and Douglas Almond, "Livestock Plants
and COVID-19 Transmission," *Proceedings of the National Academy of Sciences* 117, no. 50
(November 19, 2020), https://doi.org/10.1073/pnas.2010115117.

18. Michelle A. Waltenburg et al., "Update: COVID-19 Among Workers in Meat and
Poultry Processing Facilities—United States, April–May 2020," *Morbidity and Mortality Weekly Report* 69, no. 27 (July 10, 2020): 887–892, https://doi.org/10.15585/mmwr
.mm6927e2.

19. Lisa Dubay et al., *How Risk of Exposure to the Coronavirus at Work Varies by Race
and Ethnicity and How to Protect the Health and Well-Being of Workers and Their Families,* Urban Institute, December 2020, 51, www.urban.org/sites/default/files/publication
/103278/how-risk-of-exposure-to-the-coronavirus-at-work-varies.pdf.

20. Nils Haug et al., "Ranking the Effectiveness of Worldwide COVID-19 Government Interventions," *Nature Human Behaviour* 4, no. 12 (December 2020): 1303–1312, https://doi.org/10.1038/s41562-020-01009-0.

21. Justin Feldman, "Coronavirus Is an Occupational Disease That Spreads at Work," *Jacobin*, January 19, 2021, https://jacobinmag.com/2021/01/COVID-19-business-work-public-health; Shajia Abidi and John Gramlich, "As CDC Warned Against Holiday Travel, 57% of Americans Say They Changed Thanksgiving Plans Due to COVID-19," *Fact Tank* (blog), Pew Research Center, December 22, 2020, www.pewresearch.org/fact-tank/2020/12/22/as-cdc-warned-against-holiday-travel-57-of-americans-say-they-changed-thanksgiving-plans-due-to-COVID-19/.

22. News 8 WROC (@News_8), "Gov. Cuomo on following COVID-19 rules: 'If you're socially distant...,'" Twitter, November 18, 2020, 10:54 a.m., https://twitter.com/News_8/Status/1329135843093733378.

23. Governor Andrew M. Cuomo, "Stop Living Room Spread PSA," December 2, 2020, YouTube video, www.youtube.com/watch?v=7QGETQTOtL8.

24. Benedict Anderson, *Imagined Communities: Reflections on the Origin and Spread of Nationalism* (New York and London: Verso, 2016).

25. *Beneficial or Critical? The Heightened Need for Telework Opportunities in the Post-9/11 World: Hearing Before the Committee on Government Reform*, 108th Cong. (2004), www.govinfo.gov/content/pkg/CHRG-108hhrg96411/html/CHRG-108hhrg96411.htm.

26. Social and Demographic Trends Project, "Most Teleworkers See Online Tools as a Good Substitute for In-Person Contact; Relatively Few Have 'Zoom Fatigue,'" *Social Trends* (blog), Pew Research Center, December 4, 2020, www.pewresearch.org/social-trends/wp-content/uploads/sites/3/2020/12/PSDT_12.09.20_COVID.work-00-9.png.

27. Jamie K. McCallum, "Remote Controlled Workers," *American Prospect*, February 4, 2021, https://prospect.org/labor/remote-controlled-workers-digital-surveillance/.

28. Social and Demographic Trends Project, "Most Teleworkers See Online Tools."

29. Ruth Igielnik, "A Rising Share of Working Parents in the U.S. Say It's Been Difficult to Handle Child Care During the Pandemic," Pew Research Center, January 26, 2021, www.pewresearch.org/fact-tank/2021/01/26/a-rising-share-of-working-parents-in-the-u-s-say-its-been-difficult-to-handle-child-care-during-the-pandemic/.

30. Mark Brown, "Banksy's NHS Covid Superhero Nurse Gift Sold for Record £16.7m," *Guardian*, March 23, 2021, www.theguardian.com/artanddesign/2021/mar/23/banksys-nhs-covid-gift-superhero-nurse-sold-for-record-167m.

31. Bernadette Hogan (@bern_hogan), "#PresidentCuomo trends as governor's star status rises...," Twitter, March 22, 2020, 7:59 a.m., https://twitter.com/bern_hogan/status/1241696108776239104.

32. Russell Redman, "Grocery Worker COVID-19 Infections, Deaths Rise: UFCW Report," *Supermarket News*, April 22, 2021, www.supermarketnews.com/issues-trends/grocery-worker-COVID-19-infections-deaths-rise-ufcw-report.

33. Tracy Jan, "The Biggest Beneficiaries of the Government Safety Net: Working-Class Whites," *Washington Post*, February 16, 2017, www.washingtonpost.com/news/wonk/wp/2017/02/16/the-biggest-beneficiaries-of-the-government-safety-net-working-class-whites/.

34. Peter Ganong, Pascal Noel, and Joseph S. Vavra, "US Unemployment Insurance Replacement Rates During the Pandemic," working paper, Becker Friedman Institute, University of Chicago, August 24, 2020, https://bfi.uchicago.edu/working-paper/2020-62/.

35. Christopher Adolph et al., "The Pandemic Policy U-Turn: Partisanship, Public Health, and Race in Decisions to Ease COVID-19 Social Distancing Policies in the United States," *Perspectives on Politics*, October 1, 2021, 1–23, https://doi.org/10.1017/S1537592721002036.

Chapter 3: The Pandemic Proletariat

1. Julia Carrie Wong, "Amazon Execs Labeled Fired Worker 'Not Smart or Articulate' in Leaked PR Notes," *Guardian*, April 2, 2020, Technology, www.theguardian.com/technology/2020/apr/02/amazon-chris-smalls-smart-articulate-leaked-memo.

2. Wong, "Amazon Execs Labeled Fired Worker."

3. Wong, "Amazon Execs Labeled Fired Worker."

4. Wong, "Amazon Execs Labeled Fired Worker"; Bernie Sanders (@BernieSanders), "It's disgraceful that Amazon, which is owned by the richest man in the world…" Twitter, March 31, 2020, 6:18 p.m., https://twitter.com/BernieSanders/status/1245113355582550021.

5. Jeffrey Dastin, "Exclusive: Amazon to Deploy Masks and Temperature Checks for Workers by Next Week," Reuters, April 2, 2020, www.reuters.com/article/us-health-coronavirus-amazon-com-masks-e-idUSKBN21K1Y6.

6. Information for this statement was gathered via the link below, which has since been deleted, deemed "in violation of the Cybersecurity Law of the People's Republic of China," https://mp.weixin.qq.com/s/ahXfoPXktDnpg-62bgMGSA.

7. "How Cooperative Gig Economy Companies Managed to Flourish During the Pandemic," thetechnetwork.io, https://thetechnetwork.io/how-cooperative-gig-economy-companies-managed-to-flourish-during-the-pandemic/.

8. Megan Rose Dickey, "Gig Workers Have Created a Tool to Offer Mutual Aid During COVID-19 Pandemic," *Tech Crunch*, March 18, 2020, https://techcrunch.com/2020/03/18/gig-workers-collective-covid-19/.

9. Meagan Flynn, "They Lived in a Factory for 28 Days to Make Millions of Pounds of Raw PPE Materials to Help Fight Coronavirus," *Washington Post*, April 23, 2020, www.washingtonpost.com/nation/2020/04/23/factory-masks-coronavirus-ppe/.

10. Katie Ferrari, "GE Workers Protest, Demand to Make Ventilators," *Labor Notes*, April 13, 2020, https://labornotes.org/blogs/2020/04/ge-workers-protest-demand-make-ventilators.

11. Sarah Kliff et al., "There Aren't Enough Ventilators to Cope with the Coronavirus," *New York Times*, March 18, 2020, www.nytimes.com/2020/03/18/business/coronavirus-ventilator-shortage.html.

12. Yelena Dzhanova, "Trump Compelled These Companies to Make Critical Supplies, but Most of Them Were Already Doing It," *CNBC*, April 3, 2020, www.cnbc.com/2020/04/03/coronavirus-trump-used-defense-production-act-on-these-companies-so-far.html.

13. Jeremy Brecher, "Strike for Your Life!," *Common Dreams*, April 3, 2020, www.commondreams.org/views/2020/04/03/strike-your-life; Dan DiMaggio and Saurav Sarkar, "Walkouts Spread as Workers Seek Coronavirus Protections," *Labor Notes*, March 26, 2020, www.labornotes.org/2020/03/walkouts-spread-workers-seek-coronavirus-protections.

14. Amanda Kinnunen and Anna-Karin Gustafsson, "Relative Calm on the Industrial Action Front in 2020," *Industrial Relations and Social Dialogue* (blog), Eurofound, April 8, 2021, www.eurofound.europa.eu/publications/article/2021/relative-calm-on-the-industrial-action-front-in-2020.

15. Scott Neuman, "Essential Workers Plan May Day Strikes; Others Demand End to COVID-19 Lockdowns," NPR, May 1, 2020, www.npr.org/sections/coronavirus-live-updates/2020/05/01/848931228/essential-workers-plan-may-day-strikes-others-demand-end-to-covid-19-lockdowns; Shirin Ghaffary, "The May Day Strike from Amazon, Instacart, and Target Workers Didn't Stop Business. It Was Still a Success," *Vox*, May 1, 2020, www.vox.com/recode/2020/5/1/21244151/may-day-strike-amazon-instacart-target-success-turnout-fedex-protest-essential-workers-chris-smalls; Michael Sainato, "Strikes Erupt as US Essential Workers Demand Protection amid Pandemic," *Guardian*, May 19, 2020, www.theguardian.com/world/2020/may/19/strikes-erupt-us-essential-workers-demand-better-protection-amid-pandemic; Bridget Read, "Every Food and Delivery Strike Happening over Coronavirus," *The Cut*, May 27, 2020, www.thecut.com/2020/05/whole-foods-amazon-mcdonalds-among-coronavirus-strikes.html; Daniel A. Medina, "As Amazon, Walmart, and Others Profit amid Coronavirus Crisis, Their Essential Workers Plan Unprecedented Strike," *The Intercept*, April 28, 2020, https://theintercept.com/2020/04/28/coronavirus-may-1-strike-sickout-amazon-target-whole-foods/.

16. Tanya Modersitzki, "Perdue Farms Employees Walk Out After No Wage Increase amid COVID-19," *41NBC News/WMGT-DT*, March 23, 2020, www.41nbc.com/perdue-farms-employees-strike-no-wage-increase-amid-covid-19/.

17. Bisma Parvez, "Passengers Ride Free as Detroit Buses Back on Schedule Wednesday," *Detroit Free Press*, March 18, 2020, www.freep.com/story/news/local/michigan/wayne/2020/03/18/passengers-ride-free-detroit-ddot-buses-back-schedule-wednesday/2862877001/.

18. Ryan Basen, "Tenet Gets Big Federal $$$ but Still Cuts Employees," *MedPage Today*, July 9, 2020, www.medpagetoday.com/hospitalbasedmedicine/generalhospitalpractice/87493.

19. Basen, "Tenet Gets Big Federal $$$."

20. Steven Monacelli, "Traveling Halfway Across U.S., Striking Massachusetts Nurses Bring Fight to Dallas," *Dallas Observer*, July 8, 2021, www.dallasobserver.com/news/traveling-halfway-across-us-striking-massachusetts-nurses-bring-fight-to-dallas-12049499.

21. Dave Muoio, "Nurses Vote to End 10-Month Strike at Tenet Healthcare's St. Vincent Hospital," *Fierce Healthcare*, January 4, 2022, www.fiercehealthcare.com/hospitals/nurses-strike-tenet-healthcare-st-vincent-hospital-vote-to-end-10-month-strike-at-tenet.

22. More Perfect Union (@MorePerfectUS), "Nurses are leading a historic wave of labor organizing…" Twitter, September 7, 2020, 10:48 a.m., https://twitter.com/moreperfectus/status/1435298962026766338.

23. Frances Fox Piven and Richard Cloward, *Poor People's Movements: Why They Succeed, How They Fail* (New York: Vintage, 1978).

24. Keeanga-Yamahtta Taylor, "Did Last Summer's Black Lives Matter Protests Change Anything?," *New Yorker*, August 6, 2021, www.newyorker.com/news/our-columnists /did-last-summers-protests-change-anything.

25. "ILWU Stands Down at West Coast Ports for Historic Juneteenth Action to Honor Black Lives," ILWU, July 13, 2020, www.ilwu.org/ilwu-stands-down-at-west -coast-ports-for-historic-juneteenth-action-to-honor-black-lives/; Peter Cole, "The Most Radical Union in the U.S. Is Shutting Down the Ports on Juneteenth," *In These Times*, June 16, 2020, https://inthesetimes.com/article/juneteenth-ilwu-dockworkers-strike-ports -black-lives-matter-george-floyd.

26. Clarence Thomas, "'The Most Effective Way to Stop Police Terror Is Action at the Point of Production,'" interview by Eric Blanc, *Jacobin*, June 9, 2020, https://jacobinmag .com/2020/06/george-floyd-ilwu-work-stoppage-antiracism.

27. "ILWU Stands Down at West Coast Ports."

28. Joe DeManuelle-Hall, "West Coast Dockers Stop Work to Honor George Floyd," *Labor Notes*, June 11, 2020, https://labornotes.org/blogs/2020/06/west-coast-dockers -stop-work-honor-george-floyd; Thomas, "'The Most Effective Way to Stop Police Terror'"; "ILWU Stands Down at West Coast Ports."

29. Rachel Treisman, "Essential Workers Hold Walkouts and Protests in National 'Strike for Black Lives,'" NPR, July 20, 2020, www.npr.org/sections/live-updates-protests -for-racial-justice/2020/07/20/893316011/essential-workers-hold-walkouts-and-protests -in-national-strike-for-black-lives; Chris Brooks, "Fact Check: Have There Been 500 Wildcat Strikes in June?," *Organizing Work*, June 23, 2020, https://organizing.work/2020/06 /fact-check-have-there-been-500-wildcat-strikes-in-june/.

30. Sarah Jaffe and Michelle Chen, "Belabored Podcast #202: The Strike for Black Lives," *Dissent*, July 24, 2020, www.dissentmagazine.org/blog/belabored-podcast-202-the -strike-for-black-lives.

31. Sara Lonardo, "Tens of Thousands in 25+ Cities to Strike for Black Lives," SEIU, July 8, 2020, www.seiu.org/2020/07/tens-of-thousands-in-25-cities-to-strike-for-black-lives.

32. Miranda Matthew, "In Sports and Everywhere Else, Collective Action Can Make Change," *Jacobin*, August 28, 2020, https://jacobinmag.com/2020/08/nba-strike-milwaukee -bucks-jacob-blake.

33. Ira Winderman, "NBA Season Teetering in Wake of Boycott; Heat Playoff Run in Limbo," *Sun Sentinel*, August 26, 2020, www.sun-sentinel.com/sports/miami-heat /fl-sp-miami-heat-second-round-20200826-mgwh4fzqejglfhsuobgfhqzkwa-story.html.

34. Dan Feldman, "Andre Iguodala: 'Capitalism and Racism Go Hand in Hand. And You Can't Have One Without the Other,'" *Yahoo! Sports*, August 28, 2020, https://sports .yahoo.com/andre-iguodala-capitalism-racism-hand-202827233.html.

35. Chris Mannix, "Inside the 48 Hours That Brought Back the 2020 NBA Playoffs," *Sports Illustrated*, August 28, 2020, www.si.com/nba/2020/08/29/players-owners-agreement -successful-protest.

36. Barry Eidlin, "Last Week's Pro Athletes Strikes Could Become Much Bigger Than Sports," *Jacobin*, August 30, 2020, https://jacobinmag.com/2020/08/sports-strikes-kenosha -racial-justice.

37. Aqsa Ahmad, "With Their Wildcat Strike, NBA Players Have Pointed the Way Forward," *Jacobin*, August 29, 2020, https://jacobinmag.com/2020/08/nba-strike -lebron-iguodala-milwaukee-bucks.

38. Kevin Brower Brown, "East Bay Health Care Workers Strike Forces County to Disband the Boss," *Labor Notes*, October 9, 2020, https://labornotes.org/blogs/2020/10 /east-bay-health-care-workers-strike-forces-county-disband-boss.

39. East Bay DSA (@DSAEastBay), "Here's ER nurse, union president & EBDSA member @OaklandNurse…" Twitter, October 7, 2020, 6:32 p.m., https://twitter.com /dsaeastbay/status/1314015884491411457.

40. Alameda County Medical Center, *Alameda County Medical Center Delivery System Reform Incentive Pool Proposal for the California Section 1115 Waiver Demonstration Years Six–Ten*, California Department of Health Care Services, February 18, 2011, www.dhcs .ca.gov/Documents/1_ACMC%20DSRIP%20Proposal.pdf.

41. East Bay DSA (@DSAEastBay), "Here's ER nurse, union president & EBDSA member @OaklandNurse."

42. Brain Rinker, "Nurse Who Posted Picture of Wearing a Trash Bag Instead of PPE Was Fired," *San Francisco Business Times*, April 15, 2020, www.bizjournals .com/sanfrancisco/news/2020/04/15/nurse-who-posted-picture-of-wearing-a-trash-bag .html.

43. Hillary Clinton (@HillaryClinton), "Nurses at Mount Sinai West have resorted to wearing trash bags as protective gear…" Twitter, March 26, 2020, 10:01 a.m., https:// twitter.com/HillaryClinton/status/1243221660058206208.

44. Molly Armstrong (@heyheyitsmollya), "♪ WAP: Workers and Patients ♪ 'Workers out here, on the frontline…'" Twitter, October 30, 12:09 p.m., https://twitter.com /heyheyitsmollya/status/1322209138655391744.

45. Peter Hegarty, "Trustees Who Oversee Alameda County's Public Health Hospitals Fired," *East Bay Times*, October 21, 2020, www.eastbaytimes.com/2020/10/21 /trustees-who-oversee-alameda-countys-public-health-hospitals-ordered-to-resign.

46. Heidi Shierholz, Margaret Poydock, and Celine McNicholas, *Downturn in Strike Activity Reflects COVID-19 Recession but Fails to Capture Many Walkouts for Worker Safety*, Economic Policy Institute, February 19, 2021, www.epi.org/publication/2020-work -stoppage-report/.

47. Randi Weingarten et al., "4 Union Leaders: Coronavirus Is a Stress Test for Capitalism, and We See Encouraging Signs," *USA Today*, April 13, 2020, www.usatoday .com/story/opinion/2020/04/13/coronavirus-income-gap-economic-gains-workers -column/5130977002/.

48. Shierholz, Poydock, and McNicholas, *Downturn in Strike Activity*.

49. "We're NOT All in This Together: Reckless Protest Flaunts Brookfield's White Privilege During Pandemic," *Milwaukee Independent*, April 19, 2020, www.milwaukee independent.com/special/covid-19/not-together-reckless-protest-flaunts-brookfields -white-privilege-pandemic/.

50. Marianne Goodland, "More Than 1,000 Descend on State Capitol to Protest Stay-at-Home Orders," *Colorado Politics*, April 20, 2020, www.coloradopolitics.com /coronavirus/more-than-1-000-descend-on-state-capitol-to-protest-stay-at-home-orders -with/article_acf6b6d8-827c-11ea-9c19-f38265ba9bec.html.

51. Lisa Graves, "Who's Behind the 'Reopen' Protests?," *New York Times*, April 22, 2020, www.nytimes.com/2020/04/22/opinion/coronavirus-protests-astroturf.html; Adam Gabbat, "Thousands of Americans Backed by Rightwing Donors Gear Up for Protests," *Guardian*, April 18, 2020, www.theguardian.com/us-news/2020/apr/18/coronavirus-americans-protest-stay-at-home; City News Service, "San Diegans Plan to Protest Government-Imposed Shutdowns," *CBS8*, April 18, 2020, www.cbs8.com/article/news/local/freedom-rally/509-cffea06c-d18e-4a45-8e8a-517961c6ae5b.

52. "Labor Action Tracker," Cornell ILR School, https://striketracker.ilr.cornell.edu.

53. Michael Sainato, "'They Are Fed Up'; US Labor on the March in 2021 After Years of Decline," *Guardian*, December 21, 2021, www.theguardian.com/us-news/2021/dec/21/labor-organizing-pandemic-decline.

Chapter 4: NSFW: Not Safe for Workers

1. Martha Hostetter and Sarah Klein, "In Focus: How Unions Act as a Force for Change in Health Care Delivery and Payment," *Transforming Care* (blog), Commonwealth Fund, March 21, 2019, www.commonwealthfund.org/publications/2019/mar/focus-how-unions-act-force-change-health-care-delivery-and-payment.

2. Marianne P. Brown, "Labor's Critical Role in Workplace Health and Safety in California and Beyond—As Labor Shifts Priorities, Where Will Health and Safety Sit?," *New Solutions: A Journal of Environmental and Occupational Health Policy* 16, no. 3 (2006): 249–265, https://doi.org/10.2190/3564-11K2-2152-1J22; Sherry L. Baron et al., "Promoting Integrated Approaches to Reducing Health Inequities Among Low-Income Workers: Applying a Social Ecological Framework," *American Journal of Industrial Medicine* 57, no. 5 (2014): 539–556, https://doi.org/10.1002/ajim.22174.

3. Paul Fronstin, "The Impact of the Recession on Employment-Based Health Benefits: The Case of Union Membership," *EBRI Notes* 32, no. 7 (July 2011), http://ssrn.com/abstract=1889285.

4. Beth Malinowski, Meredith Minkler, and Laura Stock, "Labor Unions: A Public Health Institution," *American Journal of Public Health* 105, no. 2 (February 2015): 261, https://doi.org/10.2105/AJPH.2014.302309.

5. Richard B. Freeman and James L. Medoff, *What Do Unions Do?* (New York: Basic Books; 1984); Aaron Sojourner and Jooyoung Yang, "Effects of Union Certification on Workplace-Safety Enforcement: Regression-Discontinuity Evidence," *ILR Review*, September 3, 2020, https://doi.org/10.1177/0019793920953089.

6. Hostetter and Klein, "In Focus: How Unions Act as a Force for Change."

7. Alexander Hertel-Fernandez et al., *Understanding the COVID-19 Workplace: Evidence from a Survey of Essential Workforce*, Roosevelt Institute, June 2020, https://rooseveltinstitute.org/wp-content/uploads/2020/07/RI_SurveyofEssentialWorkers_IssueBrief_202006-1.pdf.

8. M. Keith Chen, Judith A. Chevalier, and Elisa F. Long, "Nursing Home Staff Networks and COVID-19," *Proceedings of the National Academy of Sciences* 118, no. 1 (December 28, 2020), https://doi.org/10.1073/pnas.2015455118; Hertel-Fernandez et

al., *Understanding the COVID-19 Workplace*; Monita Karmakar, Paula M. Lantz, and Renuka Tipirneni, "Association of Social and Demographic Factors with COVID-19 Incidence and Death Rates in the US," *JAMA Network Open* 4, no. 1 (January 29, 2021): e2036462, https://doi.org/10.1001/jamanetworkopen.2020.36462.

9. Sojourner and Yang, "Effects of Union Certification."

10. Chen, Chevalier, and Long, "Nursing Home Staff Networks and COVID-19."

11. Centers for Medicare and Medicaid Services, "COVID-19 Nursing Home Data," March 8, 2022, https://data.cms.gov/covid-19/covid-19-nursing-home-data; "AARP Nursing Home COVID-19 Dashboard," AARP Public Policy Institute, www.aarp.org /ppi/issues/caregiving/info-2020/nursing-home-covid-dashboard.html.

12. Alison C. Roxby et al., "Detection of SARS-CoV-2 Among Residents and Staff Members of an Independent and Assisted Living Community for Older Adults— Seattle, Washington, 2020," *Morbidity and Mortality Weekly Report* 69, no. 14 (April 3, 2020): 416–418, www.cdc.gov/mmwr/volumes/69/wr/mm6914e2.htm; Eric J. Chow et al., "Symptom Screening at Illness Onset of Health Care Personnel with SARS-CoV-2 Infection in King County, Washington," *JAMA* 323, no. 20 (April 17, 2020): 2087–2089, https://doi.org/10.1001/jama.2020.6637; Temet M. McMichael et al., "COVID-19 in a Long-Term Care Facility—King County, Washington, February 27–March 9, 2020," *Morbidity and Mortality Weekly Report* 69, no. 12 (March 27, 2020): 339–342, www.cdc .gov/mmwr/volumes/69/wr/mm6912e1.htm; Emily Mosites et al., "Assessment of SARS-CoV-2 Infection Prevalence in Homeless Shelters—Four U.S. Cities, March 27–April 15, 2020," *Morbidity and Mortality Weekly Report* 69, no. 17 (May 1, 2020): 521–522, www .cdc.gov/mmwr/volumes/69/wr/mm6917e1.htm.

13. Helena Temkin-Greener et al., "COVID-19 Pandemic in Assisted Living Communities: Results from Seven States," *Journal of the American Geriatrics Society* 68, no. 12 (December 2020): 2727–2734, https://doi.org/10.1111/jgs.16850; Mark Aaron Unruh et al., "Nursing Home Characteristics Associated with COVID-19 Deaths in Connecticut, New Jersey, and New York," *Journal of the American Medical Directors Association* 21, no. 7 (July 2020): 1001–1003, https://doi.org/10.1016 /j.jamda.2020.06.019; Hannah R. Abrams et al., "Characteristics of U.S. Nursing Homes with COVID-19 Cases," *Journal of the American Geriatrics Society* 68, no. 8 (August 2020): 1653–1656, https://doi.org/10.1111/jgs.16661; Priya Chidambaram, Tricia Neuman, and Rachel Garfield, *Racial and Ethnic Disparities in COVID-19 Cases and Deaths in Nursing Homes*, Kaiser Family Foundation, October 2020, www.kff.org/coronavirus-COVID-19 /issue-brief/racial-and-ethnic-disparities-in-COVID-19-cases-and-deaths-in-nursing -homes/.

14. Michael L. Barnett and David C. Grabowski, "Nursing Homes Are Ground Zero for COVID-19 Pandemic," *JAMA Health Forum* 1, no. 3 (March 2, 2020): e200369, https://doi.org/10.1001/jamahealthforum.2020.0369.

15. Adam Dean, Atheendar Venkataramani, and Simeon Kimmel, "Mortality Rates from COVID-19 Are Lower in Unionized Nursing Homes," *Health Affairs* 39, no. 11 (September 10, 2020): 1993–2001, https://doi.org/10.1377/hlthaff.2020.01011.

16. Adam Dean, Jamie McCallum, Atheendar Venkataramani, and Simeon Kimmel, "Resident Mortality and Worker Infection Rates from COVID-19 Were Lower in Unionized Nursing Homes in the United States," *Health Affairs* 41, no. 5 (May 2, 2022).

17. Peter S. Goodman, "On the Slaughterhouse Floor, Fear and Anger Remain," *New York Times*, December 19, 2021, www.nytimes.com/2021/12/29/business/meat -factories-covid.html.

18. Occupational Safety and Health Administration, "Accident Detail: Accident: 170354385—Employee Decapitated by Chain of Hide Puller Machine," US Department of Labor, June 22, 1993, www.osha.gov/pls/imis/accidentsearch.accident _detail?id=170354385; Occupational Safety and Health Administration, "Accident Detail: Accident: 881359—Employee's Arm Amputated in Meat Auger," US Department of Labor, April 7, 1995, www.osha.gov/pls/imis/accidentsearch.accident_detail?id=881359; Occupational Safety and Health Administration, "Accident Search Results," US Department of Labor, www.osha.gov/pls/imis/accidentsearch.search?sic=&sicgroup=&naics=&acc _description=&acc_abstract=&acc_keyword=%22Crushed%22&inspnr=&fatal=& officetype=&office=&startmonth=&startday=&startyear=&endmonth=&endday =&endyear=&keyword_list=on&p_start=&p_finish=5080&p_sort=event_date&p _desc=ASC&p_direction=Next&p_show=20; Peter Carlson, "Meat from the Ground Up," *Washington Post*, July 3, 2001, www.washingtonpost.com/archive/lifestyle/2001/07/03 /meat-from-the-ground-up/75e6d104-7ee9-4b13-b237-9fef578ca1b7/.

19. Taylor Telford and Kimberly Kindy, "As They Rushed to Maintain U.S. Meat Supply, Big Processors Saw Plants Become Covid-19 Hot Spots, Worker Illnesses Spike," *Washington Post*, April 25, 2020, www.washingtonpost.com/business/2020/04/25/meat -workers-safety-jbs-smithfield-tyson/.

20. "Robert Klemko and Kimberly Kindy, "About 300 Workers at a Colorado Meat Plant Have Been Infected by the Coronavirus," *Washington Post*, August 6, 2020, www .washingtonpost.com/national/he-fled-the-congo-to-work-in-a-us-meat-plant-then-he --and-hundreds-of-his-co-workers--got-the-coronavirus/2020/08/06/11e7e13e-c526 -11ea-8ffe-372be8d82298_story.html.

21. Dillon Thomas, "'It's a Joke': Family Reacts to $15,000 Fine Against Greeley's JBS Plant," *CBS Denver*, September 13, 2020, https://denver.cbslocal.com/2020/09/13 /saul-sanchez-jbs-greeley-fine-coronavirus/.

22. Danielle Wiener-Bronner, "Managers at Tyson Meat Plant Had Betting Pool on How Many Workers Would Get COVID-19, Lawsuit Alleges," CNN, November 19, 2020, www.cnn.com/2020/11/19/business/tyson-coronavirus-lawsuit/index.html.

23. Tina L. Saitone, K. Aleks Schaefer, and Daniel P. Scheitrum, "COVID-19 Morbidity and Mortality in U.S. Meatpacking Counties," *Food Policy* 101 (May 2021): 102072, https://doi.org/10.1016/j.foodpol.2021.102072.

24. Leah Douglas, "Mapping Covid-19 Outbreaks in the Food System," *Food and Environment Reporting Network*, April 22, 2020, https://thefern.org/2020/04/mapping -COVID-19-in-meat-and-food-processing-plants/.

25. Bridget Huber, "How Did Europe Avoid the COVID-19 Catastrophe Ravaging US Meatpacking Plants?," *Mother Jones*, June 13, 2020, www.motherjones.com/food /2020/06/meatpacking-plants-covid-hotspots-europe-regulations-line-speed/.

26. Colin Gordon, "The Coronavirus Wouldn't Be Decimating Meatpacking Plants If Company Bosses Hadn't Busted the Unions," *Jacobin*, May 18, 2020, https://jacobinmag .com/2020/05/iowa-upwa-meat-processing-unons-packinghouse-coronavirus.

27. Daniel Calamuci, "Return to the Jungle: The Rise and Fall of Meatpacking Work," *New Labor Forum* 17, no. 1 (Spring 2008): 66–77.

28. Calamuci, "Return to the Jungle."

29. In 1943, aided by the New Deal's National Labor Relations Act, the Congress of Industrial Organizations (CIO) incorporated PWOC as the United Packinghouse Workers of America (UPWA).

30. Calamuci, "Return to the Jungle."

31. Gordon, "The Coronavirus Wouldn't Be Decimating Meatpacking Plants."

32. Gordon, "The Coronavirus Wouldn't Be Decimating Meatpacking Plants."

33. Gordon, "The Coronavirus Wouldn't Be Decimating Meatpacking Plants."

34. "Meat Processing," America's Concentration Crisis, Open Markets Institute, accessed September 10, 2021, https://concentrationcrisis.openmarketsinstitute.org/industry/meat-processing/.

35. Romain Espinosa, Damian Tago, and Nicolas Treich, "Infectious Diseases and Meat Production," *Environmental & Resource Economics* 76 (August 2020): 1–26, https://doi.org/10.1007/s10640-020-00484-3.

36. Annelise Orleck, "Rose Schneiderman: April 16, 1882–August 11, 1972," *Shalvi/Hyman Encyclopedia of Jewish Women*, Jewish Women's Archive, https://jwa.org/encyclopedia/article/schneiderman-rose.

37. American Chemical Society, *Alice Hamilton and the Development of Occupational Medicine* (Washington, DC: American Chemical Society, September 21, 2002), www.acs.org/content/acs/en/education/whatischemistry/landmarks/alicehamilton.html.

38. Leon C. Prieto et al, "Schneiderman, Perkins, and the Early Labor Movement: An Ethic of Care Approach to Labor and Safety Reform," *Journal of Management History* 22, no. 1 (January 1, 2016): 50–72, https://doi.org/10.1108/JMH-01-2015-0003.

39. American Chemical Society, *Alice Hamilton and the Development of Occupational Medicine*.

40. Deborah Berkowitz, "OSHA Enforcement Activity Declines Under the Trump Administration," *National Employment Law Project*, June 11, 2018, www.nelp.org/publication/osha-enforcement-activity-declines-trump-administration/.

41. Occupational Safety and Health Administration, *Guidance on Preparing Workplaces for an Influenza Pandemic*, US Department of Labor, 2009, www.osha.gov/sites/default/files/publications/OSHA3327pandemic.pdf.

42. W. P. Hanage et al., "COVID-19: US Federal Accountability for Entry, Spread, and Inequities," *Harvard Center for Population and Development Studies Working Paper* 20, no. 2 (October 5, 2020), https://cdn1.sph.harvard.edu/wp-content/uploads/sites/1266/2020/10/20_covid-19_federal-response_FINAL_for-HCPDS_1001_HCPDS-working-paper_volume-20_number-2_FINAL.pdf.

43. US Department of Labor, *COVID-19: Increased Worksite Complaints and Reduced OSHA Inspections Leave U.S. Workers' Safety at Increased Risk*, February 25, 2021, www.oig.dol.gov/public/reports/oa/2021/19-21-003-10-105.pdf.

44. Chris Kirkham, "Special Report—U.S. Regulators Ignored Workers' COVID-19 Safety Complaints amid Deadly Outbreaks," Reuters, January 6, 2021, www.reuters

.com/business/healthcare-pharmaceuticals/special-report-us-regulators-ignored-workers
-COVID-19-safety-complaints-amid-2021-01-06/.

45. US Department of Labor, *COVID-19: Increased Worksite Complaints.*

46. Eli Rosenberg, "Meatpacking Workers File Lawsuit Against OSHA, Accusing
Agency of Failing to Keep Them Safe," *Washington Post*, July 24, 2020, www.washingtonpost
.com/business/2020/07/23/lawsuit-osha-safety-coronavirus/.

47. W. P. Hanage et al., "COVID-19: US Federal Accountability."

48. Deborah Berkowitz and Shayla Thompson, "OSHA Must Protect COVID Whistleblowers Who File Retaliation Complaints," National Employment Law Project, October 8, 2020, www.nelp.org/publication/osha-failed-protect-whistleblowers-filed-covid
-retaliation-complaints/.

49. Taylor Telford, "Democrat Accuses OSHA of Being 'Invisible' While Infections
Rise Among Essential Workers," *Washington Post*, June 14, 2020, www.washingtonpost
.com/business/2020/05/28/workers-safety-osha-coronavirus/.

50. Deborah Berkowitz, "Report: Number of Federal Workplace Safety Inspectors
Falls to 45-Year Low," National Employment Law Project, April 28, 2020, www.nelp.org
/news-releases/number-federal-workplace-safety-inspectors-falls-45-year-low/.

51. Elayne K. Phillips, Mark R. Conaway, and Janine C. Jagger, "Percutaneous Injuries
Before and After the Needlestick Safety and Prevention Act," *New England Journal of Medicine* 366, no. 7 (February 16, 2012): 670–671, https://doi.org/10.1056/NEJMc1110979;
Centers for Disease Control and Prevention, *Surveillance for Viral Hepatitis—United States,
2017*, November 18, 2020, www.cdc.gov/hepatitis/statistics/2017surveillance/index.htm.

52. Clark Kauffman, "Reynolds: We Can't Prioritize Iowans' Lives over Their Livelihoods," *Iowa Capital Dispatch*, May 26, 2020, https://iowacapitaldispatch.com/2020
/05/26/reynolds-we-cant-prioritize-iowans-lives-over-their-livelihoods/.

53. Adam Dean et al., "Iowa School Districts Were More Likely to Adopt COVID-19
Mask Mandates Where Teachers Were Unionized," *Health Affairs* 40, no. 8 (August
2021), https://doi.org/10.1377/hlthaff.2020.02518.

54. Jenna Gettings, "Mask Use and Ventilation Improvements to Reduce COVID-19
Incidence in Elementary Schools—Georgia, November 16–December 11, 2020," *Morbidity
and Mortality Weekly Report* 70, no. 21 (May 28, 2021): 779–784, https://doi.org/10.15585
/mmwr.mm7021e1; Helena B. Stage et al., "Shut and Re-Open: The Role of Schools in the
Spread of COVID-19 in Europe," *Philosophical Transactions of the Royal Society B: Biological
Sciences* 376, no. 1829 (July 19, 2021): 20200277, https://doi.org/10.1098/rstb.2020.0277.

55. Betsy Long, "LA Teachers Won a Safe Schools Reopening by Organizing," *Jacobin*,
April 4, 2021, https://jacobinmag.com/2021/04/la-teachers-los-angeles-school-reopening
-covid.

56. City News Service, "LA Teachers' Union Overwhelmingly Approves Plan to Return
to Classrooms," *NBC Los Angeles*, March 21, 2021, www.nbclosangeles.com/news/local
/la-teachers-union-overwhelming-approves-plan-to-return-to-classrooms/2555681/.

57. Jamie McCallum, "Getting the Common Goods," *Jacobin*, August 11, 2018, https://
jacobinmag.com/2018/08/north-carolina-teacher-union-strike-education-schools.

58. Grace Hamilton, "'Random' Searches Criminalize Students and Don't Make
Schools Safer," *UTLA*, October 20, 2017, www.utla.net/news/random-searches-criminalize
-students-and-dont-make-schools-safer.

59. "Guidance for COVID-19 Prevention in K-12 Schools," Centers for Disease Control and Prevention, accessed November 15, 2021, www.cdc.gov/coronavirus/2019 -ncov/community/schools-childcare/k-12-guidance.html; "COVID-19 Guidance for Safe Schools and Promotion of In-Person Learning," American Academy of Pediatrics, accessed November 15, 2021, www.aap.org/en/pages/2019-novel-coronavirus-covid-19-infections /clinical-guidance/covid-19-planning-considerations-return-to-in-person-education -in-schools/.

60. Brian Lopez, "Gov. Greg Abbott's Order Banning Mask Mandates in Texas Schools Faces Lawsuit, Defiance by Big-City Districts," *Texas Tribune*, August 9, 2021, www.texastribune.org/2021/08/09/texas-mask-order-schools/; María Méndez, "Austin ISD to Mandate Masks in Defiance of Gov. Greg Abbott," *Austin American-Statesman*, August 9, 2021, www.statesman.com/story/news/2021/08/09/austin-isd-issues-mask -mandate-defiance-texas-gov-greg-abbott/5545692001/; Jason Miles, "HISD Superin-tendent Stands by Decision to Implement Mask Mandate," *KHOU 11*, August 6, 2021, www.khou.com/article/news/education/hisd-superintendent-backs-mask-mandate/285 -5c96f120-4df8-4ed4-9659-f29e5e3bbb12.

61. Eliza Shapiro and Shawn Hubler, "If Teachers Get the Vaccine Quickly, Can Stu-dents Get Back to School?," *New York Times*, December 15, 2020, www.nytimes.com /2020/12/15/us/teachers-vaccine-school.html.

62. 1199SEIU Healthcare Workers (@1999SEIU), "Today, we're at NY-Presby's main campus rallying for them to hear our members voices! Educate, not mandate vaccines!," Twitter, July 22, 2021, 12:29 p.m., https://twitter.com/1199seiu/status/14182469370 19666434.

63. Rachel Siegel et al., "Millions of Workers, Businesses to Face Biden's New Coronavirus Vaccine and Testing Rules," *Washington Post*, September 10, 2021, www .washingtonpost.com/business/2021/09/10/biden-vaccine-mandate-workers-businesses/.

64. Todd E. Vachon and Michael Wallace, "Unions, Democracy, and Trump: Deconstructing the COVID-19 Vaccination Crisis of 2021," White Paper #7504, Rutgers Labor Education Action Research Network.

65. Stephen Buranyi, "Big Pharma Did Not Save the Day," *Prospect Magazine*, March 29, 2021, www.prospectmagazine.co.uk/politics/big-pharma-covid-19-vaccine-uk-revenue -stephen-buranyi; Luke Savage, "Bill Gates Chooses Corporate Patent Rights over Hu-man Lives," *Jacobin*, April 26, 2021, https://jacobinmag.com/2021/04/bill-gates-vaccines -intellectual-property-covid-patents.

66. Isaac Arnsdorf, "A Major Medical Staffing Company Just Slashed Benefits for Doctors and Nurses Fighting Coronavirus," *ProPublica*, March 31, 2020, www.propublica .org/article/coronavirus-er-doctors-nurses-benefits?token=x1WkMVQkYc7NIixUj9O EexcAEo4anmm4.

67. David Michaels and Jordan Barab, "OSHA Can Do More to Protect Americans from Covid-19," *New York Times*, January 14, 2022, www.nytimes.com/2022/01/14/opinion /supreme-court-vaccine-mandate-osha.html.

68. Benjamin C. Amick et al., "Protecting Construction Worker Health and Safety in Ontario, Canada: Identifying a Union Safety Effect," *Journal of Occupational & En-vironmental Medicine* 57, no. 12 (December 2015): 1337–1342, https://doi.org/10.1097 /JOM.0000000000000562.

69. Michael Zoorob, "Does 'Right to Work' Imperil the Right to Health? The Effect of Labour Unions on Workplace Fatalities," *Occupational and Environmental Medicine* 75, no. 10 (September 13, 2018): 736–738, https://doi.org/10.1136/oemed-2017-104747.

70. Jamie McCallum and Adam Dean, "Strong Teachers Unions and School Mask Mandates Go Together, Our Research Finds," *Washington Post*, August 20, 2021, www.washingtonpost.com/politics/2021/08/20/strong-teachers-unions-school-mask-mandates-go-together-our-research-finds/.

Chapter 5: Quitter's Paradise

1. James Freeman, "Worst Worker Shortage Ever," *Wall Street Journal*, May 6, 2021, www.wsj.com/articles/worst-worker-shortage-ever-11620319253.

2. Daniel Costa, *The H-2B Temporary Foreign Worker Program: For Labor Shortages or Cheap, Temporary Labor?*, Economic Policy Institute, January 19, 2016, www.epi.org/publication/h2b-temporary-foreign-worker-program-for-labor-shortages-or-cheap-temporary-labor/.

3. Daniel Costa, "Claims of Labor Shortages in H-2B Industries Don't Hold Up to Scrutiny: President Biden Should Not Expand a Flawed Temporary Work Visa Program," *Working Economics Blog*, Economic Policy Institute, March 9, 2021, www.epi.org/blog/claims-of-labor-shortages-in-h-2b-industries-dont-hold-up-to-scrutiny/.

4. Costa, "Claims of Labor Shortages in H-2B Industries."

5. Costa, "Claims of Labor Shortages in H-2B Industries."

6. Christine Murray, "Mexican Seafood Workers Fight Back Over U.S. Coronavirus Sacking," Reuters, June 16, 2020, www.reuters.com/article/us-usa-mexico-migrants-trfn-idUSKBN23N2MF.

7. Justin Baragona (@justinbaragona), "Laura Ingraham: 'What if we just cut off the unemployment? Hunger is a pretty powerful thing.' …" Twitter, August 12, 2021, 11:05 p.m., https://twitter.com/justinbaragona/status/1426017141724270597.

8. Christopher Rugaber and Casey Smith, "States That Cut Off of Jobless Aid See No Surge of Job Seekers," *PBS NewsHour*, October 22, 2021, www.pbs.org/newshour/economy/states-that-cutoff-of-jobless-aid-see-no-surge-of-job-seekers.

9. Jelisa Castrodale, "Diners Are Tipping Less Than They Did Before the Pandemic, Data Shows," *Food and Wine*, February 28, 2022, www.foodandwine.com/news/restaurant-tipping-rates-decline-pandemic.

10. "Act Memo: 2017 Wisconsin Act 11 [2017 Assembly Bill 25] Child Labor Law Modifications," Wisconsin Legislative Council, July 6, 2017, https://docs.legis.wisconsin.gov/2017/related/lcactmemo/act011.pdf.

11. Zahra Tayeb, "An Arkansas Restaurant Boss Is Paying His Teen Workers to Do Their Homework Before Their Shifts, in an Attempt to Retain Them During the Labor Shortage," *Yahoo News*, October 17, 2021, https://news.yahoo.com/restaurant-owner-paying-teen-workers-090842434.html.

12. Christian Spencer, "As Hiring Shortages Spread, Child Labor Laws Are Under Attack," *The Hill*, November 2, 2021, https://thehill.com/changing-america/respect/diversity-inclusion/579623-as-hiring-shortages-spread-child-labor-laws-are.

13. Noah Lanard, "You Don't Need to Freak Out About Labor Shortages," *Mother Jones*, May 18, 2021, www.motherjones.com/politics/2021/05/you-dont-need-to-freak-out-about-labor-shortages/.

14. Ioana Elena Marinescu, Daphné Skandalis, and Daniel Zhao, "Job Search, Job Posting and Unemployment Insurance During the COVID-19 Crisis," SSRN, July 30, 2020, http://dx.doi.org/10.2139/ssrn.3664265.

15. One Fair Wage and UC Berkeley Food Labor Research Center, *It's a Wage Shortage, Not a Worker Shortage: Why Restaurant Workers, Particularly Mothers, Are Leaving the Industry, and What Would Make Them Stay*, May 2021, https://onefairwage.site/wp-content/uploads/2021/05/OFW_WageShortage_F.pdf.

16. Derek Thompson, "The Great Resignation Is Accelerating," *The Atlantic*, October 15, 2021, www.theatlantic.com/ideas/archive/2021/10/great-resignation-accelerating/620382/; Josh Eidelson, "'Suicide Shifts,' 7-Day Weeks Fuel Rare Flare-Up in U.S. Strikes," *Bloomberg*, October 25, 2021, www.bloomberg.com/news/articles/2021-10-25/-suicide-shifts-7-day-weeks-fuel-rare-flare-up-in-u-s-strikes.

17. Taylor Nicole Rogers, "Reddit 'Antiwork' Forum Booms as Millions of Americans Quit Jobs," *Financial Times*, January 9, 2022, www.ft.com/content/1270ee18-3ee0-4939-98a8-c4f40940e644.

18. Kim Parker, Ruth Igielnik, and Rakesh Kochhar, "Unemployed Americans Are Feeling the Emotional Strain of Job Loss; Most Have Considered Changing Occupations," Fact Tank (blog), Pew Research Center, February 10, 2021, www.pewresearch.org/fact-tank/2021/02/10/unemployed-americans-are-feeling-the-emotional-strain-of-job-loss-most-have-considered-changing-occupations/.

19. Christina Pazzanese, "'I Quit' Is All the Rage. Blip or Sea Change?," *Harvard Gazette*, October 20, 2021, https://news.harvard.edu/gazette/story/2021/10/harvard-economist-sheds-light-on-great-resignation/.

20. Julia Raifman, Alexandra Skinner, and Aaron Sojourner, "The Unequal Toll of COVID-19 on Workers," *Working Economics Blog*, Economic Policy Institute, February 7, 2022, www.epi.org/blog/the-unequal-toll-of-covid-19-on-workers/.

21. Steven Jessen-Howard, Rasheed Malik, and MK Falgout, *Costly and Unavailable: America Lacks Sufficient Child Care Supply for Infants and Toddlers*, Center for American Progress, August 4, 2020, www.americanprogress.org/article/costly-unavailable-america-lacks-sufficient-child-care-supply-infants-toddlers/; "Child Care Sector Jobs: BLS Analysis," Center for the Study of Child Care Employment, November 8, 2021, https://cscce.berkeley.edu/child-care-sector-jobs-bls-analysis/.

22. *A Year of Strength & Loss: The Pandemic, the Economy, & the Value of Women's Work*, National Women's Law Center, March 2021, https://nwlc.org/wp-content/uploads/2021/03/Final_NWLC_Press_CovidStats_updated.pdf.

23. "Labor Force Participation Rate—Women," FRED Economic Data, August 6, 2021, https://fred.stlouisfed.org/series/LNS11300002.

24. Caitlyn Collins et al., "The Gendered Consequences of a Weak Infrastructure of Care: School Reopening Plans and Parents' Employment During the COVID-19 Pandemic," *Gender & Society* 35, no. 2 (April 2021): 180–193, https://doi.org/10.1177/08912432211001300.

25. Rasheed Malik, *Working Families Are Spending Big Money on Child Care*, Center for American Progress, June 20, 2019, www.americanprogress.org/article/working-families-spending-big-money-child-care/.

26. Jason Norlock and Matthew Stevenson, *Health Workforce 2025, Part II: Trends in the Healthcare Workforce*, Health Wealth Center, Mercer, 2016, www.imercer.com/uploads/Global/us%20healthcare%20report%20five%20states.pdf?WT.mc_id=A000436.

27. Public Health Institution, *New York City's Direct Care Workforce*, 2020, https://phinational.org/resource/new-york-citys-direct-care-workforce/.

28. Isaac Jabola-Carolus, Ilana Berger, and Julia Solow, *Essential but Undervalued: Understanding the Home Care Workforce Shortage in the Hudson Valley*, Hand in Hand: Domestic Employers Network, July 2020, https://domesticemployers.org/wp-content/uploads/2020/07/Hudson-Valley-Home-Care-Shortage-Report-10pt-1.pdf.

29. Isaac Jabola-Carolus, Stephanie Luce, and Ruth Milkman, *The Case for Public Investment in Higher Pay for New York State Home Care Workers: Estimated Costs and Savings*, Publications and Research, Graduate Center, City University of New York, March 1, 2021, https://academicworks.cuny.edu/gc_pubs/682.

30. Unemployed Action (@unemployedact), "'They ended our unemployment in June and I have put in 187 applications and resumes with 0 call backs,'" Twitter, August 29, 2021, 10:52 a.m., https://twitter.com/unemployedact/status/1431993199208189959.

31. Unemployed Action (@unemployedact), "'I've been hustling freelance jobs that pay crappy and applying for literally hundreds of jobs on LinkedIn, ZipRecruiter, Indeed...'" Twitter, August 29, 2021, 10:52 a.m., https://twitter.com/unemployedact/status/1431993200999211017.

32. Unemployed Action (@unemployedact), "'I am beyond frustrated. I used to be able to quickly land an Accounting / Bookkeeping/ Office Manager position..now I need a degree?...'" Twitter, August 29, 2021, 10:52 a.m., https://twitter.com/unemployedact/status/1431993201934491656.

33. Unemployed Action (@unemployedact), "'I had my first interview today after a year applying everywhere. unfortunately it's only part time...'" Twitter, September 2, 2021, 12:23 p.m., https://twitter.com/unemployedact/status/1433465674383327233.

34. Danny Lucia, "The Unemployed Movements of the 1930s: Bringing Misery Out of Hiding," *International Socialist Review* 71 (May 2010), https://isreview.org/issue/71/unemployed-movements-1930s/; Gordon Black, "Chapter 3: Organizing the Unemployed: The Early 1930s," *Communism in Washington State: History and Memory Project*, University of Washington, 2002, https://depts.washington.edu/labhist/cpproject/black.shtml.

35. Al Richmond, *A Long View from the Left: Memoirs of an American Revolutionary* (New York: Dell Publishing, 1975).

36. "Strike Ends at Largest U.S. Wholesale Produce Market," *New York Times*, January 22, 2021, www.nytimes.com/2021/01/22/nyregion/hunts-point-strike.html.

37. James O'Toole et al., *Work in America: Report of a Special Task Force to the Secretary of Health, Education, and Welfare*, Department of Health, Education, and Welfare Special Task Force on Work in America, December 1972, https://files.eric.ed.gov/fulltext/ED070738.pdf.

38. Jamie K. McCallum, *Worked Over: How Round-the-Clock Work Is Killing the American Dream* (New York: Basic Books, 2020).

39. Eidelson, "'Suicide Shifts,' 7-Day Weeks Fuel Rare Flare-Up."

40. Alex Press, "Workers at One of the Country's Biggest Bourbon Producers Have Been on Strike for a Month," *Jacobin*, October 14, 2021, https://jacobinmag.com/2021/10/heaven-hill-kentucky-bourbon-workers-strike-overtime-scheduling.

41. Gilbert Baez, "'These Wheels Will Not Move': Cumberland County Bus Drivers Pledge to Continue 'Sick out' Until Pay Increases," *WRAL*, November 9, 2021, www.wral.com/dozens-of-cumberland-county-school-bus-drivers-rally-to-demand-better-pay/19968878/?version=amp.

42. Kim Moody, "The Supply Chain Disruption Arrives 'Just in Time,'" *Labor Notes*, December 6, 2021, https://labornotes.org/2021/12/supply-chain-disruption-arrives-just-time.

43. Kim Moody, "Payback Time: Class Struggle Beckons the Left in 2022," *Spectre Journal*, February 16, 2022, https://spectrejournal.com/payback-time/.

44. Tyler Jett, "United Auto Workers Members Reject Second John Deere Contract Proposal, Strike Continues," *USA Today*, November 3, 2021, www.usatoday.com/story/news/nation/2021/11/03/john-deere-strike-iowa-continues-after-uaw-reject-second-contract/6263938001/; Molly Osberg, "More Than 30,000 Health Care Workers Are on the Verge of Striking," *New Republic*, November 8, 2021, https://newrepublic.com/article/164297/kaiser-permanente-nurses-union-strike.

45. Eidelson, "'Suicide Shifts,' 7-Day Weeks Fuel Rare Flare-Up."

46. Moody, "Payback Time: Class Struggle Beckons the Left in 2022."

Chapter 6: Risky Business

1. US Department of Labor, Occupational Safety and Health Administration, *Notice of Alleged Safety and Health Hazards*, March 31, 2020, www.afge.org/globalassets/documents/generalreports/coronavirus/4/osha-form-7-national-complaint.pdf.

2. WTVR CBS 6 News, "President Trump: "We are all in this together, and we'll come through…" Facebook, March 18, 2020, www.facebook.com/CBS6News/videos/president-trump-we-are-all-in-this-together-and-well-come-through-together/623850621801214/.

3. Daniel Schneider and Kristen Harknett, *Essential and Unprotected: COVID-19-Related Health and Safety Procedures for Service-Sector Workers*, The Shift Project, May 7, 2020, https://shift.hks.harvard.edu/essential-and-unprotected-covid-19-related-health-and-safety-procedures-for-service-sector-workers/.

4. Arlie Russell Hochschild, *Strangers in Their Own Land: Anger and Mourning on the American Right* (New York: The New Press, 2018); Heather Rogers, "Erasing Mossville: How Pollution Killed a Louisiana Town," *The Intercept*, November 5, 2015, https://theintercept.com/2015/11/04/erasing-mossville-how-pollution-killed-a-louisiana-town/.

5. David Leonhardt, "The Shrinking Safety Net," *New York Times*, October 29, 2006, www.nytimes.com/2006/10/29/books/review/Leonhardt.t.html.

6. Aaron E Carroll, "The Real Reason the U.S. Has Employer-Sponsored Health Insurance," *New York Times*, September 5, 2017, www.nytimes.com/2017/09/05/upshot

/the-real-reason-the-us-has-employer-sponsored-health-insurance.html; Joshua Shakin, "Tax Expenditures," Congressional Budget Office, March 17, 2017, www.cbo.gov/publication /52493.

7. Matthew Rae et al., *Long-Term Trends in Employer-Based Coverage*, Peterson-KFF Health System Tracker, April 3, 2020, www.healthsystemtracker.org/brief/long-term -trends-in-employer-based-coverage/.

8. David Blumenthal, "The Decline of Employer-Sponsored Health Insurance," *Commonwealth Fund Blog*, Commonwealth Fund, December 5, 2017, www.commonwealthfund .org/blog/2017/decline-employer-sponsored-health-insurance.

9. David Blumenthal, Lovisa Gustafsson, and Shawn Bishop, "To Control Health Care Costs, U.S. Employers Should Form Purchasing Alliances," *Harvard Business Review*, November 2, 2018, https://hbr.org/2018/11/to-control-health-care-costs-u-s-employers -should-form-purchasing-alliances.

10. Sara R. Collins, Munira Z. Gunja, and Michelle M. Doty, *Does Coverage Protect Consumers from Health Care Costs?*, Commonwealth Fund, October 18, 2017, www .commonwealthfund.org/publications/issue-briefs/2017/oct/how-well-does-insurance -coverage-protect-consumers-health-care.

11. Collins, Gunja, and Doty, *Does Coverage Protect Consumers*.

12. David Blumenthal, "The Decline of Employer-Sponsored Health Insurance," *Commonwealth Fund Blog*, Commonwealth Fund, December 5, 2017, www.commonwealthfund .org/blog/2017/decline-employer-sponsored-health-insurance.

13. Peter S. Arno and Philip Caper, "Medicare for All: The Social Transformation of US Health Care," *Health Affairs*, March 25, 2020, www.healthaffairs.org/do/10.1377 /forefront.20200319.920962/full/; Sara R. Collins, Herman K. Bhupal, and Michelle M. Doty, *Health Insurance Coverage Eight Years After the ACA: Fewer Uninsured Americans and Shorter Coverage Gaps, but More Underinsured*, Commonwealth Fund, February 2019, www.commonwealthfund.org/sites/default/files/2019-02/EMBARGOED_Collins _hlt_ins_coverage_8_years_after_ACA_2018_biennial_survey_sb_v4.pdf.

14. Blumenthal, Gustafsson, and Bishop, "To Control Health Care Costs."

15. Daniel McDermott et al., "How Has the Pandemic Affected Health Coverage in the U.S.?," *Policy Watch*, Kaiser Family Foundation, December 9, 2020, www.kff.org /policy-watch/how-has-the-pandemic-affected-health-coverage-in-the-u-s/.

16. David U. Himmelstein and Steffie Woolhandler, "Public Health's Falling Share of US Health Spending," *American Journal of Public Health* 106, no. 1 (January 2016): 56–57, https://doi.org/10.2105/AJPH.2015.302908.

17. "Table 89. Hospitals, Beds, and Occupancy Rates, by Type of Ownership and Size of Hospital: United States, Selected Years 1975–2015," CDC, 1980, www.cdc.gov/nchs /data/hus/2017/089.pdf; "Fast Facts on U.S. Hospitals, 2021," American Hospital Association, January 2021, www.aha.org/system/files/media/file/2021/01/Fast-Facts-2021 -table-FY19-data-14jan21.pdf.

18. CDC, "Table 89. Hospitals, Beds, and Occupancy Rates"; American Hospital Association, "Fast Facts on U.S. Hospitals, 2021."

19. "Health Equipment—Hospital Beds," OECD Data, OECD, 2021, http://data .oecd.org/healtheqt/hospital-beds.htm.

20. Geoffrey French et al., "Impact of Hospital Strain on Excess Deaths During the COVID-19 Pandemic—United States, July 2020–July 2021," *Morbidity and Mortality Weekly Report* 70, no. 46 (November 19, 2021): 1613–1616, http://dx.doi.org/10.15585 /mmwr.mm7046a5external icon.

21. National Nurses United, "Press Release: New Survey of Nurses Provides Frontline Proof of Widespread Employer, Government Disregard for Nurse and Patient Safety, Mainly Through Lack of Optimal PPE," press release, May 20, 2020, www .nationalnursesunited.org/press/new-survey-results.

22. "In Memoriam: Healthcare Workers Who Have Died of COVID-19," *Medscape Medical News*, April 1, 2020, www.medscape.com/viewarticle/927976#vp_1.

23. Cristina Carias et al., "Potential Demand for Respirators and Surgical Masks During a Hypothetical Influenza Pandemic in the United States," *Clinical Infectious Diseases* 60, issue suppl1 (May 2015): S42–S51, https://doi.org/10.1093/cid/civ141.

24. Mike Davis, "How a Pandemic Happens: We Knew This Was Coming," *Literary Hub*, May 18, 2020, https://lithub.com/how-a-pandemic-happens-we-knew-this-was -coming/; Jon Swaine, "Federal Government Spent Millions to Ramp Up Mask Readiness but That Isn't Helping Now," *Washington Post*, April 3, 2020, www.washingtonpost.com /investigations/federal-government-spent-millions-to-ramp-up-mask-readiness-but-that -isnt-helping-now/2020/04/03/d62dda5c-74fa-11ea-a9bd-9f8b593300d0_story.html.

25. Yea-Hung Chen et al., "Excess Mortality Associated with the COVID-19 Pandemic Among Californians 18–65 Years of Age, by Occupational Sector and Occupation: March Through October 2020," medRxiv, January 22, 2021, https://doi.org/10.1101/20 21.01.21.21250266.

26. Liz Hamel et al., "KFF COVID-19 Vaccine Monitor: June 2021," Kaiser Family Foundation, June 30, 2021, www.kff.org/coronavirus-covid-19/poll-finding/kff-covid -19-vaccine-monitor-june-2021/.

27. Samantha Artiga and Liz Hamel, "How Employer Actions Could Facilitate Equity in COVID-19 Vaccinations," *Policy Watch* (blog), Kaiser Family Foundation, May 17, 2021, www.kff.org/policy-watch/how-employer-actions-could-facilitate-equity-in-covid-19 -vaccinations/.

28. Jennifer Cohen and Yana van der Meulen Rodgers, "Contributing Factors to Personal Protective Equipment Shortages During the COVID-19 Pandemic," *Preventive Medicine* 141 (December 2020): 106263, https://doi.org/10.1016/j.ypmed.2020 .106263.

29. Job Quality Index, *The U.S. Private Sector Job Quality Index (JQI) July 2021*, JQI IP Holdings LLC, August 6, 2021, https://d3n8a8pro7vhmx.cloudfront.net/prosperous america/pages/5527/attachments/original/1628257718/JQI_Report_-_July_2021.pdf ?1628257718.

30. David Weil, *The Fissured Workplace: Why Work Became So Bad for So Many and What Can Be Done to Improve It* (Cambridge, MA: Harvard University Press, 2017).

31. David Weil, "Enforcing Labour Standards in Fissured Workplaces: The US Experience," *Economic and Labour Relations Review* 22, no. 2 (July 2011): 33–54, https://doi .org/10.1177/103530461102200203.

32. Weil, "Enforcing Labour Standards in Fissured Workplaces."

33. NTT, "NTT Shows the Value of Smart Sourcing to Businesses," press release, May 6, 2020, https://hello.global.ntt/en-us/newsroom/new-research-from-ntt-ltd-underlines-the-value-of-smart-sourcing.

34. Jon Marcus, "More Colleges and Universities Outsource Services to For-Profit Companies," *Washington Post*, January 8, 2021, www.washingtonpost.com/local/education/colleges-outsourcing-services/2021/01/07/c3f2ac6a-5135-11eb-bda4-615aaefd0555_story.html; Christina M. Jordan, "Outsourcing Legal Services During Covid-19 Pandemic," *Litigation News*, American Bar Association, June 27, 2021, www.americanbar.org/groups/litigation/publications/litigation-news/technology/outsourcing-legal-services-during-covid19-pandemic/; John Schieszer, "Medical Billing Outsourcing Is on the Rise," *Renal and Urology News*, September 28, 2021, www.renalandurologynews.com/home/departments/practice-management/medical-billing-outsourcing-can-have-financial-benefits-for-health-care-practices/.

35. Dominic Gates, "Boeing Outsourcing 600 IT Jobs to Dell," *Seattle Times*, February 3, 2021, www.seattletimes.com/business/boeing-aerospace/boeing-outsourcing-600-it-jobs-to-dell/; Tracy Rucinski and Sanjana Shivdas, "United Airlines to Outsource Catering Operations from October," Reuters, July 29, 2021, www.reuters.com/business/aerospace-defense/united-airlines-outsource-catering-operations-october-2021-07-29/.

36. Suhauna Hussain, Johana Bhuiyan, and Ryan Menezes, "How Uber and Lyft Persuaded California to Vote Their Way," *Los Angeles Times*, November 13, 2020, www.latimes.com/business/technology/story/2020-11-13/how-uber-lyft-doordash-won-proposition-22.

37. Eve Batey, "Eater Readers Overwhelmingly Oppose Prop 22," *Eater SF*, November 2, 2020, https://sf.eater.com/2020/11/2/21546110/doordash-uber-prop-22-election-2020-polling; Alex N. Press, "With Prop 22's Passage in California, Tech Companies Are Just Writing Their Own Laws Now," *Jacobin*, November 5, 2020, https://jacobinmag.com/2020/11/proposition-22-california-uber-lyft-gig-employee.

38. George Skelton, "It's No Wonder Hundreds of Millions Have Been Spent on Prop. 22. A Lot Is at Stake," *Los Angeles Times*, October 16, 2020, www.latimes.com/california/story/2020-10-16/skelton-proposition-22-uber-lyft-independent-contractors.

39. Sam Harnett, "Prop. 22 Explained: Why Gig Companies Are Spending Huge Money on an Unprecedented Measure," KQED, October 26, 2020, www.kqed.org/news/11843123/prop-22-explained-why-gig-companies-are-spending-huge-money-on-an-unprecedented-measure.

40. Alexander Sammon, "Prop 22 Is Here, and It's Already Worse Than Expected," *American Prospect*, January 15, 2021, https://prospect.org/api/content/2967b920-56ac-11eb-904a-1244d5f7c7c6/.

41. Don Seiffert, "Uber-Backed Group Says Prop 22 Ruling Won't Affect Mass. Ballot Drive," *Boston Business Journal*, August 22, 2021, www.bizjournals.com/boston/news/2021/08/22/uber-backed-group-massachusetts-prop-22-ruling.html; Nate Raymond, "Companies-Backed Massachusetts Gig Worker Ballot Measure Clears Key Hurdle," Reuters, September 1, 2021, www.reuters.com/world/us/companies-backed-massachusetts-gig-worker-ballot-measure-clears-key-hurdle-2021-09-01/; Alex N. Press, "Gig Companies Are Bringing the Disastrous Prop 22 to a State Near You," *Jacobin*, August 16, 2021, https://jacobinmag.com/2021/08/gig-tech-companies-rideshare-ride-hail-uber-lyft-prop-22-contractor-employee-worker-protections-massachusetts-bill.

42. Jamie K. McCallum, *Worked Over: How Round-the-Clock Work Is Killing the American Dream* (New York: Basic Books, 2020).

43. Frank Pega et al., "Global, Regional, and National Burdens of Ischemic Heart Disease and Stroke Attributable to Exposure to Long Working Hours for 194 Countries, 2000–2016: A Systematic Analysis from the WHO/ILO Joint Estimates of the Work-Related Burden of Disease and Injury," *Environment International* 154 (September 2021): 106595, https://doi.org/10.1016/j.envint.2021.106595.

44. Claire C. Caruso et al., *Overtime and Extended Work Shifts: Recent Findings on Illnesses, Injuries and Health Behaviors*, Centers for Disease Control and Prevention, April 2004, https://doi.org/10.26616/NIOSHPUB2004143.

45. Kristen Harknett and Daniel Schneider, "Precarious Work Schedules and Population Health, Health Affairs," February 12, 2020, www.healthaffairs.org/do/10.1377/hpb20200206.806111/full/.

46. Harknett and Schneider, *Precarious Work Schedules and Population Health*; Daniel Schneider and Kristen Harknett, "Consequences of Routine Work-Schedule Instability for Worker Health and Well-Being," *American Sociological Review* 84, no. 1 (February 1, 2019): 82–114, https://doi.org/10.1177/0003122418823184.

47. Maddy Simpson, "How Predictive Scheduling Laws Will Impact Employees During COVID-19," *Employee Benefit News*, July 20, 2020, www.benefitnews.com/news/how-predictive-scheduling-laws-will-impact-employees-during-covid-19.

48. Alexandra Berzon, Shalini Ramachandran, and Coulter Jones, "OSHA's Job Is Workplace Safety. In the Covid-19 Pandemic, It Often Struggled," *Wall Street Journal*, March 4, 2021, US, www.wsj.com/articles/oshas-job-is-workplace-safety-in-the-covid-19-pandemic-it-often-struggled-11614875112.

49. Ana Swanson and Alan Rappeport, "Businesses Want Virus Legal Protection. Workers Are Worried," *New York Times*, June 12, 2020, www.nytimes.com/2020/06/12/business/economy/coronavirus-liability-shield.html.

50. Suzanne Barlyn and John McCrank, "Sign Here First: U.S. Salons, Gyms, Offices Require Coronavirus Waivers," Reuters, June 1, 2020, www.reuters.com/article/us-health-coronavirus-disclaimers-busine-idUSKBN238298.

51. Debbie Cenziper et al., "As Nursing Home Residents Died, New Covid-19 Protections Shielded Companies from Lawsuits. Families Say That Hides the Truth," *Washington Post*, June 8, 2020, www.washingtonpost.com/business/2020/06/08/nursing-home-immunity-laws/.

52. *Special Report: Nursing Home Industry Seeks Immunity During COVID Crisis; States Are Obliging*, Center for Medicare Advocacy, May 14, 2020, https://medicareadvocacy.org/wp-content/uploads/2020/05/Special-Report-Nursing-Home-Immunity.pdf.

53. Ian R. Carrillo and Annabel Ipsen, "Worksites as Sacrifice Zones: Structural Precarity and COVID-19 in U.S. Meatpacking," *Sociological Perspectives* 64, no. 5 (May 27, 2021): 726–746, https://doi.org/10.1177/07311214211012025.

54. Jacob S. Hacker, "Average Workers Can't Bear Any More Risk," *The Atlantic*, May 31, 2020, www.theatlantic.com/ideas/archive/2020/05/average-workers-cant-bear-any-more-risk/612385/.

55. Stefan Pichler, Katherine Wen, and Nicolas R. Ziebarth, "COVID-19 Emergency Sick Leave Has Helped Flatten the Curve in the United States," *Health Affairs* 39, no. 12 (December 1, 2020): 2197–2204, https://doi.org/10.1377/hlthaff.2020.00863.

56. Pichler, Wen, and Ziebarth, "COVID-19 Emergency Sick Leave Has Helped Flatten the Curve in the United States."

57. Daniel Schneider, Kristen Harknett, and Elmer Vivas-Portillo, "Olive Garden's Expansion of Paid Sick Leave During COVID-19 Reduced the Share of Employees Working While Sick," *Health Affairs* 40, no. 8 (August 2021): 1328–1336, www.healthaffairs .org/doi/10.1377/hlthaff.2020.02320.

58. Eduardo Porter and Karl Russell, "How the American Unemployment System Failed," *New York Times*, January 21, 2021, www.nytimes.com/2021/01/21/business /economy/unemployment-insurance.html.

59. Amy Traub, *7 Things We Learned About Unemployment Insurance During the Pandemic*, National Employment Law Project, November 16, 2021, www.nelp.org /publication/7-things-we-learned-about-unemployment-insurance-during-the -pandemic/.

60. Ulrich Beck, "The Anthropological Shock: Chernobyl and the Contours of the Risk Society," *Berkeley Journal of Sociology* 32 (1987): 153–165.

Chapter 7: The Crucible of Care Work

1. "Rising Health Care Costs in California: A Worker Issue," *Health Care Blog*, UC Berkeley Labor Center, November 14, 2019, https://laborcenter.berkeley.edu/rising -health-care-costs-in-california-a-worker-issue/.

2. David Weil, *The Fissured Workplace: Why Work Became So Bad for So Many and What Can Be Done to Improve It* (Cambridge, MA: Harvard University Press, 2017).

3. Linda Delp and Katie Quan, "Homecare Worker Organizing in California: An Analysis of a Successful Strategy," *Labor Studies Journal* 27, no. 1 (Spring 2002): 1–24.

4. Delp and Quan, "Homecare Worker Organizing in California."

5. Steve Wishnia, "Health Aides Hail Bill to Ban 24-Hour Shifts," *LaborPress*, September 4, 2019, www.laborpress.org/health-aides-hail-bill-to-ban-24-hour-shifts/.

6. "Labor Standards," New York State Department of Labor, accessed September 10, 2021, https://dol.ny.gov/labor-standards-0.

7. New York State Assembly Bill A3145A, New York State Senate (February 5, 2021), www.nysenate.gov/legislation/bills/2021/a3145/amendment/a.

8. Jamie K. McCallum, *Worked Over: How Round-the-Clock Work Is Killing the American Dream* (New York: Basic Books, 2020).

9. The Ain't I a Woman Campaign?! "International Women's Day: Home Attendants Condemn 1199SEIU's Sexist and Racist Meager Settlement of 0.5% of Total," press release, 2022, www.aintiawoman.org; Caroline Lewis, "NY Home Care Workers Awarded $30 Million for Unpaid Wages," *The Gothamist*, February 28, 2022, https://gothamist .com/news/ny-home-care-workers-awarded-30-million-unpaid-wages.

10. Gabriel Winant, *The Next Shift: The Fall of Industry and the Rise of Health Care in Rust Belt America* (Cambridge, MA: Harvard University Press, 2021).

11. Helen Hester and Nick Srnicek, "The Crisis of Social Reproduction and the End of Work," *OpenMind*, BBVA, 2017, www.bbvaopenmind.com/en/articles/the-crisis -of-social-reproduction-and-the-end-of-work/.

12. Lisa M. Haddad, Pavan Annamaraju, and Tammy J. Toney-Butler, "Nursing Shortage," *StatPearls* (Treasure Island, FL: StatPearls Publishing, 2022), www.ncbi.nlm .nih.gov/books/NBK493175/.

13. Jonathan and Karin Fielding School of Public Health, "Nurse Understaffing Linked to Increased Risk of Patient Mortality," *UCLA Public Health Magazine*, June 2011, https://ph.ucla.edu/news/magazine/2011/june/article/nurse-understaffing-linked -increased-risk-patient-mortality; Roni Jacobson, "Widespread Understaffing of Nurses Increases Risk to Patients," *Scientific American*, July 14, 2015, www.scientificamerican .com/article/widespread-understaffing-of-nurses-increases-risk-to-patients/.

14. Michelle Chen, "There Is No 'Nursing Shortage.' There's Just a Good Nursing Job Shortage," *The Nation*, August 7, 2019, www.thenation.com/article/archive/health -care-medicare-nurses/.

15. "Hear Us Out Campaign Reports Nurses' COVID-19 Reality," *Newsroom*, American Association of Critical-Care Nurses, September 21, 2021, www.aacn.org/newsroom /hear-us-out-campaign-reports-nurses-covid-19-reality.

16. Ryan Basen, "Tenet Gets Big Federal $$$ but Still Cuts Employees," MedPage Today, July 9, 2020, www.medpagetoday.com/hospitalbasedmedicine/generalhospitalpractice/87493.

17. Basen, "Tenet Gets Big Federal $$$."

18. Lucy King and Jonah M. Kessel, "We Know the Real Cause of the Crisis in Our Hospitals. It's Greed," *New York Times*, January 19, 2022, Opinion, video, www.nytimes .com/video/opinion/100000008158650/covid-nurse-burnout-understaffing.html.

19. Haddad, Annamaraju, and Toney-Butler, "Nursing Shortage."

20. "Occupational Outlook Handbook," US Bureau of Labor Statistics, April 9, 2021, www.bls.gov/ooh/most-new-jobs.htm.

21. The Editors, "Who Cares for the Caregivers?," *n+1*, no. 39 (Winter 2021), www .nplusonemag.com/issue-39/the-intellectual-situation/who-cares-for-the-caregivers/.

22. Dawn Ouellette Nixon, "A Tale of Two Health Networks: How Health Care Became the Biggest Employer in the Lehigh Valley," *Lehigh Valley Business*, August 14, 2019, www .lvb.com/tale-two-health-networks-health-care-became-biggest-employer-lehigh-valley/.

23. Anne Case and Angus Deaton, *Deaths of Despair and the Future of Capitalism* (Princeton, NJ: Princeton University Press, 2020).

24. Jason E. Smith, *Smart Machines and Service Work: Automation in an Age of Stagnation* (London: Reaktion Books, 2020).

25. Gabriel Winant, *The Next Shift: The Fall of Industry and the Rise of Health Care in Rust Belt America* (Cambridge, MA: Harvard University Press, 2021).

26. Aaron Jaffe, *Social Reproduction Theory and the Socialist Horizon: Work, Power and Political Strategy* (London: Pluto Press, 2020); Nancy Fraser, "Behind Marx's Hidden Abode," *New Left Review*, no. 86 (March/April 2014), https://newleftreview.org/issues /ii86/articles/nancy-fraser-behind-marx-s-hidden-abode.

27. Nancy Fraser, "Contradictions of Capitalism and Care," *New Left Review*, no. 100 (July/August 2016), https://newleftreview.org/issues/ii100/articles/nancy-fraser -contradictions-of-capital-and-care.

28. Keith A. Bailey and James R. Spletzer, "A New Measure of Multiple Jobholding in the U.S. Economy," *Labour Economics* 71 (August 2021): 102009, https://doi.org /10.1016/j.labeco.2021.102009.

29. Sarah Foster, "Survey: As Coronavirus Spreads, Nearly 1 in 3 Americans Admit to Not Seeking Medical Care Due to Cost," *Personal Finance* (blog), Bankrate, March 12, 2020, www.bankrate.com/surveys/health-care-costs/.

30. Ruth Wilson Gilmore, *Golden Gulag: Prisons, Surplus, Crisis, and Opposition in Globalizing California* (Berkeley: University of California Press, 2017).

31. Jane Slaughter, "Detroit Bus Drivers Win Protections Against Virus Through Strike," *Labor Notes*, March 18, 2020, https://labornotes.org/blogs/2020/03/detroit-bus-drivers -win-protections-against-virus-through-strike; Charisse Jones, "GE Workers Demand to Save Jobs, Make Ventilators to Fight Coronavirus Pandemic," *USA Today*, April 8, 2020, www .usatoday.com/story/money/2020/04/08/covid-19-ge-workers-stage-protests-demanding -make-ventilators/2973582001/; Greg Ryan, "Labor Unions Demand GE Make Ventilators Using Laid-off Workers," *Boston Business Journal*, March 30, 2020, www.bizjournals .com/boston/news/2020/03/30/labor-unions-demand-ge-make-ventilators-using-laid.html; Megan Cassella, Nicole Gaudiano, and MacKenzie Mays, "Teachers Unions Test Goodwill with Strike Threats, Hardball Negotiations," POLITICO, August 18, 2020, www.politico .com/news/2020/08/18/teachers-unions-school-reopening-coronavirus-397997.

32. Heidi Shierholz et al., *Why Unions Are Good for Workers—Especially in a Crisis like COVID-19: 12 Policies That Would Boost Worker Rights, Safety, and Wages*, Economic Policy Institute, August 25, 2020, www.epi.org/publication/why-unions-are-good-for -workers-especially-in-a-crisis-like-covid-19-12-policies-that-would-boost-worker-rights -safety-and-wages/; "Verizon Unions Win Model Paid Leave Policy for Coronavirus— Will Other Unions Demand the Same?," *Labor Notes*, March 18, 2020, https://labornotes .org/blogs/2020/03/verizon-union-wins-model-paid-leave-policy-coronavirus-will -other-unions-demand-same.

33. Ashley Yung, "Union Members Advocate for Childcare Benefits as the Pandemic Continues to Disproportionately Affect Female Faculty," *Columbia Daily Spectator*, March 18, 2021, www.columbiaspectator.com/news/2021/03/17/union-members-advocate -for-childcare-benefits-as-the-pandemic-continues-to-disproportionately-affect-female -faculty/.

34. Hester and Srnicek, "The Crisis of Social Reproduction."

35. Jill Lepore, "What Our Contagion Fables Are Really About," *New Yorker*, March 23, 2020, www.newyorker.com/magazine/2020/03/30/what-our-contagion-fables -are-really-about.

36. Lepore, "What Our Contagion Fables Are Really About."

37. *America's Hidden Common Ground on the Coronavirus, Part 1*, Public Agenda, April 3, 2020, www.publicagenda.org/reports/americas-hidden-common-ground-on-covid-19 -results-from-a-public-agenda-usa-today-ipsos-snapshot-poll/.

Chapter 8: The Pandemic Pendulum

1. Aaron Sojourner (@aaronsojourner), "Public feeling towards labor unions is more positive than in any year on record back over half a Century…" Twitter, March 26, 2021, 6:46 a.m., https://twitter.com/aaronsojourner/status/1375443938396409861.

2. Tom Rosentiel, *How a Different America Responded to the Great Depression*, Pew Research Center, December 14, 2010, www.pewresearch.org/2010/12/14/how-a-different -america-responded-to-the-great-depression/.

3. Claire Cain Miller, "The World 'Has Found a Way to Do This': The U.S. Lags on Paid Leave," *New York Times*, October 25, 2021, www.nytimes.com/2021/10/25/upshot /paid-leave-democrats.html/.

4. Stefan Pichler, Katherine Wen, and Nicolas R. Ziebarth, "COVID-19 Emergency Sick Leave Has Helped Flatten the Curve in the United States," *Health Affairs* 39, no. 12 (October 15, 2020), https://doi.org/10.1377/hlthaff.2020.00863.

5. Karl Polanyi, *The Great Transformation* (Boston: Beacon, 2001).

6. Tim Arango, "Ady Barkan Won't Let Dying Stop His Activism," *New York Times*, September 19, 2019, www.nytimes.com/2019/09/19/us/ady-barkan-activist-medicare.html.

7. Michelle Chen, "There Is No 'Nursing Shortage.' There's Just a Good Nursing Job Shortage," *The Nation*, August 7, 2019, www.thenation.com/article/archive/health-care -medicare-nurses/; "Union Endorsers," Unions for Single Payer Health Care, https:// unionsforsinglepayer.org/union_endorsers/.

8. Jason Lemon, "Medicare for All Would Save $450 Billion Annually While Preventing 68,000 Deaths, New Study Shows," *Newsweek*, February 18, 2020, www.newsweek .com/medicare-all-would-save-450-billion-annually-while-preventing-68000-deaths -new-study-shows-1487862.

9. Diane Archer, "22 Studies Agree: 'Medicare for All' Saves Money," *The Hill*, February 24, 2020, https://thehill.com/blogs/congress-blog/healthcare/484301-22-studies -agree-medicare-for-all-saves-money.

10. Christopher Cai et al., "Projected Costs of Single-Payer Healthcare Financing in the United States: A Systematic Review of Economic Analyses," *PLOS Medicine* 17, no. 1 (January 15, 2020): e1003013, https://doi.org/10.1371/journal.pmed.1003013; Charles Blahous, "The Costs of a National Single-Payer Healthcare System," *Mercatus Working Paper*, Mercatus Center at George Mason University, July 2018, www.mercatus.org/system /files/blahous-costs-medicare-mercatus-working-paper-v1_1.pdf.

11. Eagan Kemp, "Why Medicare for All, Not a Public Option, Is the Best Solution," Public Citizen, www.citizen.org/article/why-medicare-for-all-not-a-public-option -is-the-best-solution/.

12. Roosa Tikkanen and Melinda K. Abrams, *U.S. Health Care from a Global Perspective, 2019*, Commonwealth Fund, January 30, 2020, www.commonwealthfund.org /publications/issue-briefs/2020/jan/us-health-care-global-perspective-2019.

13. Stan Dorn and Rebecca Gordon, "The Catastrophic Cost of Uninsurance: COVID-19 Cases and Deaths Closely Tied to America's Health Coverage Gaps," Resources, Families USA, March 4, 2021, https://familiesusa.org/resources/the-catastrophic-cost-of-uninsurance -covid-19-cases-and-deaths-closely-tied-to-americas-health-coverage-gaps/; Walker Bragman and David Sirota, "The Corporate Deterrent to More Vaccinations," *Daily Poster*, August 24, 2021, www.dailyposter.com/the-corporate-deterrent-to-more-vaccinations/.

14. Alison P. Galvani et al., "Improving the Prognosis of Health Care in the USA," *The Lancet* 395, no. 10223 (February 2020): 524–533, https://doi.org/10.1016/s0140 -6736(19)33019-3.

15. MaryBeth Musumeci, "How Could $400 Billion New Federal Dollars Change Medicaid Home and Community-Based Services?," *Medicaid*, Kaiser Family Foundation, July 16, 2021, www.kff.org/medicaid/issue-brief/how-could-400-billion-new-federal-dollars-change-medicaid-home-and-community-based-services/.

16. Alexia Fernández Campbell, "Kamala Harris Just Introduced a Bill to Give Housekeepers Overtime Pay and Meal Breaks," *Vox*, July 15, 2019, www.vox.com/2019/7/15/20694610/kamala-harris-domestic-workers-bill-of-rights-act.

17. Jori Kandra et al., *Domestic Workers Chartbook: A Comprehensive Look at the Demographics, Wages, Benefits, and Poverty Rates of the Professionals Who Care for Our Family Members and Clean Our Homes*, Economic Policy Institute, May 14, 2020, www.epi.org/publication/domestic-workers-chartbook-a-comprehensive-look-at-the-demographics-wages-benefits-and-poverty-rates-of-the-professionals-who-care-for-our-family-members-and-clean-our-homes/.

18. Kandra et al., *Domestic Workers Chartbook*; Campbell, "Kamala Harris Just Introduced a Bill."

19. Marilyn A. Brown and Majid Ahmadi, "Would a Green New Deal Add or Kill Jobs?," *Scientific American*, December 17, 2019, www.scientificamerican.com/article/would-a-green-new-deal-add-or-kill-jobs1/.

20. Christopher Flavelle, "Work Injuries Tied to Heat Are Vastly Undercounted, Study Finds," *New York Times*, July 15, 2021, Climate, www.nytimes.com/2021/07/15/climate/heat-injuries.html; Erika Mahoney, "Farm Workers Face Double Threat: Wildfire Smoke and COVID-19," NPR, September 7, 2020, www.npr.org/2020/09/07/909314223/farm-workers-face-double-threat-wildfire-smoke-and-covid-19; Whitney Kimball, "Amazon's New Safety Crisis Could Be Heat Waves," *Gizmodo*, June 29, 2021, https://gizmodo.com/amazons-new-safety-crisis-could-be-heat-waves-1847188930.

21. Naomi Klein, "Care and Repair: Left Politics in the Age of Climate Change," *Dissent*, Winter 2020, www.dissentmagazine.org/article/care-and-repair-left-politics-in-the-age-of-climate-change.

22. IWL Rutgers, "Care Work Is Climate Work: A Series on the Green New Deal," November 14, 2019, YouTube video, www.youtube.com/watch?v=SdQPyGxLLUA.

23. IWL Rutgers, "Care Work Is Climate Work."

24. Ai-jen Poo, "The Pandemic Offers a Chance to Reimagine Caregiving," *The Nation*, January 4, 2021, www.thenation.com/article/society/pandemic-caregiver-biden/.

25. Jamie K. McCallum, *Worked Over: How Round-the-Clock Work Is Killing the American Dream* (New York: Basic Books, 2020).

26. McCallum, *Worked Over*.

27. Ben Casselman and Ella Koeze, "More Phone Calls, Less Shopping: How the Pandemic Changed American Lives, Down to the Minute," *New York Times*, July 22, 2021, www.nytimes.com/2021/07/22/business/economy/how-we-spend-our-days.html.

28. Jose Maria Barrero, Nicholas Bloom, and Steven Davis, "60 Million Fewer Commuting Hours per Day: How Americans Use Time Saved by Working from Home," *VoxEU*, September 23, 2020, https://voxeu.org/article/how-americans-use-time-saved-working-home.

29. "The Quarantine Weekly Update: World VPN Use Skyrockets, US Workday up 3 Hours, and Why You Should Call That Weird Cousin," *NordLayer*, NordVPN Teams,

March 25, 2020, https://nordvpnteams.medium.com/the-quarantine-weekly-update-world
-vpn-use-skyrockets-us-workday-up-3-hours-and-why-you-should-1f875507739b.

30. Frank Pega et al., "Global, Regional, and National Burdens of Ischemic Heart Disease and Stroke Attributable to Exposure to Long Working Hours for 194 Countries, 2000–2016: A Systematic Analysis from the WHO/ILO Joint Estimates of the Work-Related Burden of Disease and Injury," *Environment International* 154 (September 1, 2021): 106595, https://doi.org/10.1016/j.envint.2021.106595.

31. Christine Ro, "How Overwork Is Literally Killing Us," *BBC*, May 19, 2021, www.bbc.com/worklife/article/20210518-how-overwork-is-literally-killing-us.

32. Sammy Westfall, "Japan Proposes Four-Day Workweek as Idea Gains Purchase amid Pandemic," *Washington Post*, June 24, 2021, www.washingtonpost.com/world/2021/06/24/japan-four-day-work-week/.

33. Paulina Villegas and Hannah Knowles, "Iceland Tested a 4-Day Workweek. Employees Were Productive—and Happier, Researchers Say," *Washington Post*, July 7, 2021, www.washingtonpost.com/business/2021/07/06/iceland-four-day-work-week/; Antonia Noori Farzan, "Spain Will Experiment with Four-Day Workweek, a First for Europe," *Washington Post*, March 15, 2021, www.washingtonpost.com/world/2021/03/15/spain-four-day-workweek/.

34. Lisa Thompson, "Federal Art Project (FAP) (1935)," Living New Deal, November 18, 2016, https://livingnewdeal.org/glossary/federal-art-project-fap-1935-1943/.

35. Michael Goldfield and Cody R. Melcher, "Moments of Rupture: The 1930s and the Great Depression," *Convergence*, November 9, 2021, https://convergencemag.com/articles/moments-of-rupture-the-1930s-and-the-great-depression/.

36. Jane McAlevey, "How Workers Can Win in 2022," *The Nation*, December 27, 2021, www.thenation.com/article/society/labor-strikes-workers-unions/.

37. Ben Burgis, "Capitalism Isn't Working. But What Would a Viable Socialist System Look Like?," *Jacobin*, May 21, 2020, https://jacobinmag.com/2020/05/capitalism-socialism-cooperatives-market-nhs-democracy; Ben Burgis, "Yes, Socialism Would Handle the Coronavirus Pandemic Better Than Capitalism," *Jacobin*, May 24, 2020, https://jacobinmag.com/2020/05/socialism-coronavirus-pandemic-capitalism-nationalization.

38. Kat Devlin, Shannon Schumacher, and J. J. Moncus, *Many in Western Europe and U.S. Want Economic Changes as Pandemic Continues*, Pew Research Center, April 22, 2021, www.pewresearch.org/global/2021/04/22/many-in-western-europe-and-u-s-want-economic-changes-as-pandemic-continues/.

39. Ady Barkan, "Talking Socialism: 'Injustice Is Interconnected but So Is Freedom': Ady Barkan Talks to Democratic Left," interview by Chris Lombardi, *Democratic Left*, Fall 2021, https://democraticleft.dsausa.org/issues/fall-2021/barkan/?fbclid=IwAR0OS NiehDYvrVysH1V8IrNHmikxp7PXij1Sh-EvJ3DgAfCCFD_r7hHQZLk.

40. "Employee Benefits in the United States News Release," Bureau of Labor Statistics, September 23, 2021, www.bls.gov/news.release/ebs2.htm; Drew Desilver, "As Coronavirus Spreads, Which U.S. Workers Have Paid Sick Leave—and Which Don't?," *Fact Tank* (blog), Pew Research Center, March 12, 2020, www.pewresearch.org/fact-tank/2020/03/12/as-coronavirus-spreads-which-u-s-workers-have-paid-sick-leave-and-which-dont/.

Conclusion: Morbid Symptoms

1. Here I am channeling Tony Judt, *Ill Fares the Land* (New York: Penguin Books, 2011).

2. Ben Casselman, "America Is on a Road to a Better Economy. But Better for Whom?," *New York Times*, May 21, 2021, www.nytimes.com/2021/05/18/magazine/stimulus-us-economy.html.

3. Ben Casselman and Sydney Ember, "Omicron's Economic Toll: Missing Workers, More Uncertainty and Higher Inflation (Maybe)," *New York Times*, January 24, 2022, www.nytimes.com/2022/01/24/business/economy/omicron-economy.html.

4. "Sparrow Caregivers Announce Informational Picket to Demonstrate for Safe Staffing and a Fair Contract," MI Nurses Association, October 21, 2021, www.minurses.org/news/sparrow-caregivers-announce-picket/.

INDEX

JAMIE K. MCCALLUM is professor of sociology at Middlebury College. He is the author of *Worked Over* and *Global Unions, Local Power*, which won the American Sociological Association's prize for the best book on labor. His work has appeared in scholarly journals and popular outlets such as the *Washington Post, Mother Jones, Dissent,* and *Jacobin*. He lives in Weybridge, Vermont.